DISCOURSE ANALYSIS

Routledge English Language Introductions cover core areas of language study and are one-stop resources for students.

Assuming no prior knowledge, books in the series offer an accessible overview of the subject, with activities, study questions, sample analyses, commentaries and key readings – all in the same volume. The innovative and flexible 'two dimensional' structure is built around four sections – introduction, development, exploration and extension – which offer self-contained stages for study. Each topic can also be read across these sections, enabling the reader to build gradually on the knowledge gained. Each book in the series has a companion website with extra resources for teachers, lecturers and students.

Discourse Analysis:

❏ provides an accessible introduction and comprehensive overview of the major approaches and methodological tools used in discourse analysis;
❏ introduces both traditional perspectives on the analysis of texts and spoken discourse as well as more recent approaches that address technologically mediated and multi-modal discourse;
❏ incorporates practical examples using real data from conversational interaction, ceremonial vows, dating adverts, social media such as Facebook, blogs and MSN, films such as *When Harry Met Sally*, popular music lyrics and newspaper articles on areas as diverse as international political incidents and Lady Gaga;
❏ includes key readings from leading scholars in the field, such as James Paul Gee, Michael Halliday, Henry G. Widdowson, Dell Hymes, Harvey Sacks and Ron Scollon;
❏ offers a wide range of activities, questions and points for further discussion;
❏ is supported by a companion website www.routledge.com/cw/jones featuring extra activities, additional guidance, useful links and multimedia examples including sound files, YouTube and videos.

This title will be essential reading for students undertaking research within the areas of English language, linguistics and applied linguistics.

Rodney Jones is Associate Head of the Department of English at City University of Hong Kong, China.

ROUTLEDGE ENGLISH LANGUAGE INTRODUCTIONS

SERIES CONSULTANT: PETER STOCKWELL

Peter Stockwell is Professor of Literary Linguistics in the School of English Studies at the University of Nottingham, UK, where his interests include sociolinguistics, stylistics and cognitive poetics. His recent publications include *Language in Theory*, Routledge 2005 (with Mark Robson), *Cognitive Poetics: An Introduction*, Routledge 2002, *The Poetics of Science Fiction, Investigating English Language* (with Howard Jackson), and *Contextualized Stylistics* (edited with Tony Bex and Michael Burke).

SERIES CONSULTANT: RONALD CARTER

Ronald Carter is Professor of Modern English Language in the School of English Studies at the University of Nottingham, UK. He is the co-series editor of the Routledge Applied Linguistics Series, series editor of Interface and was co-founder of the Routledge Intertext series.

OTHER TITLES IN THE SERIES:

Introducing English Language
Louise Mullany and Peter Stockwell

Language and Power
Paul Simpson and Andrea Mayr

Language and Media
Alan Durant and Marina Lambrou

Sociolinguistics
Peter Stockwell

Pragmatics and Discourse
Joan Cutting

Grammar and Vocabulary
Howard Jackson

Psycholinguistics
John Field

World Englishes
Jennifer Jenkins

Practical Phonetics and Phonology
Beverley Collins and Inger Mees

Stylistics
Paul Simpson

Language in Theory
Mark Robson and Peter Stockwell

Child Language
Jean Stilwell Peccei

Introducing English Language
Louise Mullany and Peter Stockwell

Researching English Language
Alison Sealey

English Grammar
Roger Berry

DISCOURSE ANALYSIS

A resource book for students

RODNEY JONES

Routledge
Taylor & Francis Group

LONDON AND NEW YORK

First published 2012
by Routledge
2 Park Square, Milton Park, Abingdon, Oxon, OX14 4RN

Simultaneously published in the USA and Canada
by Routledge
711 Third Avenue, New York, NY 10017

Routledge is an imprint of the Taylor & Francis Group, an informa business

British Library Cataloguing in Publication Data
A catalogue record for this book is available from the British Library

Library of Congress Cataloging-in-Publication Data
Jones, Rodney H.
  Discourse analysis: a resource book for students/Rodney Jones.
    p. cm. — (Routledge English Language Introductions)
  Includes bibliographical references and index.
  Discourse analysis.   I. Title.
P302.J66 2012
401'.41—dc23
                                                    2011028880

ISBN: 978–0–415–60999–9 (hbk)
ISBN: 978–0–415–61000–1 (pbk)

Typeset in Minion
by RefineCatch Limited, Bungay, Suffolk

Printed and bound in Great Britain by
CPI Antony Rowe, Chippenham, Wiltshire

HOW TO USE THIS BOOK

The Routledge English Language Introductions are 'flexi-texts' that you can use to suit your own style of study. The books are divided into four sections:

A: Introduction – sets out the key concepts for the area of study. The units of this section take you through the foundational concepts, providing you with an initial toolkit for your own study. By the end of the section, you will have a good overview of the whole field.

B: Development – adds to your knowledge and builds on the key ideas already introduced. Units in this section also introduce key analytical tools and techniques. By the end of this section, you will already have a good and fairly detailed grasp of the field and will be ready to undertake your own exploration and thinking.

C: Exploration – provides examples of language data and guides you through your own investigation of the topic or area. The units in this section will be more open-ended and exploratory and you will be encouraged to try out your ideas and think for yourself, using your newly acquired knowledge.

D: Extension – offers you the chance to compare your expertise with key readings in the area. These are taken from the work of important writers and are provided with guidance and questions for your further thought. You can read this book like a traditional textbook, 'vertically' straight through from beginning to end. So you would establish a broad sense of the key ideas by reading through section A, and deepen your knowledge by reading section B. Section C would then present you with one or more activities to test out different aspects of your broad knowledge. Finally, having gained a good level of competence, you can read the section D articles and follow up the further reading.

However, the Routledge English Language Introductions have been designed so that you can read them in another dimension, 'horizontally' across the numbered units. For example, units A1, B1, C1 and D1 constitute a strand first introducing a topic, then developing your knowledge, then testing out and exploring some key ideas and finally offering you a key case study to read. The strand across A2, B2, C2, D2 and the other strands 3, 4, 5 and so on all work in the same way. Reading across the strands will take you rapidly from the key concepts of a specific topic to a level of expertise in that precise topic, all with a very close focus. You can match your way of reading with the best way that you work. The glossarial index at the end together with the suggestions for further reading for each strand will help to keep you orientated. Each textbook has a supporting website with extra commentary, suggestions, additional material and support for teachers and students.

DISCOURSE ANALYSIS

This book covers the vast field of discourse analysis. Strand 1 gives a general introduction to the field, and the following strands are broadly arranged across three areas. Strands 1 to 4 cover the study of written discourse, examining cohesion and coherence, the social functions of texts and the ways ideology is expressed in written texts. Strands 5 to 7 focus more on spoken discourse and more interactive written discourse such as that which occurs in computer-mediated communication, examining how conversations are structured and how conversational participations strategically construct identities and activities in their talk, as well as how social contexts affect the way utterances are produced and interpreted. The last three strands focus on three relatively new approaches to discourse: mediated discourse analysis, an approach which examines, among other things, the way media affect the kinds of discourse we can produce and what we can do with it; multimodal discourse analysis, an approach which considers modes of communication beyond spoken and written language such as images and gestures; and corpus-assisted discourse analysis, an approach which uses computers to aid in the analysis of large collections of texts or transcripts.

Discourse analysis is a diverse and rapidly developing field: nearly every observation we have made about discourse in this book is open to debate and nearly every analytical technique we have introduced is open to criticism or further refinement. The real aim of this book is to provide you with the basic background to be able to engage in these debates and to assemble a toolkit of analytical techniques that best fit your needs. If you wish to know more about the ways discourse analysis fits into or relates to other approaches to the study of English, there are other books in the RELI series such as *Introducing English Language: A resource book for students* by Louise Mullany and Peter Stockwell, *Pragmatics and Discourse: A resource book for students* by Joan Cutting, and *Language and Power: A resource book for students* by Paul Simpson and Andrea Mayr.

The RELI books do not aim to replace your teacher or lecturer, but instead they offer both student and expert a resource for you to adapt as you think most appropriate. You will want to take issue with what is presented here, test out the assumptions and – we hope – feel motivated to read and explore further. Space is always space for tutors to mediate the material and for students to explore beyond the book.

CONTENTS

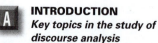

EXPLORATION
Analysing discourse

 EXTENSION
Readings in discourse analysis

LIST OF FIGURES AND TABLES

Figures

Tables

ACKNOWLEDGEMENTS

I wish to thank all of my colleagues at City University of Hong Kong for their valuable suggestions and support while I was writing this book, and especially my students with whom I have tried out this material over the years and who have given me valuable feedback on it. Particular thanks go to Danyal Freeman and Peter Stockwell for their close reading and insightful suggestions.

The Newsweek/Daily Beast Company LLC, Screenshot from *the Daily Dish* http://www.theatlantic.com/daily-dish/archive/2011/02/-our-family-isnt-so-different-from-any-other-iowan-family/176329/ (C3)

Cheryn-ann Chew, Screenshot from blog http://calciumblock.diaryland.com/, used with permission. (C3)

China shuns US mediation in its island dispute with Japan, *CNN International*, 3 November 2010, http://articles.cnn.com/2010–11–03/world/china.japan.disputed.islands_1_island-dispute-diaoyu-islands-beijing-and-tokyo?_s=PM:WORLD

China: Trilateral talks merely US wishful thinking, *China Daily*, 2 November 2010, http://www.chinadaily.com.cn/china/2010–11/02/content_11491199.htm (C4)

MSN Messenger emoticons. Microsoft Corporation. Used with permission from Microsoft. (C6)

Wacoal Butterfly Bra ad, Wacoal Holdings Corporation. All Rights Reserved. (C9)

Harris, Zellig (1952) Discourse Analysis, *Language 28* (1) 1–30. Language by LINGUISTIC SOCIETY OF AMERICA. © 2012. Reproduced with permission of LINGUISTIC SOCIETY OF AMERICA in the format Textbook via Copyright Clearance Center.

Widdowson, Henry (1973) An Applied Linguistic Approach To Discourse Analysis. Ph.D. thesis, Department of Linguistics, University of Edinburgh. Reproduced with kind permission of the author.

Gee, James Paul (2010) *Introduction to Discourse Analysis* 3rd Edition. London: Routledge. (p. 28–29). Reproduced with permission.

Halliday, Michael and Hasan, R. (1976). *Cohesion in English* London: Pearson Education Ltd (pp 1–6). Reproduced with permission.

Rumelhart, D. (1975) Notes on a schema for stories. In D. Bobrow and A. Collins (Eds.), *Representation and Understanding: Studies in Cognitive Science*, pp 211–216. New York: Academic Press. © Elsevier 2011.

Swales, John (1990) *Genre Analysis*. Cambridge: Cambridge University Press. © Cambridge University Press 1990, reproduced with permission.

Bhatia, V. K. (1997) The power and politics of genre. *World Englishes 16*(3): 359–371. Copyright © 1997 John Wiley & Sons. Reproduced with permission.

Fairclough, Norman (1992) *Discourse and Social Change*. Cambridge: Polity Press. © Polity Press. Reproduced with permission.

Gee, James Paul (1996) Social Linguistics and Literacies, pp 69–73 and 77–79. London: Taylor and Francis. Reproduced with permission.

Austin, J. L. (1962) *How to Do Things with Words*. Oxford: Oxford University Press. By permission of Oxford University Press.

Schegloff, E. A. and Sacks, H. (1973) Opening up closings. *Semiotica* 7: 289–327. Reproduced by permission of De Gruyter.

Tannen, Deborah and Wallat, Cynthia (1987) Interactive frames and knowledge schemas in interaction: examples from a medical examination/interview. *Social Psychology Quarterly* 50(2): 205–16. Reproduced with kind permission of Deborah Tannen and the American Sociological Association

Hymes, Dell (1986) Models of the interaction of language and social life, *Directions in Sociolinguistics*, John J. Gumperz and Dell Hymes (eds.) Oxford: Blackwell. Copyright © 2011 Blackwell Publishing Ltd. Reproduced with permission of Blackwell Publishing Ltd.

Saville-Troike, Muriel (2003) *The Ethnography of Communication*. Oxford: Blackwell. Copyright © 2011 Blackwell Publishing Ltd. Reproduced with permission of Blackwell Publishing Ltd.

Starbucks Coffee Company, text from coffee sleeve. © 2005 Starbucks Coffee Company. All rights reserved.

Excerpts from *When Harry Met Sally* (1988), granted courtesy of Warner Bros. Entertainment Inc.

United Press Syndicate for Fig. A5.1, Calvin and Hobbs. Reprinted with permission. All rights reserved.

Scollon, R. (2001). *Mediated discourse: The nexus of practice*. London: Routledge. (D8)

Kress, Gunther and van Leeuwen, Theo (2006). *Reading images: the grammar of visual design* (2nd ed.). London and New York: Routledge. Reproduced with permission.

Norris, S. (2004). *Analyzing multimodal interaction: A methodological framework*. London: Routledge. (A9) Reproduced with permission.

Baker, P. and McEnery, T. (2005). A corpus-based approach to discourses of refugees and asylum seekers in UN and newspaper texts. *Journal of Language and Politics* 4(2), 97–226. (D10) With kind permission by John Benjamins Publishing Company. Amsterdam Philadelphia. www.benjamins.com

Section A

INTRODUCTION

KEY TOPICS IN THE STUDY OF DISCOURSE ANALYSIS

A1   WHAT IS DISCOURSE ANALYSIS?

Our first step in the study of discourse analysis has to be figuring out exactly what we mean by **discourse** and why it is so important to learn how to analyse it.

In one sense we can say that discourse analysis is the study of language. Many people would define discourse analysis as a sub-field of linguistics, which is the scientific study of language. Linguistics has many sub-fields, each of which looks at a different aspect of language. **Phonology** is the study of the sounds of languages and how people put them together to form words. **Grammar** is the study of how words are put together to form sentences and spoken utterances. And **discourse analysis** is the study of the ways sentences and utterances are put together to make texts and interactions and how those texts and interactions fit into our social world.

But discourse analysis is not *just* the study of language. It is a way of looking at language that focuses on how people use it in real life to do things such as joke and argue and persuade and flirt, and to show that they are certain kinds of people or belong to certain groups. This way of looking at language is based on four main assumptions. They are:

1 *Language is ambiguous.* What things mean is never absolutely clear. All communication involves interpreting what other people mean and what they are trying to do.
2 *Language is always 'in the world'.* That is, what language means is always a matter of where and when it is used and what it is used to do.
3 *The way we use language is inseparable from who we are and the different social groups to which we belong.* We use language to display different kinds of social identities and to show that we belong to different groups.
4 *Language is never used all by itself.* It is always combined with other things such as our tone of voice, facial expressions and gestures when we speak, and the fonts, layout and graphics we use in written texts. What language means and what we can do with it is often a matter of how it is combined with these other things.

The ambiguity of language

Everyone has had the experience of puzzling over what someone – a lover or a parent or a friend – 'really meant' by what he or she said. In fact, nearly all communication contains some elements of meaning that are not expressed directly by the words that are spoken or written. Even when we think we are expressing ourselves clearly and directly, we may not be. For example, you may want to borrow a pen from someone and express this desire with the question, 'Do you have a pen?' Strictly speaking, though, this question does not directly communicate that you need a pen. It only asks if the other person is in possession of one. In order to understand this question as a request, the other person needs to undertake a process of 'figuring out' what you meant, a process which in this case may be largely unconscious and automatic, but which is, all the same, a process of interpretation.

So, we can take as a starting point for our study of discourse analysis the fact that *people don't always say what they mean, and people don't always mean what they say*. This is not because people are trying to trick or deceive each other (though sometimes they are), but because language is, by its very nature, ambiguous. To say exactly what we mean all the time would be impossible: first, because as poets, lovers and even lawyers know, language is an imperfect tool for the precise expression of many things we think and feel; and second, because whenever we communicate we always mean to communicate more than just one thing. When you ask your friend if he or she has a pen, for example, you mean to communicate not just that you need a pen but also that you do not wish to impose on your friend or that you feel a bit shy about borrowing a pen, which is one of the reasons why you approach the whole business of requesting indirectly by asking if they have a pen, even when you know very well that they have one.

Language in the world

One of the most important ways we understand what people mean when they communicate is by making reference to the social context within which they are speaking or writing. The meaning of an utterance can change dramatically depending on who is saying it, when and where it is said, and to whom it is said. If a teacher asks a student who is about to take an examination the same question we discussed above, 'Do you have a pen?' it is rather unlikely that this is a request or that the teacher is a bit shy about communicating with the student. Rather, this utterance is probably designed to make sure that the student has the proper tool to take the examination or to inform the student that a pen (rather than a pencil) must be used.

In other words, when we speak of discourse, we are always speaking of language that is in some way *situated*. Language is always situated in at least four ways. First, language is situated within the material world, and where we encounter it, whether it be on a shop sign or in a textbook or on a particular website will contribute to the way we interpret it. Second, language is situated within relationships; one of the main ways we understand what people mean when they speak or write is by referring to who they are, how well we know them and whether or not they have some kind of power over us. Third, language is situated in history, that is, in relation to what happened before and what we expect to happen afterwards. Finally, language is situated in relation to other language – utterances and texts always respond to or refer to other utterances and texts; that is, everything that we say or write is situated in a kind of network of discourse.

Language and social identity

Not only is discourse situated partly by who says (or writes) what to whom, but people – the 'whos' and the 'whoms' who say or write these things – are also situated by discourse. What I mean by this is that whenever people speak or write, they are, through their discourse, somehow demonstrating who they are and what their relationship is to other people. They are enacting their identities.

The important thing about such identities is that they are multiple and fluid rather than singular and fixed. The identity I enact at the dance club on Friday night is not the same identity I enact at the office on Monday morning. The reason for this is not that I change my personality in any fundamental way, but rather that I change the way I use language.

Language and other modes

Changing the way I use language when I enact the identity of a dance club diva or a yoga teacher or a university professor, of course, is not enough to fully enact these identities. I also have to dress in certain ways, act in certain ways and hang out in certain places with certain people. In other words, language alone cannot achieve all the things I need to do to be a certain kind of person. I always have to combine that language with other things such as fashion, gestures and the handling of various kinds of objects.

Partially because of its roots in linguistics, discourse analysts used to focus almost exclusively on written or spoken language. Now, people are increasingly realising not just that we communicate in a lot of ways that do not involve language, but that in order to understand what people mean when they use language, we need to pay attention to the way it is combined with other communicative **modes** such as pictures, gestures, music and the layout of furniture.

So what good is discourse analysis?

Given these four principles, we can begin to understand some of the reasons why learning how to analyse discourse might be useful. The chief reason is that we *already* engage in discourse analysis all the time when we try to figure out what people mean by what they say and when we try to express our multiple and complicated meanings to them. Much of what you learn in this book will be about making processes that already take place beneath the surface of your consciousness more explicit. But what is the point of that, you might ask, if all of this communication and interpretation is going on so smoothly without us having to attend to it? The fact is, however, it is not. None of us is immune to misunderstandings, to offending people by saying the wrong thing, to struggling to get our message across, or to being taken in by someone who is trying somehow to cheat us. Hopefully, by understanding how discourse works, we will be able to understand people better and communicate more effectively.

Studying discourse analysis, however, can teach you more than that. Since the way we use discourse is tied up with our social identities and our social relationships, discourse analysis can help us to understand how the societies in which we live are put together and how they are maintained through our day-to-day activities of speaking, writing and making use of other modes of communication. It can help us to understand why people interact with one another the way they do and how they exert power and influence over one another. It can help us to understand how people view reality differently and why they view it that way. The study of discourse analysis, then, is not just the study of how we use language. It is also indirectly the study of politics, power, psychology, romance and a whole lot of other things.

👁 **Look deeper into why people don't say what they mean or mean what they say online.**

TEXTS AND TEXTURE

Discourse analysts analyse 'texts' and 'conversations'. But what is a 'text' and what is a 'conversation'? What distinguishes texts and conversations from random collections of sentences and utterances? These are the questions taken up in this section. For now we will mostly be considering written texts. Conversations will be dealt with in later units.

Consider the following list of words:

- ❏ milk
- ❏ spaghetti
- ❏ tomatoes
- ❏ rocket
- ❏ light bulbs.

You might look at this list and conclude that this is not a text for the simple reason that it 'makes no sense' to you – that it has no **meaning**. According to the linguist M.A.K. Halliday, meaning is the most important thing that makes a text a text; it has to *make sense*. A text, in his view, is everything that is meaningful in a particular situation. And the basis for *meaning* is *choice* (Halliday, 1978: 137). Whenever I choose one thing rather than another from a set of alternatives (yes or no, up or down, red or green), I am making meaning. This focus on meaning, in fact, is one of the main things that distinguishes Halliday's brand of linguistics from that of other linguists who are concerned chiefly with linguistic *forms*. Historically, the study of linguistics, he points out (1994: xiv), first involved studying the way the language was put together (syntax and morphology) *followed by* the study of meaning. In his view, however, the reverse approach is more useful. As he puts it, 'A language is . . . *a system of meanings*, accompanied by forms through which the meanings can be expressed' [emphasis mine].

So one way you can begin to make sense of the list of words above is to consider them as a series of choices. In other words, I wrote 'milk' instead of 'juice' and 'spaghetti' instead of 'linguini'. There must be some reason for this. You will still probably not be able to recognise this as a text because you do not have any understanding of what motivated these choices (why I wrote down these particular words) and the relationship between one set of choices (e.g. 'milk' vs. 'juice') and another.

It is these two pieces of missing information – the *context* of these choices and the *relationships* between them – which form the basis for what is known as **texture** – that quality that makes a particular set of words or sentences a *text* rather than a random collection of linguistic items. A language speaker's 'ability to discriminate between a random string of sentences and one forming a discourse', Halliday explains, 'is due to the inherent texture in the language and to his awareness of it' (Halliday 1968: 210). According to this formulation, there are two important things that make a text a text. One has to do with features inherent in the language itself (things, for example, such as grammatical 'rules'), which help us to understand the relationship among the different words and sentences and other elements in the text. It is these features that help you to figure out the relationship between the various sets of choices (either lexical or grammatical) that you encounter. The problem with the text above is that there is not much in the language itself that helps you to do this. There are, however, two very basic things that help you to establish a connection among these words. The first is the fact that they appear in a list – they come one after another. This very fact helps to connect them together because you automatically think that they would not have been put together in the same list if they did not have something to do with one another.

Another 'internal' thing that holds these words together as a potential text is that they are similar; with the exception of 'light bulbs', they all belong to the same *semantic field* (i.e. words having to do with food). In fact, It is because of words such as 'milk' and 'tomatoes' that you are able to infer that what is meant by the word 'rocket' is 'rocket lettuce' (or *arugula*) rather than the kind of rocket that shoots satellites into space. This semantic relationship among the words, however, is probably still not enough for you to make sense of this list as a text as long as you are relying only on features that are intrinsic to the language. The reason for this is that there are no grammatical elements that join these words together. It would be much easier for you to understand the relationship among these words if they appeared in a conversation like this:

A: What do we need to get at the shop?
B: Well, we need some milk. And I want to make a salad, so let's get some tomatoes and rocket. And, oh yeah, the light bulb in the living room is burnt out. We'd better get some new ones.

In this conversation, the relationship between the different words is much clearer because new words have been added. One important word that joins these words together is 'and', which creates an *additive* relationship among them, indicating that they are all part of a cumulative list. Other important words are 'we' and 'need'. The verb 'need' connects the things in the list to some kind of *action* that is associated with them and the word 'we' connects them to some people who are also involved in this action.

This second part of Halliday's formulation has to do with something that cannot be found in the language itself, but rather exists inside the minds of the people who are perceiving the text, what Halliday calls an *awareness* of the conventions of the language (and, by extension, broader conventions of communication in a given society) which helps us to work out the relationships among words, sentences, paragraphs, pictures and other textual elements, as well as relationships between these combinations of textual elements and certain social situations or communicative purposes. These conventions give us a kind of 'framework' within which we can fit the language. The framework for the text above, for example, is 'a shopping list'. As soon as you have that framework, this list of words makes perfect sense as a text. In fact, you do not even need to refer back to the conversation above to understand what the text means and how it will be used. All of the information about what people do with shopping lists is already part of your **common knowledge** (the knowledge you share with other people in society).

There is still one more thing that helps you to make sense of this as a text, and that has to do with the connections that exist between this particular collection of words and other texts that exist outside of it. For example, this text might be related to the conversation above. In fact, it might be the result of that conversation: 'A' might have written down this list as 'B' dictated it to him or her. It might also be related to other texts, like a recipe for rocket salad 'B' found in a cookbook. Finally, when A and B go to the supermarket, they will connect this text to still other texts like signs advertising the price of tomatoes or the label on the milk carton telling them the expiry date. In other words, all texts are somehow related to other texts, and sometimes, in order to make sense of them or use them to perform social actions, you need to make reference to these other texts.

To sum up, the main thing that makes a text a text is *relationships* or *connections*. Sometimes these relationships are between words, sentences or other elements *inside* the text. These kinds of relationships create what we refer to as **cohesion**. Another kind of relationship exists between the text and the person who is reading it or using it in some way. Here, meaning comes chiefly from the background knowledge the person has about certain social conventions regarding texts as well as the social situation in which the text is found and what the person wants to do with the text. This kind of relationship creates what we call **coherence**. Finally, there is the relationship between one text and other texts in the world that one might, at some point, need to refer to in the process of making sense of this text. This kind of relationship creates what we call **intertextuality**.

👁 **Look deeper into what makes a text a text online.**

TEXTS AND THEIR SOCIAL FUNCTIONS   A3

In the previous unit I talked about how the internal structure of a text and the expectations we have about it contribute to a text's *texture*. In this section I will explore how the structures and expectations associated with different kinds of texts contribute to how they function in the social world – how they help to define social activities and the groups of people who take part in them.

Different patterns of texture are associated with different types of text. Newspaper articles, for example, tend to favour particular kinds of cohesive devices and are structured in a conventional way with a summary of the main points in the beginning and the details coming later (see C2). To understand why such textual conventions are associated with this type of text, however, we need to understand something about the people who produce and consume it and what they are *doing* with it. The study of the social functions of different kinds of texts is called **genre analysis**.

The notion of **genre** is probably familiar to you from your experience as a movie-goer. Different films belong to different genres: there are westerns, love stories, horror movies, thrillers, 'chick flicks' and many other film genres. Before we go to the movies, we always have some idea about the film we are about to see based on the genre that it belongs to. These expectations include ideas about the kind of story the film will tell and the kinds of characters it will include. At the same time, of course, not all films fit neatly into genres. We might go to a film called *Scary Movie* and find that it is actually a comedy, or we might expect a film like *Brokeback Mountain*, whose poster portrays cowboys, to be a western, only to find that it is also a love story. In fact, one thing that makes such films so successful is that they creatively confound our expectations by mixing different genres together.

The notion of *genre* in discourse analysis goes beyond examining the conventional structures and features of different kinds of texts to asking what these structures and features can tell us about the people who use the texts and what they are using them to do. Bhatia (1993: 13) defines genre as follows:

> (A genre is) a recognisable communicative *event* characterised by a set of *communicative purposes* identified and mutually understood by members of the community in which it occurs. Most often it is highly structured and *conventionalised* with *constraints* on allowable contributions in terms of their intent, positioning, form and functional value. These constraints, however, are often *exploited by expert members* of the discourse community to achieve private intentions within the framework of the socially recognised purpose(s). [emphasis mine]

There are three important aspects to this definition which need to be further explained: first, that genres are not defined as types of text but rather as types of **communicative event**; second, that these events are characterised by **constraints** on what can and cannot be done within them; and third, that *expert* users often *exploit* these constraints in creative and unexpected ways.

Genres are communicative events

While it might not seem unusual to refer to spoken genres such as conversations and debates and political speeches as 'events', thinking of written texts such as newspaper articles, recipes and job application letters as 'events' might at first seem rather strange. We are in many ways accustomed to thinking of texts as 'objects'. Seeing them as 'events', however, highlights the fact that all texts are basically instances of people doing things with or to other people: a newspaper article is an instance of someone *informing* someone else about some recent event; a recipe is an instance of someone *instructing* another person how to prepare a particular kind of food; and a job application letter is an instance of someone *requesting* that another person give him or her a job. As Martin (1985: 250) points out, 'genres are how things get done, when language is used to accomplish them'.

Of course, most texts are not just trying to get only one thing done. The **communicative purposes** of texts are often multiple and complex. A recipe, for example, may be *persuading* you to make a certain dish (or to buy a certain product with which to make it) as much as it is *instructing* you how to do it, and a newspaper article might be attempting not just to *inform* you about a particular event, but also to somehow affect your opinion about it. The different people using the text might also have different purposes in mind: while a job applicant sees his or her application letter as a way to convince a prospective employer to hire him or her, the employer might see the very same application letter as a means of 'weeding out' unsuitable candidates.

Conventions and constraints

Because genres are about 'getting things done', the way they are structured and the kinds of features they contain are largely determined by what people want to do with them. The kinds of information I might include in a job application, for example, would be designed to convince a prospective employer that I am the right person for the job. This information would probably not include my recipe for chocolate brownies or my opinion about some event I read about in a newspaper. Genres, therefore, come with 'built-in' *constraints* as to what kinds of things they can include and what kinds of things they cannot, based on the activity they are trying to accomplish.

These constraints govern not just *what* can be included, but also *how* it should be included. In my job application letter, for example, I would probably want to present the information in a certain order, beginning by indicating the post I am applying for, and then going on to describe my qualifications and experience, and ending by requesting an appointment for an interview. Putting this information in a different order, for example, waiting until the end of the letter to indicate the post for which I am applying, would be considered odd. The order in which I do things in a genre, what in genre analysis is called the '**move structure**' of a particular genre, often determines how successfully I am able to fulfil the communicative purpose of the genre.

But what is important about these conventions and constraints is not only that they make communicative events more efficient, but also that they demonstrate that the person who produced the text knows 'how we do things'. Prospective employers read application letters not just to find out what post an applicant is applying for and what qualifications or experience that person has, but also to find out if that person knows how to write a job application letter. In other words, the ability to successfully produce this type of genre following particular conventions is taken as an indication that the writer is a 'certain kind of person' who 'knows how to communicate like us'. In fact, for some employers, the qualifications that applicants demonstrate through successfully producing this genre are far more important than those they describe in the letter itself.

Creativity

That is not to say that all job application letters, or other genres such as newspaper articles and recipes, are always exactly the same. As the 'hybrid' films described above tell us, often the most successful texts are those which defy conventions and push the boundaries of constraints. Expert producers of texts, for example, sometimes mix different kinds of text together, or embed one genre into another, or alter the moves that are included or the order in which they are presented. Of course, there are limitations to how much a genre can be altered and still be successful at accomplishing what its producers want to accomplish. There are always risks associated with being creative.

There are several important points to be made here. The first is that such creativity would not be possible without the existence of conventions and constraints, and the reason innovations can be effective is that they exploit previously formed expectations. The second is that such creativity must itself have some relationship to the communicative purpose of the genre and the context in which it is used. Writing a job application letter in the form of a sonnet, for example, may be more effective if I want to get a job as an editor at a literary magazine than if I want to get a job as a software engineer. Finally, being able to successfully defy convention is very much a matter of and a marker of expertise: in order to break the rules effectively, you must also be able to show that you have mastered the rules.

Discourse communities

It should be clear by now that at the centre of the concept of genre is the idea of *belonging*. We produce and use genres not just in order to get things done, but also to show ourselves to be members of particular groups and to demonstrate that we are qualified to participate in particular activities. Genres are always associated with certain groups of people that have certain common goals and common ways of reaching these goals.

John Swales calls these groups **discourse communities**. In the excerpt from his book *Genre Analysis* (1990) which is included in D3, he describes a number of features that define discourse communities, among which are that they consist of 'expert' members whose job it is to socialise new members into 'how things are done', that members have ways of regularly communicating with and providing feedback to one another, and that members tend to share a certain vocabulary or 'jargon'. The two most important characteristics of discourse communities are that members have common goals and common means of reaching those goals (genres). These goals and the means of reaching them work to reinforce each other. Every time a member makes use of a particular genre, he or she not only moves the group closer to the shared goals, but also validates these goals as worthy and legitimate and shows him or herself to be a worthy and legitimate member of the group.

Thus, genres not only link people together, they also link people with certain activities, identities, roles and responsibilities. In a very real way, then, genres help to regulate and control what people can do and who people can 'be' in various contexts.

This regulation and control is exercised in a number of ways. First of all, since the goals of the community and the ways those goals are to be accomplished are 'built in' to the texts that members of a discourse community use on a daily basis, it becomes much more difficult to question those goals. Since mastery of the genre is a requirement for membership, members must also 'buy into' the goals of the community. Finally, since texts always create certain kinds of relationships between those who have produced them and those who are using them, when the conventions and constraints associated with texts become fixed and difficult to change, these roles and relationships also become fixed and difficult to change. When looked at in this way, genres are not just 'text types' that are structured in certain ways; they are important tools through which people, groups and institutions define, organise and structure social life.

👁 **Look deeper into the idea of discourse communities online.**

DISCOURSE AND IDEOLOGY   A4

In the last two units I looked at the ways texts are structured and the social functions they fulfil for different groups of people. In this section I will examine how texts promote certain points of view or versions of reality. I will focus on four things:

1   the ways authors create 'versions of reality' based on their choice of words and how they combine words together;
2   the ways authors construct certain kinds of relationship between themselves and their readers;
3   the ways authors appropriate the words of other people and how they represent those words; and
4   the ways authors of texts draw upon and reinforce the larger systems of belief and knowledge that govern what counts as right or wrong, good or bad, and normal or abnormal in a particular society.

Whether we are aware of it or not, our words are never neutral. They always represent the world in a certain way and create certain kinds of relationship with the people with whom we are communicating. For this reason, texts always to some degree promote a particular **ideology**. An *ideology* is a specific set of beliefs and assumptions people have about things such as what is good and bad, what is right and wrong, and what is normal and abnormal. Ideologies provide us with models of how the world is 'supposed to be'. In some respects ideologies help to create a shared worldview and sense of purpose among people in a particular group. Ideologies also limit the way we look at reality and tend to marginalise or exclude altogether people, things and ideas that do not fit into these models.

All texts, even those that seem rather innocuous or banal, somehow involve these systems of inclusion and exclusion. Often when you fill out a form, such as a university application form, for example, or an application for a driver's licence, you are asked to indicate whether you are married or single. One thing that this question does is reinforce the idea that your marital status is an important aspect of your identity (although it may have very little bearing on whether or not you are qualified to either study in university or drive a car). Another thing it does is limit this aspect of your identity to one of only two choices. Other choices such as divorced, widowed or in a civil partnership are often not offered, nor are choices having to do with other important relationships in your life, such as your relationship with your parents or your siblings. In China, such forms often ask this question slightly differently, offering the categories of 結婚 ('married') or 未婚 ('single', or literally 'not yet married'). These two choices not only exclude people in the kinds of relationships mentioned above but also people such as Buddhist monks and 'confirmed bachelors' who have no intention of getting married. They also promote the idea that being married is somehow the 'natural' or 'normal' state of affairs.

In such cases, it is fair to ask how much you are answering questions about yourself, and how much the forms themselves are constructing you as a certain kind of person by enabling some choices and constraining others. In other words, are you filling out the form, or is the form filling out you?

'Whos doing whats'

The linguist Michael Halliday (1994) pointed out that whenever we use language we are always doing three things at once: we are in some way representing the world, which he called the **ideational** function of language; we are creating, ratifying or negotiating our relationships with the people with whom we are communicating, which he called the **interpersonal** function of language; and we are joining sentences and ideas together in particular ways to form cohesive and coherent texts, which he called the **textual** function of language. All of these functions play a role in the way a text promotes a particular ideology or worldview. In A2 we looked at the *textual* function, discussing how different ways of connecting ideas together and of structuring them based on larger sets of expectations help us to make sense of texts, but can also reinforce certain assumptions about people, things and ideas and how they are linked together. In this section the *ideational* and the *interpersonal* functions of language will be the focus.

According to Halliday, we represent the world through language by choosing words that represent people, things or concepts (**participants**), and words about what these participants are *doing* to, with, or for one another (**processes**). All texts contain these two elements: *participants* and *processes*. James Paul Gee (2010) calls them 'whos doing whats'.

Rather than talking about texts representing reality, however, it might be better to talk about texts 'constructing' reality, since, depending on the words they choose to represent the 'whos doing whats' in a particular situation, people can create very different impressions of what is going on. First of all, we might choose different words to represent the same kinds of participant. In traditional church wedding ceremonies in many places, for example, the convener of the ceremony (often a priest or a minister), after the couple have taken their vows, will pronounce them 'man and wife'. By using different kinds of words to describe the groom and the bride, this utterance portrays them as two different kinds of people, and as fundamentally unequal. This choice of words gives to the 'man' an independent identity, but makes the woman's (the 'wife's') identity contingent on her relationship to the man. Nowadays, many churches have changed their liturgies to make this 'I now pronounce you husband and wife' in order to present the two individuals as more equal.

The words we use for processes and how we use them to link participants together can also create different impressions of what is going on. One of the key things about *processes* is that they always construct a certain kind of *relationship* between participants. Halliday calls this relationship **transitivity**. An important aspect of transitivity when it comes to ideology has to do with which participants are portrayed as performing actions and which are portrayed as having actions performed to or for them. In the same kinds of traditional church weddings described above, after pronouncing the couple 'man and wife' the convener might turn to the man and say, 'you may now kiss the bride'. Making the male participant the *actor* in the process (kissing) constructs him as the person 'in charge' of the situation, and the woman as a passive recipient of his kiss, thus reinforcing many assumptions about the roles of men and women, especially in romantic and sexual relationships, which are still deeply held in some societies. As with the statement 'I now pronounce you man and wife', in many places this has changed in recent years, with the couple either simply kissing after the declaration of marriage or the convener saying something like 'you may now kiss each other'.

Relationships

Another important way texts promote ideology is in the *relationships* they create between the people who are communicating, what Halliday calls the *interpersonal* function of language. We construct relationships through words we choose to express– things such as certainty and obligation (known as the system of **modality** in a language). The traditional priest or minister described above, for example, typically says 'you may now kiss the bride', rather than 'kiss the bride!', constructing the action as a matter of permission rather than obligation and constructing himself or herself as someone who is there to assist them in doing what they want to do rather than to force them to do things they do not want to do.

Another way we use language to construct relationships is through the style of speaking or writing that we choose. To take the example of the convener of the wedding ceremony again, he or she says, 'you many now kiss the bride', rather than something such as 'why don't you give her a kiss!' This use of more formal language helps create a relationship of respectful distance between the couple and the convener and maintains an air of seriousness in the occasion.

Halliday sees the degree of 'formality' of language as a matter of what he calls **register**, the different ways we use language in different situations depending on the topic we are communicating about, the people with whom we are communicating, and the channel through which we are communicating (e.g. formal writing, instant messaging, face-to-face conversation) (see A7).

Like genres, registers tend to communicate that we are 'certain kinds of people' and show something about the relationships we have with the people with whom we are communicating. Most people, for instance, use a different register when they are talking or writing to their boss than when they are talking or writing to their peers. The American discourse analyst James Paul Gee refers to these different ways of speaking and writing as **social languages** (see D4).

Intertextuality

As I have mentioned before, texts often refer to or somehow depend for their meaning on other texts. We called the relationship texts create with other texts *intertextuality*, and intertextuality is another important way ideologies are promoted in discourse.

According to the Russian literary critic Mikhail Bakhtin, all texts involve some degree of intertextuality. We cannot speak or write, he argues, without borrowing the words and ideas of other people, and nearly everything we say or write is in some way a response to some previous utterance or text and an anticipation of some future one.

When we appropriate the words and ideas of others in our texts and utterances, we almost always end up communicating how we think about those words and ideas (and the people who have said or written them) in the way we represent them. We might, for example, quote them verbatim, paraphrase them, or refer to them in an indirect way, and we might characterise them in certain ways using different 'reporting' words such as 'said', or 'insisted', or 'claimed'.

In the 1980s the British singer Sir Elton John sang a song called 'Kiss the Bride' in which the singer talks about attending the wedding of his old girlfriend for whom he still has romantic feelings. In the 'version of reality' constructed by this song, the words 'I wanna kiss the bride' refer to the convener of a marriage ceremony saying to the groom 'you may now kiss the bride'. While the singer appropriates verbatim the words of the convener, by positioning himself as the 'kisser' of a bride who is not 'his', he transforms these words, using them to undermine rather than ratify the marriage that is being performed.

Intertextuality does not just involve mixing other people's words with ours. It can also involve mixing genres (see section A3) and mixing social languages. In the excerpt from James Paul Gee reprinted in section D4, for example, he examines how the authors of the label on an aspirin bottle mix together different social languages.

Discourses

It should be quite clear by now that even a seemingly innocent phrase such as 'you may now kiss the bride' can be seen as *ideological*. That is to say, it promotes what James Paul Gee calls **cultural models** (see B2) – 'frozen theories' or generalisations about the world and how people should behave, in this case generalisations about brides and grooms and men and women and how they are supposed to act in the context of marriage. Cultural models serve an important role in helping us make sense of the texts and the situations that we encounter in our lives. At the same time, however, they also function to exclude certain people or certain ways of behaving from our consideration.

Cultural models are not random and free floating. They are parts of larger systems of knowledge, values and social relationships that grow up within societies and cultures which Gee calls '**Discourses**' (with a capital 'D'). Other people have used different terms. The French philosopher Michel Foucault calls these systems '**orders of discourse**', and gives as examples things such as 'clinical discourse, economic discourse, the discourse of natural history, psychiatric discourse' (1972: 121).

The phrase 'you may now kiss the bride', then, does not just reinforce a theory about how brides and grooms are supposed to act *during* a marriage ceremony, but also invokes broader theories about marriage gender relations, love, sex, morality and economics. All of these theories are part of a system of discourse which we might call the 'discourse of marriage'.

According to Foucault, 'discourses' can exert a tremendous power over us by creating constraints regarding how certain things can be talked about and what counts as 'knowledge' in particular contexts. At the same time, it is also important to remember that discourses are complex and often contain internal contradictions. They also change over time. In pre-nineteenth-century Europe, for example, the strongest values promoted in the discourse of marriage were those of duty and commitment. Most marriages were arranged and divorce was illegal in many countries. The contemporary discourse of marriage in Europe and many other places has changed considerably, emphasising more the values of love and personal fulfilment.

👁 **Look deeper into ideology, cultural models and discourses online.**

SPOKEN DISCOURSE   A5

So far we have been focusing mostly on the analysis of written texts. In this section we will begin to consider some of the special aspects of spoken discourse. In many ways, speech is not so different from writing. When people speak they also produce different kinds of *genres* (such as casual conversations, debates, lectures and speeches of various kinds) and use different kinds of *registers* or *social languages*. They also promote particular versions of reality or *ideologies*. But there are some ways in which speech is very different from writing.

First of all, speech is more interactive. While we do often expect and receive feedback for our writing, especially when it comes to new media genres such as blogs, this feedback is usually delayed. When we speak we usually do so in 'real time' with other people, and we receive their responses to what we have said right away. As we carry on conversations, we decide what to say based on what the previous speaker has said as well as what we expect the subsequent speaker to say after we have finished speaking. We can even alter what we are saying as we go along based on how other people seem to be reacting to it. Similarly, listeners can let us know immediately whether they object to, or do not understand, what we are saying. In other words, conversations are always *co-constructed* between or among the different parties having them.

Second, speech tends to be more transient and spontaneous than writing. When we write, we often plan what we are going to write carefully, and we often read over, revise and edit what we have written before showing it to other people. Because writing has a certain 'permanence', people can also read what we have written more carefully. They can read it quickly or slowly, and they can re-read it as many times as they like. They can also show it to other people and get their opinions about it. Speech, on the other hand, is usually not as well planned as writing. While some genres such as formal speeches and lectures are planned, most casual conversation is just made up as we go along. It is also transient; that is to say, our words usually disappear the moment we utter them. This makes listening in some ways more challenging than reading. Unless our words are recorded, people cannot return to them, save them or transport them into other contexts. While they might be able to remember what we have said and repeat it to other people, it is never exactly the same as what we have actually said.

Finally, speech tends to be less explicit than writing. The reason for this is that when we are speaking, we often also depend on other methods of getting our message across. We communicate with our gaze, our gestures, our facial expressions and the tone of our voice. When we are writing we do not have these tools at our disposal, and so we often need to depend more on the words themselves to express our meaning. Speech also usually takes place in some kind of physical context which participants share, and often the meaning of what we say is dependent on this context. We can use words such as 'this' and 'that' and 'here' and 'there' and expect that the people we are speaking to can understand what we are talking about based on the physical environment in which the conversation takes place.

Of course, there are many kinds of speech that do not share all of the features we have discussed above. People engaged in telephone conversations, for example, like readers and writers, are situated in different places and cannot rely on physical cues such as gestures and facial expressions to convey meaning, although their conversations are still interactive. When people speak to us through television and cinema, on the other hand, while we can see their gestures and facial expressions, we cannot usually respond to what they are saying in real time. There are also certain kinds of conversations that share features of both speech and writing. Instant messaging and text-based computer chats, for example, are, like speech, interactive and usually fairly unplanned, while at the same time, like writing, they involve a certain amount of permanence (the words we write remain in chat windows for some time after we have written them and may be stored as 'history files'). They also lack the non-verbal cues that are part of physical co-presence. This type of mediated communication will be considered later. In this unit the focus is mainly on real-time, face-to-face interaction.

Making sense of conversations

The main problem that people have when communicating with spoken discourse is that quite often *people do not mean what they say, and people do not say what they mean*. In the first unit we gave the example of someone asking to borrow a pen with the words 'Do you have a pen?' and pointed out that, strictly speaking, this utterance is really a question about whether or not someone possesses a pen rather than a request to borrow one. Similarly, in the comic strip below (Figure A5.1), when Calvin's mother says 'What are you doing to the coffee table?!' she is not so much asking a question as she is expressing shock and disapproval – offering a rebuke. The humour in Calvin's response lies in the fact that he has taken her utterance to be a question rather than a rebuke. Interestingly, we regard Calvin, who operates on the principle that people should mean what they say, as the uncooperative party in this conversation rather than his mother, who, strictly speaking, does not say what she means.

Figure A5.1 Calvin and Hobbes (© 1985 Watterson. Dist. by Universal Uclick. Reprinted with permission. All rights reserved.)

Although there is also a certain amount of ambiguity in written language, this problem is much more common in spoken language due in part to its inexplicit, context-specific nature. And so, the problem is, if people do not say what they mean or mean what they say, how are we able to successfully engage in conversations with one another?

This problem is exasperated by the fact that we have to make decisions about what we think people mean rather quickly in conversations in order for the conversations to proceed smoothly, which increases the chances for misunderstanding.

In order to understand how conversation participants deal with this problem, I will be drawing on two different analytical traditions, one with its roots in philosophy and the other with its roots in sociology. These two traditions are called **pragmatics** and **conversation analysis**.

Pragmatics is the study of how people use words to accomplish actions in their conversations: actions such as requesting, threatening and apologising. It aims to help us understand how people figure out what actions other people are trying to take with their words and respond appropriately. It has its roots primarily in the work of three philosophers of language: Herbert Paul Grice, John Austin and John Searle.

Conversation analysis, on the other hand, comes out of a tradition in sociology called ethnomethodology, which focuses on the 'methods' ordinary members of a society use to interact with one another and interpret their experience. It was developed by three sociologists, Harvey Sacks, Emanuel Schegloff and Gail Jefferson, and studies the procedural rules that people use to cooperatively manage conversations and make sense of what is going on.

Because these two analytical frameworks come out of such different intellectual traditions, they approach the problem discussed above in two very different ways. With its roots in philosophy, *pragmatics* tends to approach the problem as a matter of *logic*, asking what conditions need to be present for a participant in a conversation to logically conclude that a given utterance has a certain meaning (or pragmatic 'force'). With its roots in sociology, conversation analysis approaches the problem not as one of abstract logic, but as one of locally contingent action. According to this perspective, people make sense of what other people say not by 'figuring it out' logically, but by paying attention to the local conditions of the conversation itself, especially the sequence of utterances.

Rather than being mutually exclusive, these two approaches represent two different windows on the phenomenon of conversation, with each illuminating a different aspect of it. In the units that follow, even more perspectives will be introduced that focus on different aspects of spoken interaction. Taking these various perspectives together will lead to a rich and comprehensive understanding of what people are doing when they engage in conversation and how they cope with the unique challenges of spoken discourse as well as more interactive written discourse such as some forms of computer-mediated communication.

👁 **Look deeper into the differences between pragmatics and conversation analysis online.**

A6 STRATEGIC INTERACTION

When we have conversations with others, we are always engaged in some kind of activity – we are arguing, or flirting, or commiserating, or gossiping, or doing other things with our conversations, and a big part of understanding what somebody means is understanding what he or she is 'doing' and what is 'going on' in the social situation that the conversation is part of. At the same time, we also use conversations to show that we are certain kinds of people and to establish and maintain certain kinds of relationships with the people with whom we are talking. Understanding who somebody is 'trying to be' in a conversation is also an important part of understanding what they mean by what they say.

We do not, however, engage in these activities and construct these identities all by ourselves. We must always negotiate 'what we are doing' and 'who we are being' with the people with whom we are interacting. The methods we use to engage in these negotiations are called **conversational strategies**.

In this unit we will focus on two basic kinds of conversational strategies: **face strategies** and **framing strategies**. Face strategies have to do primarily with showing who we are and what kind of relationship we have with the people with whom we are talking. Framing strategies have more to do with showing what we are doing in the conversation, whether we are, for example, arguing, teasing, flirting or gossiping.

These two concepts for analysing how we manage conversations come from an approach to discourse known as **interactional sociolinguistics**, which is concerned with the sometimes very subtle ways people signal and interpret what they think they are doing and who they think they are being in social interaction. It is grounded in the work of the anthropologist John Gumperz (1982a, 1982b) who drew on insights from anthropology and linguistics as well as the fields of pragmatics and conversation analysis which were introduced in the previous unit. One of the most important insights Gumperz had was that people belonging to different groups have different ways of signalling and interpreting cues about conversational identity and conversational activities, and this can sometimes result in misunderstandings and even conflict. Not surprisingly, interactional sociolinguistics has been used widely in studies of intercultural communication, including some of the early studies by Gumperz himself on communication between Anglo-British and South Asian immigrants to the UK.

Another important influence on interactional sociolinguistics comes from the American sociologist Erving Goffman, who, in his classic book *The Presentation of Self in Everyday Life* (1959), compared social interaction to a dramatic performance. Social actors in everyday life, he argued, like stage actors, use certain 'expressive equipment' such as costumes, props and settings to perform certain 'roles' and 'routines'. Our goal in these performances is to promote our particular 'line' or version of who we are and what is going on. Most of the time, other people help us to maintain our line, especially if we are willing to help them to maintain theirs. Sometimes, however, people's 'lines' are not entirely compatible, which means they need to negotiate an acceptable common 'line' or else risk spoiling the performance for one or more of the participants.

It was Goffman who contributed to discourse analysis the concepts of **face** and **frames**. By 'face' he meant 'the positive social value a person effectively claims for himself by the line others assume he has taken' (1967: 41). In other words, for Goffman a person's 'face' is tied up with how successful he or she is at 'pulling off' his or her performance and getting others to accept his or her 'line'. What he meant by 'frames' was 'definitions of a situation (that) are built up in accordance with principals of organisation which govern events'. The concept of 'framing' relates to how we negotiate these 'definitions of situations' with other people and use them as a basis for communicating and interpreting meaning.

Showing who we are: face strategies

Social identity is a complex topic and one that will be further explored in the coming units. For now the focus will be on one fundamental aspect of identity: the fact that our identities are always constructed *in relation to* the people with whom we are interacting. Some people are our friends, and others are complete strangers. Some people are our superiors and others are our subordinates. When we talk, along with conveying information about the topic about which we are talking, we always convey information about how close to or distant from the people with whom we are talking we think we are, along with information about whether we are social equals or whether one has more power than the other. The strategies we use to do this are called face strategies.

The concept of 'face' in its more everyday sense will be familiar to many readers. The term is often used to denote a person's honour or reputation. Many cultures have the notions of 'giving' people face (helping them to maintain a sense of dignity or honour) and of 'losing face' (when people, for some reason or another, suffer a loss of dignity or honour). Interactional sociolinguists, however, have a rather more specific definition of face. They define it as 'the negotiated public image mutually granted to each other by participants in a communicative event' (Scollon *et al.* 2012).

There are three important aspects to this definition: The first is that one's face is one's public image rather than one's 'true self'. This means that the social image that constitutes face is not the same in every interaction in which we engage. We 'wear' different faces for different people. The second important aspect of this definition is that this image is 'negotiated'. That is to say, it is always the result of a kind of 'give and take' with the person or people with whom we are interacting, and throughout a given interaction the image that we present and the images others project to us may undergo multiple adjustments. Finally, this image is 'mutually granted'. In other words, successfully presenting a certain face in interaction depends on the people with whom we are interacting cooperating with us. This is because face is the aspect of our identity which defines us *in relation* to others. If one person's idea of the relationship is different from the other person's idea, chances are one or the other will end up 'losing face'. And so, in this regard, the everyday ideas of 'giving face' and 'losing face' are also quite important in this more specialised definition of face.

There are basically two broad kinds of strategies we use to negotiate our identities and relationships in interaction. The first we will call **involvement strategies**. They are strategies we use to establish or maintain closeness with the people with whom we are interacting – to show them that we consider them our friends. These include things such as calling people by their first names or using nicknames, using informal language, showing interest in someone by, for example, asking personal questions, and emphasising our common experiences or points of view. While such strategies can be used to show friendliness – as we will see in the next section – they can also be used to assert power over people. Teachers, for example, often use such strategies when interacting with young students, and bosses sometimes use them when interacting with their employees.

The second class of face strategies is known as **independence strategies**. These are strategies we use to establish or maintain distance from the people with whom we are interacting either because we are not their friends, or, more commonly, because we wish to show them respect by not imposing on them. They include using more formal language and terms of address, trying to minimise the imposition, being indirect, apologising and trying to depersonalise the conversation (see Table A6.1).

These two kinds of face strategy correspond to two fundamentally and, in some ways, contradictory social needs that all humans experience: we all have the need to be liked (sometimes referred to as our **positive face**) and we all have the need to be respected (in the sense of not being imposed on or interfered with – sometimes referred to as our **negative face**). When we interact with others, we must constantly attend to their need to be liked and respected, and constantly protect our own need to be liked and respected (Brown and Levinson 1987). How we balance and negotiate these needs in communication is fundamental to the way we show who we are in relation to the people around us.

In any given interaction we are likely to use a combination of both of these strategies as we negotiate our relationships with the people with whom we are interacting. In section B we will go into more detail about how we decide which of these strategies to use, when and with whom.

Table A6.1 Face strategies

Involvement strategies	Independence strategies
Using first names or nicknames (*Hey, Rodders!*)	Using titles (*Good afternoon, Professor Jones.*)
Expressing interest (*What have you been up to lately?*)	Apologising (*I'm terribly sorry to bother you.*)
Claiming a common point of view (*I know exactly what you mean.*)	Admitting differences (*Of course, you know much more about it than I do.*)
Making assumptions (*I know you love lots of sugar in your coffee.*)	Not making assumptions (*How would you like your coffee today?*)
Using informal language (*Gotta minute?*)	Using formal language (*Pardon me, can you spare a few moments?*)
Being direct (*Will you come?*)	Being indirect and hedging (*I wonder if you might possibly drop by.*)
Being optimistic (*I'm sure you'll have a great time.*)	Being pessimistic (*I'm afraid you'll find it a bit boring.*)
Being voluble (talking a lot)	Being taciturn (not talking much)
Talking about 'us'	Talking about things other than 'us'

Showing what we are doing: framing strategies

In order to understand one another, we have to interpret what other people say in the context of some kind of overall activity in which we are mutually involved. One could think of many examples of utterances whose meanings change based on what the people are doing when they utter them. The meaning of the utterance by a doctor of the phrase, 'please take off your clothes' is different if uttered in the context of a medical examination or in the context of his or her apartment. For different kinds of activities we have different sets of expectations about what kinds of things will be said and how those things ought to be interpreted. We call these sets of expectations *frames*.

Goffman took his idea of frames from the work of the anthropologist Gregory Bateson, who used it to explain the behaviour of monkeys he had observed at the zoo. Sometimes, he noticed, the monkeys displayed hostile signals, seemingly fighting with, or attempting to bite, one another. It soon became clear to him, however, that the monkeys were not actually fighting; they were playing. It then occurred to him that they must have some way of communicating to one another how a particular display of aggression should be interpreted, whether as an invitation to fight or an invitation to play.

We bring to most interactions a set of expectations about the overall activity in which we will be engaged, which Goffman called the **primary framework** of the interaction. When we are a patient in a medical examination, for example, we expect that the doctor will touch us, and we interpret this behaviour as a method for diagnosing our particular medical problem. When we attend a lecture, we do so with an idea of what the activities of delivering a lecture and of listening to a lecture involve.

Interaction, however, hardly ever involves just one activity. We often engage in a variety of different activities within the primary framework. While lecturing, for example, a lecturer might give explanations, tell jokes or even rebuke members of the audience if they are not paying attention. Similarly, medical examinations might include multiple frames. In the reading in D6, for example, Deborah Tannen and Cynthia Wallat analyse how a doctor uses a 'playing' frame while examining a young child, and then switches back to a 'consultation' frame when talking with the child's mother. These smaller, more local frames are called **interactive frames**. When we are interacting with people, we often change what we are doing within the broader primary framework and, like Bateson's monkeys, we need ways to signal these 'frame changes' and ways to negotiate them with the people with whom we are interacting.

👁 **Look deeper into the work of Erving Goffman online.**

A7 **CONTEXT, CULTURE AND COMMUNICATION**

What is context?

By now it should be clear that what an utterance means and the effect it has on a hearer depends crucially on the circumstances under which it is uttered. The different approaches to spoken discourse we have considered so far all focus on different aspects of these circumstances. Pragmatics focuses on the intentions of speakers and the immediate conditions under which utterances are produced (including the knowledge, goals and status of those who produce them). Conversation analysis takes a rather narrower view, focusing on how talk occurring immediately before and immediately after utterances creates the circumstances for particular meanings to be produced. Finally, interactional sociolinguistics examines how utterances are interpreted based on the relationship of the participants and what they think they are doing, which are negotiated using *face* strategies and *contextualisation cues*. In this section we will take a wider view of the circumstances in which conversations occur, taking into account broader aspects of the situation as well as the 'cultural' norms and expectations of the people involved.

The idea that the meaning of utterances depends on the **context** in which they are produced can be traced back to the anthropologist Bronislow Malinowski and his 1923 paper, 'The problem of meaning in primitive languages', in which he argued that we cannot understand the words spoken by members of societies very different from our own through mere translation. We must also have an understanding of the situation in which the words were spoken and the significance of various relationships and activities in that situation to the speakers. In other words, meaning is transmitted not just through words, but through the ways words are embedded into social relationships, social goals and activities, histories, and the beliefs, values and ideologies of a particular cultural group.

The problem with this idea is determining exactly which aspects of the situation or of 'cultural knowledge' need to be taken into account in the production and interpretation of utterances. 'Context' could mean practically anything from the place and time of day of an utterance, to the colour of the clothing that the speakers are wearing, to speakers' political views or religious beliefs. How does the discourse analyst figure out which aspects of context are relevant to the production and interpretation of discourse and which are not? More to the point, how do people immersed in conversation figure this out?

Since Malinowksi, a number of scholars have proposed models to address this question. The linguist John Firth (1957), for example, proposed that context can be divided into three components:

1   the relevant features of participants, persons, personalities;
2   the relevant objects in the situation;
3   the effect of the verbal action.

Although Firth's formulation highlights what are undoubtedly central aspects of context, one nevertheless wonders why some elements are included and others are not. Why, for example, is the setting or time not part of his model? Furthermore, while one of the most important aspects of Firth's model is his insight that only those things that are 'relevant' to the communication being analysed should be considered context, he does not fully explain how such relevance is to be established.

Perhaps the most famous model of context is that developed by the linguist Michael Halliday, whose ideas about the structure of texts and the functions of language were discussed in units A2 and A4. Halliday, drawing heavily on the work of both Malinowski and Firth, also proposed a three-part model of context. For him, context consists of:

1   field: the social action that is taking place;
2   tenor: the participants, their roles and relationships;
3   mode: the symbolic or rhetorical channel and the role which language plays in the situation.

It is these three aspects of context, Halliday says, that chiefly determine the *register* people use when they speak or write (see A4).

Halliday's model of context, however, suffers some of the same problems as Firth's: without clearer definitions of the three categories, the analyst is unsure where to fit in things such as the social identities of participants and their membership in certain social groups (are these subsumed under 'role' or can they be seen as part of field?), or why things such as the physical mode (or channel), the rhetorical form (or genre) and the role language plays in the situation should be subsumed under the same category (van Dijk 2008). Furthermore, like Firth, he fails to fully address the issue of exactly what makes some contextual features 'relevant' to speakers and others not.

Context and competence

Halliday explains context from an essentially linguistic point of view, seeing it as part of a language's system of 'meaning potential'. 'There is no need to bring in the question of what the speaker knows,' he writes; 'the background to what he does is *what he could do – a potential*, which is objective, not a competence, which is subjective' (1978: 38, emphasis mine). In sharp contrast to this position is that of the linguistic anthropologist Dell Hymes, for whom the notion of 'competence' is central to a model of context he called **the ethnography of speaking**, or, as it is sometimes called, **the ethnography of communication**.

In his work, Hymes focuses on the interaction between language and social life – the ways using and understanding language are related to wider social and cultural knowledge. Knowledge or mastery of the linguistic system alone, he insists, is not sufficient for successful communication. People also need to know and master various rules, norms and conventions regarding *what* to say to *whom, when, where* and *how* – which he calls **communicative competence**. He writes:

> The sharing of grammatical (variety) rules is not sufficient. There may be persons whose English I can grammatically identify but whose messages escape me. I may be ignorant of what counts as a coherent sequence, request, statement requiring an answer, requisite or forbidden topic, marking of emphasis or irony, normal duration of silence, normal level of voice, etc., and have no metacommunitative means or opportunity for discovering such things.
>
> (Hymes 1974: 49)

The question Hymes asks is: 'What kinds of things do participants in particular activities or *speech events* need to know in order to demonstrate that they are competent members of a particular *speech community*?' What he means by *speech community* is not just a group of people who speak the same language, but a group of people who share the rules and norms for using and interpreting at least one language variety *in particular contexts*.

Like Halliday and Firth, Hymes developed a model of what he considered to be the essential elements of context. Rather than just three components, however, Hymes's consists of eight, each component beginning with one of the letters of the word 'SPEAKING':

- ❏   S stands for *setting*
- ❏   P stands for *participants*
- ❏   E stands for *ends*
- ❏   A stands for *act sequence*
- ❏   K stands for *key*
- ❏   I stands for *instrumentalities*
- ❏   N stands for *norms of interaction*
- ❏   G stands for *genre*.

One might point out that, although Hymes's model seems more 'complete', it suffers from the same fundamental problem as those of Firth and Halliday: why are some elements included and others not? Why are there only eight elements rather than nine or ten, and why are they divided up the way they are? The crucial difference between this model and the others is that, for Hymes, these elements do not represent objective features of context, but rather represent more subjective features of *competence*, the kinds of things about which speakers need to know to be considered competent communicators by other members of their group.

For Hymes, then, the 'subjective' nature of context is not the weakness of his model, but, in a way, the whole point of it. Even when the 'objective' aspects of context – the status of the participants, the nature of the activity and the semiotic modes being used – remain the same, expectations about who should say what to whom, when, where and how will still vary across different communities of speakers.

An understanding of the communicative competence necessary in a particular speech community in order to participate in a particular speech event cannot be acquired with reference to the linguistic system alone, or simply through the analysis of texts or transcripts of conversations. This is because what is of importance is not just the meanings people communicate and how they are communicated, but the meaning *communication itself* has for them in different situations with different people. Understanding this requires a different approach to the analysis of discourse, an approach which is summed up in the word *ethnography*.

Ethnography is a research method developed in the field of anthropology which is concerned with describing the lived experiences of people in particular social groups. It involves not just analysing the texts and talk that they produce from a distance, but actually spending time with them, observing them as they use language, and talking to them at length about the meanings they ascribe to different kinds of utterance and different kinds of behaviour.

These methods are not just used in the approach to discourse developed by Hymes and his students. Many of the approaches to discourse discussed earlier have also begun to incorporate ethnographic fieldwork: genre analysts, for example, typically interview members of discourse communities about the kinds of text they use and how they use them; critical discourse analysts are increasingly focusing not just on how producers of texts express ideology and reproduce power relations, but also on how readers respond to and sometimes contest these ideological formations; and issues of cross-cultural pragmatics are increasingly being explored through ethnographic methods.

👁 **Look deeper into the question of context online.**

MEDIATED DISCOURSE ANALYSIS   A8

So far this book has presented different methods for the analysis of written and spoken discourse. These methods include ways to understand how texts and conversations are put together and how people make sense of them, as well as how people use them to manage their activities and identities and to advance their ideological agendas. We have also explored how context, from the narrow context of the immediate situation to the broader context of culture, can affect the ways discourse is produced and interpreted.

In this unit we will step back and attempt to answer a more fundamental question in discourse analysis: 'How do we determine what texts or conversations are worth analysing in the first place?'

We are literally surrounded by discourse. In the course of a single day the number of words we speak and hear and the number of texts that pass before our eyes, from emails to advertising billboards to shop receipts, is mind-boggling. In the excerpt reprinted in D8, Ron Scollon talks about just some of the texts and spoken language involved in the simple activity of having a cup of coffee at Starbucks. These include things such as conversations between customers and the cashier, the communication between the cashier and the person making the coffee, the chatting that occurs between the people sitting at tables and lounging on sofas throughout the shop, the writing on the paper cups out of which they are drinking their beverages, the menu posted on the wall above the counter, the name badges that the employees wear, the magazines and newspapers provided for patrons to read, and the various advertisements and posters hanging on the walls around the shop, to mention only a few. There is also a whole host of texts and conversations that have contributed to this moment of drinking coffee that are not immediately visible: training manuals and work schedules for employees, orders and invoices for bulk coffee beans, and conversations and text messages between friends planning when and where they might meet up for a cup of coffee.

Given this complex situation, the most important question for a discourse analyst is: Where do I start? Which texts or utterances should I commence analysing? For most discourse analysts the answer to this question is: 'Whatever *I* happen to be interested in.' Thus, analysts interested in casual conversation might focus on the talk that goes on between friends sitting at tables, analysts interested in promotional discourse might zero in on the advertising posters or menu which inform patrons of the 'drink of the month', and those interested in the speech event of the 'service encounter' might want to record or observe people ordering and paying for their coffee.

In principle there is nothing wrong with this 'analyst-centred' approach. From it we can learn quite a lot about things such as casual conversation, promotional discourse and service encounters. What we might miss, however, is an understanding of what the *practice* of 'having a cup of coffee at Starbucks' is really like for the *actual participants* involved, what this practice means to them, how they go about performing it and how it fits into their lives.

Mediated discourse analysis, the perspective on discourse that is the topic of this unit, approaches the problem of 'which discourse to analyse' by asking the simple question: 'What's going on here?' and then focusing on whatever texts, conversations or other things play a part in 'what's going on'.

Of course, the answer to that question might not be very simple. For one thing, it is likely to be different depending on whom you ask: for a customer, it might be 'having a cup of coffee'; for a worker, it might be 'taking orders' or 'making coffee' or 'bussing tables' or more generally 'making a living'; for a government health inspector, it might be determining whether the shop complies with government regulations when it comes to hygiene and food safety.

The focus of mediated discourse analysis is trying to understand the relationships between 'what's going on' and the discourse that is available in the situation to perform these 'goings on'. Certain kinds of discourse make certain kinds of actions easier to perform and other kinds more difficult to perform. But it is also interested in the relationship between these actions and the *social identities* of the people involved. The point is not just that cashiers or customers need to use certain kinds of discourse to perform certain kinds of actions, but that it is chiefly by using these different kinds of discourse to perform these actions that they *enact* their identities as cashiers and customers and health inspectors. That is to say, we associate different kinds of actions and different kinds of discourse with different kinds of people. We might find it odd to see someone who is wearing a badge and uniform reading a newspaper and drinking a cup of coffee at one of the tables, or a customer inspecting the cleanliness of the espresso machine.

The point, then, is not that some discourse is more important than other discourse. Rather, the point is that to really understand how discourse is relevant to 'real life', we have to try to understand how different texts and conversations are linked, sometimes directly and sometimes indirectly, to the concrete, real-time actions that are going on in coffee shops and classrooms and offices and on street corners at particular moments, and how these linkages work to create social identities (such as 'friends', 'colleagues', 'teachers', 'cashiers' and 'customers') and social practices (such as 'teaching a lesson' or 'having a cup of coffee').

Discourse and action

One of the definitions of discourse given in the very first unit of this book was that discourse is 'language in use' or, to put it another way, 'language in action'. Nearly all of the approaches to discourse analysis we have discussed are concerned in some way with the relationship between language and action. According to speech act theory (see A5 and B5), for example, people use language in order to accomplish particular actions such as requesting, apologising and warning, and according to genre analysis (see A3 and B3), the structure of genres is crucially determined by the actions that users are attempting to accomplish with them within particular discourse communities.

Mediated discourse analysis has a similar focus on action, but, whereas these other approaches start with the discourse and ask what kinds of social action speakers or writers can accomplish with it, mediated discourse analysis starts with *actions* and asks what role discourse plays in them.

This may seem to be a rather small distinction, but it is actually a crucial one, because it avoids the assumption that discourse (rather than other things such as espresso machines and coffee cups) is necessarily the most important cultural tool involved in the action. It also reminds us that just because a piece of discourse *might* be used to perform certain kinds of action, the way people *actually* use it may be to perform actions which we may not have expected. People might just as easily use a newspaper to wrap fish and chips as to find out about the latest news from Parliament. One's relationship status on Facebook, as we will see in unit C8, might just as easily be used to *avoid* giving information about one's relationship status as to give it.

Thus, the unit of analysis in mediated discourse analysis is not the 'utterance' or 'speech act' or 'adjacency pair' or 'conversation' or 'text', but rather the *mediated action*, that is, the action that is *mediated* through these discursive tools or other tools that may have nothing to do with language. Such an analysis begins with two questions: 'What is the action going on here? and 'How does discourse figure into this action?'

The answer to the question 'What is the action going on here?' might have a very complex answer. As mentioned above, it might be different for different people, and even for the same person, it might depend on how broadly or narrowly they are focusing on what they are doing. The person operating the espresso machine at Starbucks, for example, might say she's 'working' or 'making a cappuccino' or 'steaming milk'.

What this tells us is that actions are always dependent on other actions that occur before them and are likely to occur after them, and that whatever one identifies as an action can always be divided up into smaller and smaller actions. In other words, actions are always related to other actions in complex patterns. Often these patterns, such as the sequence of smaller actions and how they combine to make larger actions, become conventionalised in the same way that genres of written and spoken discourse can become conventionalised. When this happens, we refer to these patterns of actions as *social practices*.

Part of what a mediated discourse analyst focuses on is how small, discrete actions such as handing money to a cashier or steaming milk in a stainless steel pitcher come to be habitually joined with other actions and regarded by participants as the *social practices* of 'having a cup of coffee' or 'making a cappuccino'. In particular they are interested in the role discourse plays in creating and sustaining these *social practices*.

Like other analysts, then, mediated discourse analysts, through their interest in *social practices*, are concerned with the *ideological* dimension of discourse, or what James Paul Gee refers to as 'Discourses with a capital D'. When chains of actions occur over and over again in the same way in the same kinds of situation involving the same kinds of people, they become *social practices*, and thus begin to exert control over the people who carry them out: people come to be expected to do things in a certain way and the things that they do come to be associated with the kinds of social identities they are able to claim. Discourse of all kinds, from training manuals to health regulations to conversations, plays a crucial role in this process. In contrast to other approaches concerned with the ideological nature of discourse, however, mediated discourse analysis does not focus so much on how discourse itself expresses ideology, but rather how it is used to help create and maintain the *practices* that come to exert control over us.

👁 **Look deeper into the idea of 'social practices' online.**

A9   MULTIMODAL DISCOURSE ANALYSIS

In the first unit of this book I said that one of the fundamental principles of discourse analysis is that discourse includes more than just language. It also involves things such as non-verbal communication, images, music and even the arrangement of furniture in rooms and the spaces created by architectural structures. I elaborated on this point a bit further in my examination of spoken discourse, first noting how non-verbal cues can serve to signal the 'frames' within which an utterance is meant to be interpreted, and later how the larger physical and cultural context including such things as setting, participants and communication media can affect how language is produced and understood. This point was taken even further in the last section in the discussion of mediated discourse analysis, in which I pointed out that language is only one of many 'cultural tools' with which people take actions, and warned that focusing on language alone at the expense of these other tools can result in a distorted picture of 'what's going on'.

This unit introduces an approach to discourse called **multimodal discourse analysis**, which focuses more directly on these other tools or 'modes' of communication. Multimodal discourse analysts see discourse as involving multiple modes which often work together. In a face-to-face conversation, for example, people do not just communicate with spoken language. They also communicate through their gestures, gaze, facial expressions, posture, dress, how close or far away they stand or sit from each other, and many other things. Similarly, 'written texts' rarely consist only of words, especially nowadays. They often include pictures, charts or graphs. Even the font that is used and the way paragraphs are arranged on a page or screen can convey meaning.

The point of multimodal discourse analysis is not to analyse these other modes *instead* of speech and writing, but to understand how different modes, including speech and writing, work together in discourse. The point is also not to study some special kind of discourse – 'multimodal discourse' – but rather to understand how *all* discourse involves the interaction of multiple modes.

The idea of a **communicative mode** (sometimes called a **semiotic mode**) should not be confused with the notion of 'modality' in linguistics (the way we express possibility and obligation in language, discussed in B4), or with Halliday's use of the term 'mode' in his model of context (discussed in A7). What is meant by 'mode' in the context of *multimodal discourse analysis* is a system for making meaning. So we can speak, for example, of the modes of speech, writing, gesture, colour, dress, and so on. Any system of signs that are used in a consistent and systematic way to make meaning can be considered a mode.

Modes should also not be confused with **media**, which are the material carriers of modes. Telephones, radios and computers are all *media* which can carry the *mode* of spoken language. They can also carry other modes, such as music, and, in the case of computers and some mobile telephones, written text and pictures.

Multimodal discourse analysis can generally be divided into two types: one which focuses on 'texts' such as magazines, comic books, web pages, films and works of art, and the other which focuses more on social interaction (sometimes referred to as **multimodal interaction analysis**).

Perhaps the most influential approach to the multimodal analysis of texts has grown out of the study of **systemic functional grammar** as it was developed by M.A.K. Halliday, whose work we have already discussed at length (see A2, A4). Halliday's view is that grammar is a system of 'resources' for making meaning shaped by the kinds of things people need to *do* with language. Those applying this framework to multimodal discourse analysis propose that other modes such as images, music and architecture also have a kind of 'grammar'. In other words, their components can be organised as networks of options that users choose from in order to realise different meanings.

The most famous application of this idea is the book *Reading Images: The grammar of visual design*, first published in 1996 by Gunther Kress and Theo van Leeuwen, an excerpt from which is reprinted in D9. Before the publication of this book, most of those involved in the analysis of images assumed that their interpretation depended on their interaction with language – that images themselves were too 'vague' to be understood on their own. In contrast, Kress and van Leeuwen show that, while in many texts images and language work together, images are not dependent on written text, but rather have their own way of structuring and organising meaning – their own 'grammar'. This approach has also been applied to other modes such as music (van Leeuwen 1999), architecture (O'Toole 1994), colour (van Leeuwen 2011), hypermedia (Djonov 2007) and mathematical symbolism (O'Halloran 2005).

It is important to note, however, that this approach does *not* involve simply applying the 'grammatical rules' derived from the study of language to other modes. Instead, each mode is seen to have its own special way of organising meaning, and it is the task of the analyst to discover what that system is, independent of other systems.

The second approach to multimodal discourse analysis grows more out of traditions associated with the analysis of spoken discourse, especially conversation analysis (see A5), interactional sociolinguistics (see A6) and the ethnography of speaking (see A7). Some of the more recent work in what has come to be known as *multimodal interaction analysis* (Norris 2004) has also been influenced by meditated discourse analysis (see A8).

In analysing multimodality in interaction, analysts pay attention to many of the same kinds of things they do when they analyse spoken language, especially **sequentiality**, how elements are ordered in relation to one another, and **simultaneity**, how elements that occur at the same time affect one another. A multimodal discourse analyst, for example, might look for patterns in the ordering of non-verbal behaviour in a conversation, such as the role that things such as gaze play in the regulation of turn taking, or at how the meanings of utterances are affected by non-verbal behaviour such as gestures of facial expressions, which often serve to contextualise utterances (see A6).

One of the key preoccupations of multimodal interaction analysis is the fact that when we are interacting we are almost always involved in multiple activities. We might, for example, be chatting with a friend at the beauty salon, leafing through a magazine and checking the mirror to see what is going on with our hair all at the same time. Multimodal interaction analysis gives us a way to examine how people use different communicative modes to manage simultaneous activities and to communicate to others something about how they are distributing their attention.

It is important to mention that both of these approaches have been applied to both static texts and dynamic interactions. Approaches based on systemic functional grammar have been used to analyse things such as gestures and gaze, and multimodal interaction analysis has been applied to more static texts such as advertisements. Furthermore, with the increasing popularity of interactive text-based forms of communication such as instant messaging, blogs and social networking sites, discourse analysts often find that they need to focus *both* on patterns and structures in the organisation of elements in texts *and* on the sequentiality and simultaneity of actions as people interact using these texts (see, for example, Jones 2005, 2009a, 2009b).

As new forms of media are developed which allow people to mix modes of communication in new ways over time and space, our whole idea of what we mean by a text or a conversation is beginning to change. If, for example, as we discussed in unit A2, *texture* is a result of elements such as clauses, sentences and paragraphs being connected together in various ways using *cohesive devices*, then it would make sense to consider not just a particular web page, but an entire website consisting of numerous pages joined together by hyperlinks as a kind of 'text'. We might also be tempted to consider as part of this text other websites outside of the primary site to which this text hyperlinks, and, before long, following this logic, we might end up with the idea that the entire Internet can on some level be considered a single text.

Similarly, our notion of conversations is changing. Not only are computer-mediated conversations often written rather than spoken, but they may extend over days or even months on discussion forums or Facebook walls, accompanied by things such as photos and video clips rather than gestures and facial expressions. Furthermore, conversations often travel across communication media and modes. You might, for example, begin a conversation with a friend over lunch, continue it later in the afternoon using text messages, carry on chatting about the same topic through the telephone or instant messaging in the evening, and resume the conversation the next morning over coffee at Starbucks.

These changes associated with multimedia and multimodality present challenges for communicators and discourse analysts alike. Because different modes and media alter the kinds of meanings we can make, we need to learn to adjust our discourse in different ways every time we move from one mode to another and from one medium to another. This phenomenon is known as **resemiotisation** – the fact that the meanings that we make change as they are shaped by the different modes we use as social practices unfold. The discourse analyst Rick Iedema (2001) gives as an example of *resemiotisation* the way meanings associated with the building of a new wing of a hospital changed as they were expressed orally in planning meetings, then later in the written language of reports, and still later in the graphic language of architectural drawings, and finally in the materiality of bricks and mortar.

The most important point multimodal discourse analysts make is that modes can never really be analysed in isolation from other modes (although this is, as we have seen in this book, what most discourse analysts do with the modes of spoken and written language). Not only do modes always interact with other modes in texts and interaction, but authors and conversational participants often shift from foregrounding one mode or set of modes, to foregrounding other modes or sets of modes, and in doing so, alter the 'meaning potential' of the communicative environment.

CORPUS-ASSISTED DISCOURSE ANALYSIS   A10

So far all of the approaches to discourse analysis we have considered involve analysing a relatively small number of texts or interactions at one time. In fact, the focus of most discourse analysis is on looking very closely at one or a small number of texts or conversations of a particular type, trying to uncover things such as how the text or conversation is structured, how writers/speakers and readers/listeners are constructed, how the text or conversation promotes the broader ideological agendas of groups or institutions, and how people actually use the text or conversation to perform concrete social actions.

Corpus-assisted discourse analysis is unique in that it allows us to go beyond looking at a small number of texts or interactions to analysing a large number of them and being able to compare them with other texts and conversations that are produced under similar or different circumstances. It also allows us to bring to our analysis some degree of 'objectivity' by giving us the opportunity to test out the theories we have formulated in our close analysis of a few texts or conversations on a much larger body of data in a rather systematic way.

A **corpus** is basically a collection of texts in digital format that it is possible to search through and manipulate using a computer program. There are a number of large corpora, such as the British National Corpus, which is a very general collection of written and spoken texts in English. You can also find general corpora of texts produced in different varieties of English and also other languages. There are also a large number of specialised corpora available, that is, collections of particular kinds of text such as business letters or academic articles. There are even multimodal corpora in which not just verbal data but also visual data are collected and tagged.

Normally, corpora are used by linguists in order to find out things about the grammatical and lexical patterns in particular varieties of language or particular kinds of text. A lot of what we know about the differences among the different varieties of English (such as British English, American English and Australian English) or among different registers comes from the analysis of corpora. Corpora have also played an important role in *forensic linguistics* (the use of linguistics to solve crimes): linguists sometimes, for example, compare the features in a piece of writing to those in a corpus of texts by a particular author in order to answer questions about authorship.

Discourse analysts have only recently started using corpora, and the number of discourse analytical studies that rely heavily on corpora is still relatively small. The reasons for this have to do with the way discourse analysts have traditionally viewed what they do. As we said in the beginning of this book, discourse analysts are not just interested in linguistic forms and patterns but also in how language is actually used in concrete social situations. Computer analysis using large corpora seems to go against this key aim: texts in corpora are taken out of their social contexts, and even the information we often get from the analysis, which usually consists of things such as lists of frequently used words or phrases, is often presented outside of the context of the texts in which these words and phrases occur.

Other than this, the analysis of corpora also presents other problems for discourse analysts. As we asserted at the beginning of our study of discourse analysis: 'People don't always say what they mean, and people don't always mean what they say.' A big part of discourse analysis, in fact, is figuring out what people mean when they do not say (or write) it directly. Any method which takes language and its meaning at face value is of limited use to discourse analysts. Words and phrases, as we have seen, can have multiple meanings depending on how they are used in different circumstances by different people, and just because a word is used frequently, does not mean it is particularly important. Often the most important meanings that we make are implicit or stated indirectly.

Despite these potential problems, however, the *computer-assisted* analysis of corpora can still be a very valuable tool for discourse analysts. The key word in this phrase is *assisted*. The computer analysis of corpora cannot be used by itself to *do* discourse analysis. But it can *assist* us in doing discourse analysis in some very valuable ways.

First, it can help us to see the data that we are analysing from a new perspective. Often seeing your data broken down into things such as concordances or frequency lists can help you to see things that you missed using more traditional discourse analytical techniques.

Second, it can help us to see if we can generalise our theories or observations about certain kinds of text or certain kinds of interaction. If you find certain features in a business email you are analysing, the most you can say is that this particular email has these features and that these features function in the particular social situation from which the email comes in a certain way. If, however, you have access to a large number of similar emails, or emails from the same company, then you can start to make generalisations about the kinds of features that are common to business emails, or the kinds of features that are common to emails in this particular company. This has obvious applications to *genre analysis* in which the analyst is interested in identifying certain conventions of language use associated with particular kinds of text.

Finally, and most importantly, the analysis of corpora can help us to detect what we have been calling 'Discourses with a capital D' – systems of language use that promote particular kinds of ideologies and power relationships. One of the biggest problems we have as discourse analysts is that, while we want to make some kind of connection between the texts and conversations that we are analysing and larger 'Discourses' – such as the 'Discourse of medicine' or the 'Discourse of racism' – we are usually just guessing about whether or not these discourses actually exist and what kinds of ideologies, power relationships and linguistic strategies they entail. These are usually quite educated guesses that we make based on world knowledge, scholarly research, common sense and the analysis of lots of different texts over a long period of time. The analysis of large corpora, however, gives us a more empirical way to detect trends in language use – how words and phrases tend to reoccur – across a large number of texts, which might signal a 'Discourse', and also to detect if and how such language use changes over time (Baker 2005, 2006).

The study by Baker and McEnery (2005) on the portrayal of refugees and asylum-seekers in public discourse, an excerpt of which is reprinted in unit D10, is a good example of how corpus-assisted analysis can help to uncover patterns of language use that point to the existence of different 'Discourses' associated with a particular issue. Other examples include Hardt-Mautner's 1995 study of British newspaper editorials on the European Union, Rey's 2001 study of gender and language in the popular US television series *Star Trek*, and Baker's (2005) study of the various 'Discourses' surrounding male homosexuality in Britain and America.

Of course, being able to detect 'Discourses' through the computer analysis of corpora requires the creative combination of multiple analytical procedures, and it also necessarily involves a large amount of interpretative work by the analyst.

Corpus-assisted discourse analysis is not a science, it is an art, and perhaps the biggest danger of employing it is that the analyst comes to see it as somehow more 'scientific' than the close analysis of texts just because computers and quantification are involved. The computer analysis of corpora does not provide discourse analysts with answers. Rather, it provides them with additional information to make their educated guesses even more educated and their theory building more evidence based.

Theory or method?

One of the differences between corpus-assisted discourse analysis and the other approaches to discourse we have presented in this book is that, while approaches such as genre analysis, conversation analysis and the ethnography of speaking each explicitly advance a particular theory of discourse, corpus-assisted discourse analysis is often seen to be 'theory neutral'. That is, it is viewed more as a method for assisting in the application of different theories. Thus, one can use corpora in doing genre analysis, conversation analysis, pragmatics or critical discourse analysis.

Here, however, it would be useful to recall some of the points made in the discussion of *mediated discourse analysis* in unit A8 about the nature of *cultural tools*. Since all tools make certain kinds of action easier and others more difficult, there is really no such thing as an ideologically neutral tool. The computer-assisted analysis of corpora has certain *affordances* and *constraints* which make it more compatible with some approaches to discourse and less compatible with others. In particular, while it seems especially suited for approaches which concern themselves with the ways texts and conversations are structured or patterned (such as genre analysis and conversation analysis), it is perhaps less suitable for approaches which focus more on the social context of communication (such as the ethnography of speaking).

👁 **Look deeper into the applications of the analysis of corpora to discourse analysis online.**

Section B

DEVELOPMENT
APPROACHES TO
DISCOURSE ANALYSIS

B1 THREE WAYS OF LOOKING AT DISCOURSE

Over the years people have approached the study of discourse in many different ways, and in this section you will explore some of these ways of analysing discourse and learn how to apply them to texts and conversations from your own life. People who analyse discourse have basically gone about it from three different perspectives based on three different ideas about what discourse is.

Some have taken a *formal* approach to discourse, seeing it simply as 'language above the level of the clause or sentence'. Those working from this perspective often try to understand the kinds of rules and conventions that govern the ways we join clauses and sentences together to make texts.

Others take a more *functional* approach, defining discourse as 'language in use'. This perspective leads to questions about how people use language to do things such as make requests, issue warnings and apologise in different kinds of situations and how we interpret what other people are trying to do when they speak or write.

Finally, there are those who take what we might call a *social* approach, conceiving discourse as a kind of social practice. The way we use language, they point out, is tied up with the way we construct different social identities and relationships and participate in different kinds of groups and institutions. It is tied up with issues of what we believe to be right and wrong, who has power over whom, and what we have to do and say to 'fit in' to our societies.

Although these three different approaches to discourse are often treated as separate, and are certainly associated with different historical traditions and different individual discourse analysts, the position I will be taking in this book is that good discourse analysis requires that we take into account all three of these perspectives. Instead of three separate definitions of discourse, they are better seen as three interrelated aspects of discourse. The way people use language cannot really be separated from the way it is put together, and the way people use language to show who they are and what they believe cannot be separated from the things people are using language to do in particular situations.

Language above the clause

The use of the term 'discourse' to mean language above the level of the sentence or the clause probably originated with the linguist Zellig Harris, who, back in the 1950s, wanted to take the study of linguistics to a new level. Before this, linguists had come a long way in understanding how sounds are put together to form words and how words are put together to form sentences. What Harris wanted to do was to understand how sentences are put together to form texts.

The idea that texts could be analysed in terms of their formal structure was actually very popular in the early and mid-twentieth century, even before Harris invented the term 'discourse analysis', especially in the field of literature. One group of literary critics called the Russian Formalists, for example, tried to apply the same kinds of methods people used to analyse the grammar of sentences to analysing stories and novels. Perhaps the most famous was Vladimir Propp, who tried to come up with a 'grammar of stories' by studying Russian folk tales.

The method that Harris proposed for the analysis of discourse, which he called **distributional analysis**, was not much different from how people go about doing grammatical analysis. The idea is to identify particular linguistic features and determine how they occur in texts relative to other features, that is, which features occur next to other features or 'in the same environment' with them. However, as you will see from the excerpt from Harris's seminal paper reprinted in D1, his ambitions went beyond simply understanding how linguistic features are distributed throughout texts. He was also interested in understanding how these features correlate with non-linguistic behaviour beyond texts, that is, how the form that texts take is related to the social situations in which they occur. It was really left to discourse analysts who came after him, however, to figure out exactly how the relationship between texts and the social contexts in which they are used could be fruitfully studied.

When focusing on the formal aspect of discourse, we are mostly interested in how the different elements of texts or conversations are put together to form unified wholes. In this respect, we usually look for two kinds of things. We look for linguistic features (words and grammar), which help to link different parts of the text or conversation together, and we look at the overall pattern of the text or conversation. We can refer to these two things as: 1) *cohesion* – how pieces of the text are 'stuck together'; and 2) *coherence* – the overall pattern or sequence of elements in a text or conversation that conforms to our expectations about how different kinds of texts or interactions ought to be structured (see A2). I will deal with these two concepts in more detail in the next unit.

Language in use

The second aspect of discourse that discourse analysts focus on is how people actually use language to get things done in specific contexts. In fact, as was pointed out in section A1, it is often very difficult to understand what a piece of language means without referring to the social context in which it is being used and what the person who is using it is trying to do.

This view of discourse grew out of the work of a number of important scholars including Michael Halliday, whose approach to the study of grammar differed markedly from earlier approaches by focusing less on the forms language takes and more on the social functions accomplished by language (see A2), and the work of the British philosophers John L. Austin and Paul Grice, who laid the foundation for what we call *pragmatics* (the study of how people do things with language) (see A5). Another important figure who promoted this view of discourse is the applied linguist H.G. Widdowson, who approached the whole problem of language use from the perspective of language learning, noting that learning a foreign language requires more than just learning how to make grammatical sentences; it also involves being able to use the language to accomplish things in the world.

There are a number of ways to study language in use. One way is to consider discourse itself as a kind of action, and to explore how, when we say things or write things, we are actually *doing* things such as apologising, promising, threatening or making requests (see A5). Another way to consider language in use is to examine how different kinds of discourse make certain kinds of actions or activities either easier or more difficult to perform (see A8). Finally, we might consider how people use discourse strategically to try to communicate their interpretation of a situation or to manage their relationships with the people with whom they are communicating (see A6).

Language and 'social practice'

The third aspect of discourse has to do with the role of language in 'social practice'. Language is seen not just as a system for making meaning, but as part of larger systems through which people construct social identities and social realities. Different people use language in different ways. An English teacher talks differently than a hip-hop artist. These different ways of talking help to show who we are and also reflect our different ideas about the world, different beliefs and different values.

This view of discourse probably owes the most to the French philosopher Michel Foucault, who argued that discourse is the main tool through which we construct 'knowledge' and exert power over other people. Different kinds of discourse (or 'discourses') are associated with different kinds of people and different 'systems of knowledge'. Foucault spoke, for example, of 'clinical discourse, economic discourse, the discourse of natural history, (and) psychiatric discourse' (1972: 121). The American discourse analyst James Paul Gee uses a capital 'D' to distinguish this view of discourse from the others we have talked about. For him, **Discourses** are 'ways of being in the world, or forms of life which integrate words, acts, values, beliefs, attitudes, and social identities' (1996: 127).

This aspect of discourse leads us to explore how people use language to advance certain versions of reality and certain relationships of power, and also how our beliefs, values and social institutions are constructed through and supported by discourse. A central principle of this view of discourse is that discourse is always 'ideological', meaning that discourse always has 'an agenda', that it always ends up serving the interests of certain people over those of others (see A4).

As stated above, it is difficult to look at discourse in any meaningful way from only one of these perspectives. Simply looking at how texts are put together, for example, while it may be interesting, has limited practical value. At the same time, you cannot really make broad statements about 'power' or 'ideology' in a text without first understanding some basic things about how the text is put together and how people are actually using it in specific social contexts to perform specific actions.

◉ **Look deeper into the different perspectives on discourse online.**

B2   **COHESION AND COHERENCE**

One of the most basic tasks for a discourse analyst is to figure out what makes a text a text and what makes a conversation and conversation, in other words, to figure out what gives texts and conversations *texture. Texture*, as I said in unit A2, comes from *cohesion* and *coherence. Cohesion* primarily has to do with linguistic features in texts, and *coherence* has to do with the kinds of 'frameworks' with which readers approach texts and what they want to use texts to do.

This last statement is perhaps a bit misleading, possibly making you think that, when it comes to cohesion, the reader doesn't have to do any work, and in the case of coherence the expectations in the mind of the reader are more important than what is actually in the text. This is not the case. In fact, what creates cohesion is not just the linguistic features within the text, but the fact that these features lead readers to perform certain mental operations – to locate and take note of earlier or later parts of the text as they are going through it.

For example, if I were to say, 'Lady Gaga doesn't appeal to me, but my sister loves her,' in order to understand the meaning of 'her' in the second clause, you have to do some mental work. Not only do you need to refer back to the first clause, you also have to be smart enough to know that 'her' refers to Lady Gaga and not my sister. Thus, cohesion is the quality in a text that forces you to look either backward or forward in the text in order to make sense of the things you read, and it is through your acts of looking backward and forward that the text comes to take on a quality of connectedness.

Similarly, to say that *coherence* is a matter of the 'frameworks' or sets of expectations that we bring to texts, does not mean that what is actually in the text is any less important. Concrete features must exist in the text which 'trigger' those expectations. For example, for me to interpret a text as a shopping list, it must have a certain structure (a list), certain kinds of words (generally nouns), and those words must represent things that I am able to purchase (as opposed to abstract things such as 'world peace' or unaffordable items such as the Golden Gate Bridge).

Cohesion

Halliday and Hasan (whose work is excerpted in D2) describe two broad kinds of linguistic devices that are used to force readers to engage in this process of backward and forward looking which gives texts a sense of connectedness. One type depends on grammar (which they call **grammatical cohesion**) and the other type depends more on the meanings of words (which they call **lexical cohesion**).

Devices used to create grammatical cohesion include:

❑ **conjunction** (using 'connecting words')
❑ **reference** (using a pronoun to refer to another word)
❑ **substitution** (substituting one word or phrase for another word or phrase)
❑ **ellipses** (leaving something out).

Lexical cohesion involves the **repetition** of words or of words from the same **semantic field** (e.g. milk, tomatoes, rocket).

Conjunction refers to the use of various 'connecting words' (such as conjunctions like *and* and *but* and conjunctive adverbs like *furthermore* and *however*) to join together clauses and sentences. Conjunction causes the reader to look back to the first clause in a pair of joined clauses to make sense of the second clause. The important thing about these 'connecting words' is that they do not just establish a relationship between the two clauses, but that they tell us what kind of relationship it is.

'Connecting words', then, can be grouped into different kinds depending on the relationship they establish between the clauses or sentences that they join together. Some are called **additive**, because they add information to the previous clause or sentence. Examples are 'and', 'moreover', 'furthermore', 'in addition', 'as well'. Others are called **contrastive** because they set up some kind of contrast with the previous sentence or clause. Examples are 'but', 'however'. Still others are called **causative** because they set up some kind of cause and effect relationship between the two sentences or clauses. Examples of these are 'because', 'consequently', 'therefore'. Finally, some are called **sequential** because they indicate the order facts or events come in. Examples are 'firstly', 'subsequently', 'then' and 'finally'. In the two examples below, the first uses a contrastive connective and the second uses a causative connective.

He liked the exchange students. She, *however*, would have nothing to do with them.

He liked the exchange students. She, *therefore*, would have nothing to do with them.

All connecting words cause the reader to look back to a previous clause (or sentence) in order to understand the subsequent clause (or sentence), and the kind of connecting word used guides the reader in understanding the relationship between two clauses (or sentences). In the first example given above, the word *however* causes the reader to look back at the first sentence to find out what the difference is between her and him. In the second example, the word *therefore* causes the reader to look back at the first sentence to find out *why* she won't have anything to do with the exchange students.

Another very common way we make our texts 'stick together' is by using words that refer to words we used elsewhere in the text. This kind of cohesive device is known as *reference*. The two examples above, besides using connecting words, also use this device. The word 'them' in the second sentence refers back to 'the exchange students' in the first sentence, and so, to make sense of it, the reader is forced to look back. 'He' and 'she' are also pronouns and presumably refer to specific people who are probably named at an earlier point in the longer text from which these sentences were taken. The word or group of words that a pronoun refers to is called its **antecedent**. What reference does, then, is help the reader to keep track of the various participants in the text as he or she reads (Eggins 1994: 95).

There are basically three kinds of reference:

1   **anaphoric** reference – using words that point back to a word used before:

After Lady Gaga appeared at the MTV Music Video Awards in a dress made completely of meat, *she* was criticised by animal rights groups.

2   **cataphoric** reference – using words that point forward to a word that has not been used yet:

When *she* was challenged by reporters, Lady Gaga insisted that the dress was not intended to offend anyone.

3   **exophoric** reference – using words that point to something outside the text (reference):

If *you* want to know more about this controversy, *you* can read the comments people have left on animal rights blogs.

The definite article ('the') can also be a form of *anaphoric* reference in that it usually refers the reader back to an earlier mention of a particular noun.

Lady Gaga appeared in a dress made completely of meat. *The* dress was designed by Franc Fernandez.

Substitution is similar to reference except rather than using pronouns, other words are used to refer to an *antecedent*, which has either appeared earlier or will appear later. In the sentence below, for example, the word *one* is used to substitute for *dress*.

Besides wearing a meat dress, Lady Gaga has also worn a hair *one*, which was designed by Chris March.

Substitution can also be used to refer to the verb or the entire predicate of a clause, as in the example below.

If Lady Gaga was intending to shock people, she succeeded in *doing so*.

Ellipsis is the omission of a noun, verb or phrase on the assumption that it is understood from the linguistic context. In order to fill in the gap(s), readers need to look back to previous clauses or sentences, as in the example below.

There is much to support the view that it is clothes that wear us, and *not we, them*.

(Virginia Woolf)

All of the devices mentioned above are examples of *grammatical cohesion*, the kind of cohesion that is created because of the *grammatical relationships* between words. Lexical cohesion occurs as a result of the *semantic* relationship between words. The simplest kind of lexical cohesion is when words are repeated. But a more common kind is the repetition of words related to the same subject. We call these 'chains' of similar kinds of words that run through texts **lexical chains**. In the following text, for example, besides the use of reference (who, it, she), the clauses are held together by the repetition of the verb 'to wear' and of other words having to do with clothing and fashion ('bikini', *Vogue* – a famous fashion magazine, 'dress' and 'outfits').

Lady Gaga, who came under fire recently for *wearing* a meat *bikini* on the cover of *Vogue* Hommes Japan, *wore* a raw meat *dress* at last night's VMAs. It was one of many *outfits* she *wore* throughout the night.

(Oldenberg 2010)

Taken together, these words form a *lexical chain*, which helps to bind the text together. *Lexical chains* not only make a text more cohesive but also highlight the topic or topics (such as 'fashion', 'entertainment', 'technology') that the text is about – and so can provide context for determining the meaning of ambiguous words (such as 'rocket' in the example of the shopping list given in A2). In fact, searching for lexical chains is one of the main techniques used in computer-automated text categorisation and summarisation.

Coherence

As the shopping list we discussed in A2 illustrates, what makes a text a text is often as much a matter of the interpretative framework that the reader brings to the text as it is of anything internal to the text. The relationship between the words 'tomatoes' and 'rocket' becomes meaningful to a reader based on his or her understanding of what a shopping list is and what it is used for. This aspect of texture is known as *coherence*, and it has to do with our expectations about the way elements in a text ought to be organised and the kinds of social actions (such as shopping) that are associated with a given text.

The text in Figure B2.1 is a good example of how we sometimes need to apply our experience with past texts and with certain conventions that have grown up in our society in order to understand new texts we encounter.

Figure B2.1 Advertisement for Body Coach.Net (Duval Guillaume, Brussels, Belgium)

For most people, as soon as they see the words 'before' and 'after', a certain body of knowledge is 'triggered' based on texts they have seen in the past which contain these words such as advertisements for beauty products. In such texts, 'before' is usually portrayed as 'bad' and 'after' is usually portrayed as 'good', and the product being advertised is portrayed as the 'agent' that causes the transformation from 'before' to 'after'. This structure is a variation on what Michael Hoey (1983) has called the 'Problem–Solution' pattern, which underlies many texts from business proposals to newspaper editorials.

The challenge this ad presents for the reader is that there is no explicit information about what is meant by 'before' and 'after' other than a curved line drawn down the centre of the page. In order to interpret this line, we must make reference to the smaller words in the lower right corner which give the name of the advertiser: Body Coach.Net, and the slogan: 'For a perfect body'. This information creates for readers an interpretive framework based on their knowledge of the kind of business such a company might be engaged in and cultural notions of what a 'perfect body' might look like. Once this framework is triggered, most readers have no trouble interpreting the space formed on the 'before' side of the ad as portraying the stomach of an overweight person, and the space formed on the 'after' side as the 'hourglass' shape associated (at least in the culture in which this ad appeared) with female beauty, and of the company – Body Coach.Net and the product that it sells – as the agents of this transformation.

There are a number of different kinds of interpretative frameworks that we use to make sense of texts. One kind, which we will discuss further in the next section, we might call a **generic framework**. This kind of framework is based on the expectations we have about different kinds of texts, the kinds of information we expect to encounter in texts of different kinds and the order in which we expect that information to be presented, along with other kinds of lexical or grammatical features we expect to encounter. In the example above, for instance, it is partially our knowledge of the structure of 'before and after ads' that helps us to make sense of this particular ad.

Part of what forms such *generic frameworks* is that different parts of a text are not just grammatically and lexically related, but that they are *conceptually* and *procedurally* related – in other words, that they appear in a certain logical or predictable sequence. Texts following the 'Problem–Solution' pattern, for example, begin by presenting a problem and then go on to present one or more solutions to the problem. This important principle in discourse analysis has its origins largely in cognitive science and early research in artificial intelligence by people such as Schank and Abelson (1977), who pointed out that many human activities are governed by conventional, sequentially ordered, multi-step procedures (which they called 'scripts'), and Rumelhart (1975), who pointed out that, in a similar way, texts such as narratives also exhibit conventional structures based on predictable sequences of actions and information (which he called 'schema'). An excerpt from Rumelhart's classic article 'Notes on a Schema for Stories' is reprinted in D2.

But not all of the knowledge we use to make sense of texts comes from our knowledge about the conventions associated with different kinds of text. Some of this knowledge is part of larger conceptual frameworks that we build up based on our understanding of how the world works. I will use the term **cultural models** to describe these frameworks. James Paul Gee (2010) calls *cultural models* 'videotapes in the mind' based on experiences we have had and depicting what we take to be *prototypical* (or 'normal') people, objects and events. To illustrate the concept he points out that we would never refer to the Pope as a 'bachelor', even though the Pope, as an unmarried adult male, fulfils the conditions for the dictionary definition of the word, because he does not fit into our *cultural model* of what a bachelor is.

Cultural models regarding both the kind of work 'coaches' do and about what constitutes a 'perfect body' are central to our ability to interpret the ad above, and especially for our understanding of the meaning of the two shapes formed by the line drawn down the centre of the page.

The important thing to remember about *cultural models* (and, for that matter, *generic frameworks*) is that they are *cultural*. In other words, they reflect the beliefs and values of a particular group of people in a particular place at a particular point in history. The ad reprinted above would be totally incomprehensible for people in many societies outside of our own because they would not share either the knowledge of 'before and after ads' or the beliefs about physical attractiveness that we have. It is even more important to remember that such texts do not just reflect such expectations, values and beliefs, but also *reinforce* them. Every time we encounter a text like the one above, these generic frameworks and cultural models and the habitual ways of looking at the world associated with them are strengthened.

👁 **Find more examples of cohesion and coherence online.**

B3   **ALL THE RIGHT MOVES**

Texts that are structured according to particular *generic frameworks* are called genres. But genres are more than just texts; they are means by which people *get things done*, and the way they are structured depends crucially on what the particular people using a genre want or need to do. In other words, what determines the way a particular genre is put together is its *communicative purpose*, and so this must be the central focus in analysing genres.

Usually, the overall communicative purpose of a genre can be broken down into a number of steps that users need to follow in order to achieve the desired purpose – rather like the steps in a recipe – and typically the most important constraints and conventions regarding how a genre is structured involve: 1) which steps must be included; and 2) the order in which they should appear. In the field of *genre analysis* these steps are known as **moves**.

John Swales, the father of genre analysis, illustrated the idea of *moves* in his analysis of introductions to academic articles. Instead of asking the traditional question: 'how is this text structured?', Swales asked 'What do writers of such texts need to *do* in order to achieve their desired purpose?' (which, in the case of an introduction to an academic article, is mainly getting people to believe that the article is worth reading). In answering this question, Swales identified four *moves* characteristic of such texts. An introduction to an academic article, he said, typically:

1   *establishes the field* in which the writer of the study is working;
2   *summarises the related research* or interpretations on one aspect of the field;
3   *creates a research space* or interpretive space (a 'niche') for the present study by indicating a gap in current knowledge or by raising questions; and
4   *introduces the study* by indicating what the investigation being reported will accomplish for the field (adapted from Swales 1990).

Of course, not all introductions to academic articles contain all four of these moves in exactly the order presented by Swales. Some article introductions may contain only some of these moves, and some might contain different moves. Furthermore, the ways these moves are *realised* might be very different for articles about engineering and articles about English literature. The point that Swales was trying to make, however, was not that these moves are universal or in some way *obligatory*, but that these are the *prototypical* moves one would expect to occur in this genre, and understanding these default expectations is the first step to understanding how 'expert users' might creatively flout these conventions.

At the same time, it is important to remember that not all genres are equally 'conventionalised'; while some genres have very strict rules about which moves should be included and what order they should be in, other genres exhibit much more variety (see for example the weblog entries discussed in C3).

One genre which has a particularly consistent set of communicative moves is the genre of the 'personal advertisement' (sometimes called the 'dating advertisement') which sometimes appears in the classified sections of newspapers and, increasingly, on online social media and dating sites. The following is an example given by Justine Coupland in her 1996 study of dating advertisements in British newspapers:

> Sensual, imaginative brunette, 25, artistic, intelligent, with a sense of humour. Enjoys home life, cooking, sports, country life. No ties, own home. Seeking a tall, strong, intelligent fun companion with inner depth for passionate, loving romance, 25–35. Photo guarantees reply. Must feel able to love Ben my dog too. London/anywhere.
>
> (Coupland 1996: 187)

Advertisements like this tend to consist of five moves:

1   The advertiser *describes himself or herself* ('Sensual, imaginative brunette . . .').
2   The advertiser *describes the kind of person he or she is looking for* ('Seeking tall, strong, intelligent . . .').
3   The advertiser *describes the kind of relationship or activities he or she wishes to engage in* with the target ('for passionate, loving romance').
4   The advertiser *gives additional information*, makes a humorous remark or issues a challenge ('Photo guarantees reply. Must feel able to love Ben my dog too').
5   The advertiser *indicates how he or she can be contacted* (by, for example, giving a telephone number, an email address, or a post office box – this move is not present in the excerpt Coupland gives, but was presumably present in some form in the original ad).

Of course, as we will see below, dating ads in other contexts might have slightly different move structures, but all of these moves will likely be present in one form or another. The reason for this is that these moves (especially 1, 2, 3 and 5) are essential if the overall communicative purpose of finding a partner is to be achieved.

Such ads also tend to have certain regularities in style and the kind of language that is used to realise these five moves. If they appear in newspapers, for example, they are often written in a kind of telegraphic style, which omits non-essential function words (since advertisers usually have a word limit or are charged by the word). In most cases, self-descriptions and other descriptions contain information about things such as age, appearance and personality expressed in lists of positive adjectives (such as 'young', 'fit', 'fun-loving') and the goal is almost always a romantic or sexual relationship or activities (such as 'opera', 'candlelight dinners', 'quiet evenings at home') which are normally associated with or act as euphemisms for sex or romance.

In a sense, such advertisements not only serve the communicative purpose of individual members of a discourse community to find suitable partners, but they also serve to define and reinforce the values of the discourse community as a whole regarding what kinds of partners and activities are considered desirable. Therefore, being able to compose such ads successfully is not just about portraying oneself as desirable, but also about portraying oneself as a competent member of a particular community of users.

Of course, many different kinds of discourse communities use this genre for different purposes, and so one might identify 'sub-genres' of the personal advertisement for communities of heterosexual singles, gay men, seniors and any number of other groups, each with different conventions and constraints on what kind of information should be included and how it should be structured. One such 'sub-genre' is the matrimonial advertisement found in communities of south Asians, an example of which is given below:

> A well-settled uncle invites matrimonial correspondence from slim, fair, educated South Indian girl, for his nephew, 25 years, smart, M.B.A., green card holder, 5'6". Full particulars with returnable photo appreciated.
>
> (Nanda 2000: 196–204)

The most obvious difference in this ad from the first example given is that the advertiser is not the person who will be engaging in the sought-after relationship, but rather a family member acting as an intermediary. Another important difference has to do with the kinds of information included in the descriptions. Ads of this sub-genre often include information such as immigration status, educational attainment, income, caste and religion, information that is not a common feature of dating ads in other communities.

Another rather unique sub-genre of personal ads are ads placed by lesbians in search of reproductive partners, such as those examined by Susan Hogben and Justine Coupland in their 2000 study. Here is an example of such an ad:

> Loving, stable lesbian couple require donor. Involvement encouraged but not essential. HIV test required. London. BoxPS34Q.
>
> (Hogben and Coupland 2000: 464)

What is interesting about this ad and many of those like it is that there is no elaborate description of the kind of person sought or what he or she is sought for beyond the use of the term 'donor', a term which, in this community, presumably communicates all of the necessary information. Another interesting aspect of this sub-genre is that the 'commenting move', a move which in typical heterosexual dating ads is usually of the least consequence, in these ads often includes vital information about legal and health issues that are central to the practice of surrogate parenthood.

The most important point we can take from these two examples is that generic variation is not just a matter of the different values or styles of different discourse communities, but is also very often a function of differences in the overall *communicative purpose* of the sub-genre (finding a sexual partner, a wife, a reproductive partner).

Bending and blending

Despite the stylistic variety in personal advertisements among different discourse communities, this genre nevertheless remains very conventionalised, with fairly strict constraints on what is considered a relevant contribution. Advertisers must describe themselves, describe the kind of person they are seeking and describe the kind of relationship they want to have. Ironically, however, the strongly conventionalised nature of this genre, the fact that nearly all examples of it have more or less the same structure, has the potential to work against the overall communicative purpose, which is attracting the attention of interested (and interesting) readers. Consequently, it is not uncommon for 'expert users' of this genre to try to make their ads stand out by 'playing with' the conventions of the genre.

One way of 'playing with' generic conventions, which Bhatia (1997) calls **genre bending**, involves flouting the conventions of a genre in subtle ways which, while not altering the move structure substantially, make a particular realisation of a genre seem creative or unique. One way writers of personal advertisements sometimes bend this genre is by flouting the expectations for self-aggrandisement associated with it. The following example comes from a study of gay personal ads in Hong Kong:

> CHINESE, 20, STILL YOUNG, but not good-looking, not attractive, not sexy, not hairy, not fit, not tall, not experienced, not mature, not very intelligent but Thoughtful and Sincere, looking for friendship and love.
>
> (Jones 2000: 46)

Another way of 'playing with' generic conventions is to mix the conventions of one genre with another, a process which Bhatia (1997) refers to as **genre blending**. In the following example from Coupland's study, for instance, the advertiser blends the conventions of the dating ad genre with the conventions of another genre, namely ads for automobiles:

> CLASSIC LADY limousine, mint condition, excellent runner for years seeks gentleman enthusiast 45+ for TLC and excursions in the Exeter area BOX 555L.
>
> (Coupland 1996: 192)

Ironically, what both of these writers are doing by flouting the conventions of the genre is subtly distancing themselves from the discourse community of users while at the same time identifying with it. This seemingly odd strategy is less surprising when one considers that most people who post such ads feel some ambivalence about identifying themselves as members of the community of people who have resorted to such means to find a partner. By 'playing with' the genre they succeed in resisting the commodifying nature of the genre (Coupland 1996) and humanising themselves, one through modesty and the other through humour. It is a way of saying, 'even though I am posting a personal ad, I am not the usual kind of person who posts such ads'.

While membership in other discourse communities does not usually involve the same kind of ambivalence, 'tactical' aspects of using genres such as *bending* and *blending* are common in nearly all communities and, indeed, are often markers of users' expertise. Of course, in order for blending to be effective it must result in some sort of enhancement that contributes to the overall communicative purpose being achieved more effectively or more efficiently. Similarly, when *bending* a genre, one must be careful not to bend it to the point of breaking. Whether a particular use of a genre is considered a creative innovation or an embarrassing failure is ultimately a matter of whether or not the original communicative purpose of the genre is achieved.

Modes, media and context

A number of other important factors determine how genres are used and how they change. One, which we deal with in more detail in A9 and B9, has to do with the different *modes* (e.g. writing, graphics, video) that are available for constructing the genre. Another, which we will discuss in B8, has to do with the media through which genres are produced and distributed.

Both of these factors are important in relation to the genre we have been discussing, personal advertisements, given the fact that recently this genre has, to a large extent, migrated online. Nowadays it is more likely that one would encounter such an advertisement on the Internet than in a newspaper. As a result of this migration, the genre itself has changed dramatically.

First, it has changed in terms of the different modes that are available to users to realise the moves discussed above. Because it is so easy to upload digital photographs and even video, self-descriptions in online personal advertisements are not dependent on text alone.

Second, websites that host such advertisements often require users to fill out web forms, which specify exactly which information should be included and render that information in a predetermined format. Such standardisation leads to more uniformity, but also makes it easier for users to electronically search through thousands of ads using keywords.

Third, Internet-based dating advertisements include all kinds of ways for the advertiser and target to interact, including sending online messages, engaging in real-time video chat or exchanging forms of communication unique to this medium such as virtual 'kisses', 'pokes', 'hugs', 'winks' and 'hearts' (see Jones 2009a).

Finally, with the development of mobile technologies, users of such genres can access them anywhere through their mobile phones and use GPS tools to search for suitable partners within a certain radius of their present location.

The point is that genres inevitably change, either because the communicative goals of users change or because technologies for the production or distribution of texts introduce new, more efficient ways of fulfilling old communicative goals. Every time a genre changes, however, new sets of conventions and constraints are introduced, and users need to invent new ways to operate strategically within these constraints and to *bend* or *blend* the genre in creative ways.

👁 **Find more examples of move analysis online.**

CONSTRUCTING REALITY   B4

Participants and processes

In unit A4 I argued that no text is ideologically 'neutral' – that all texts promote certain kinds of beliefs about the world and certain kinds of power relationships between people. The main ways authors of texts promote ideologies is by constructing versions of reality in which certain kinds of *participants* are excluded, and those that are included are linked to each other in certain relationships, often based on the actions (*processes*) they are portrayed as engaging in.

Different kinds of processes link participants in different ways. As I discussed in A1, processes involving some kind of physical action link participants in ways in which one participant is portrayed as doing something to or for the other (**action processes**). Processes involving saying or writing, on the other hand, often link participants so that one participant takes the position of the speaker or writer and the other takes the position of the listener or reader (**verbal processes**). Processes involving thinking and feeling link participants to ideas or emotions in various ways (**mental processes**).

Participants can also be linked in ways that show their relationship with each other (**relational processes**): they might be portrayed as equal or equivalent with linking verbs such as 'to be' or 'to seem' (as in 'this ice cream is my dinner'); one participant might be portrayed as possessing another with words such as 'to have' or 'to contain' (as in 'this ice cream contains nuts'); and participants might be linked to each other in other kinds of relationship such as cause and effect with words such as 'to cause', 'to lead to' or 'to result in' (as in 'ice cream leads to obesity').

Finally, processes themselves can sometimes be transformed into participants and linked to other participants or other processes (as in 'eating ice cream caused my divorce'). In this last example, one process, the action of eating ice cream, is linked in a cause-and-effect relationship with another process, the speaker's getting divorced from his or her spouse. Turning a process into a participant is known as **nominalisation** and is often a characteristic of technical or academic texts.

The ideology of warnings

One example of how participants and processes can be combined in texts to create certain versions of reality can be found in the warning labels that most governments require to appear on cigarette packets. These requirements did not always exist, and when the US government first instituted them in 1966, there was fierce negotiation between legislators and tobacco companies, which at that time still had considerable influence with the government, regarding how the warnings should be worded. The first warning labels that appeared on cigarettes in the US read:

Caution: Cigarette Smoking May be Hazardous to Your Health

Here, the process type used is relational ('to be'), linking the _nominalised_ process of smoking cigarettes to a possible attribute: 'hazardousness'. This link is weakened by the use of the modal verb 'may', which reduces the certainty of the statement. One can almost hear the voice of the government competing with the voice of the tobacco companies in this statement, the one working to claim that cigarette smoking is risky and the other working to undermine this claim.

In 1970, the US Congress passed new legislation, which revised the warning to read:

Warning: The Surgeon General Has Determined that Cigarette Smoking is Dangerous to Your Health

The first difference we can notice about this statement is that it is now characterised as a 'warning' rather than just a 'caution'. The second thing we can notice is that the participants and processes have changed. Now the main participant is no longer the nominalised process of 'cigarette smoking' but a person, the surgeon general, the chief medical officer of the United States, engaged in a mental process, that of 'determining'. The statement in the previous warning about cigarettes being hazardous has itself become a participant, the thing that the surgeon general has determined, and has been slightly modified, the relational link becoming more certain ('is' rather than 'may be'), and the attribute changed to 'dangerous'.

On the one hand, it is easy to see how this warning is in some ways stronger than the previous one: 'dangerous' seems more serious than 'hazardous' and the voice of the surgeon general seems to add authority to the statement. On the other hand, the statement about the risk of cigarette smoking is no longer the main clause of the sentence, but has been 'demoted' to the status of a participant. In other words, while the previous warning was about cigarette smoking and its 'hazardousness', this sentence is about the surgeon general and what he (at the time, a man) had determined.

In 1985, the warning label was again changed to read:

SURGEON GENERAL'S WARNING: Smoking Causes Lung Cancer, Heart Disease, Emphysema, and May Complicate Pregnancy.

Here, the main participant is once again the nominalised process 'smoking', but a new process has been introduced, the process of 'causing'. This process is also a relational one, but it portrays a different kind of relationship. Rather than simply talking about an attribute of smoking, it places smoking in a cause and effect relationship with a number of serious diseases ('lung cancer', 'heart disease' and 'emphysema'). Smoking's relationship with 'pregnancy', however, is more uncertain. First, the modal verb 'may' weakens the relationship created by the process. Second, the process itself, also one of causation ('complicate' means 'to cause to be complicated'), is much more vague. It is uncertain exactly how pregnancy might be made 'complicated' and what the implications of that might be.

It is interesting to note that the cigarette warnings mandated by the government in the United States, the country where most of the world's biggest tobacco companies are based, tend to portray cigarettes as either having certain attributes (being 'harmful') or being in certain other kinds of relationships with other participants rather than *doing* things *to* people. Although 'cause' may seem to be about doing something, it is actually more about the relationship between two things, one thing leading to another thing. Warnings used in other countries, on the other hand, often use *action processes*. One warning used in Australia, for example, is:

Smoking harms unborn babies.

Here 'smoking' is portrayed as doing something (harming) *to* someone (unborn babies). Similarly, since 2003, cigarettes in the European Union have carried warnings such as:

Smoking seriously harms you and others around you.
Smoking while pregnant harms your child.

and the direct and unambiguous statement:

Smoking Kills

In the examples above it is clear how the use of different kinds of participants and processes constructs very different versions of the risk of cigarette smoking. At the same time, it is important to caution that searching for ideology in texts is usually not simple or straightforward. One cannot, for example, say that certain process types or other grammatical features such as nominalisation *always* result in certain kinds of effects. Rather, grammar is a *resource* that authors draw upon to represent reality in particular ways.

Constructing relationships

Constructing reality is not just a matter of representing what is going on. It is also a matter of the author of a text constructing a certain kind of relationship with the reader or listener and communicating something about the relevance of what is going on to him or her. As stated before, one way this is done is to use the language's system of *modality*. The use of the modal verb 'may' in the statement 'Cigarette smoking may be hazardous to your health' discussed above, for example, creates in the reader some doubt about the certainty of the statement.

Another way authors might construct a relationship with readers is through the use of pronouns such as 'you' and 'we'. By using the possessive pronoun 'your' in the above statement, for example, the authors of the statement make the potential 'hazardousness' of cigarette smoking relevant to readers. Similarly, the statement, 'Smoking seriously harms you and others around you' makes the harm of cigarettes directly relevant by making the reader a participant in the statement and, particularly, the participant to which the act of 'harming' is being done. This statement also constructs readers as socially responsible by implying that they would not only wish to avoid harm to themselves, but also harm to those around them. An even more striking example of this technique can be seen in the Australian warning label below:

Protect children: don't make them breathe your smoke.

In this example the message is also personalised by making the reader a participant. In contrast to the warning above, however, which positions the reader as a victim of cigarette smoking, this warning positions the reader as the potential agent of harm, making children breathe smoke which is explicitly portrayed as 'belonging to' him or her.

Finally, texts create relationships between authors and readers through the use of what we have been calling 'social languages'. Consider the two examples below:

1) Smoking when pregnant harms your baby (European Union).
2) SURGEON GENERAL'S WARNING: Smoking By Pregnant Women May Result in Fetal Injury, Premature Birth, And Low Birth Weight (United States).

Both of these examples are about the same thing: smoking by pregnant women. This first text, however, constructs a reader who is herself a pregnant woman, whereas the second constructs a reader who, while he or she may be interested in 'pregnant women', may not be one. Furthermore, the first example uses common, everyday language and few nominalisations, constructing the author as a person not so different from the reader, someone akin to a friend or a relative. The second example, on the other hand, uses very dense scientific language and nominalisations such as 'fetal injury' in which the process of 'harming' from the first example is transformed into a noun, and the participant 'your baby' is transformed into an adjective modifying that noun ('fetal'). This sort of language constructs the author as some kind of expert, perhaps a doctor or a research scientist, and creates a considerable distance between him or her and the reader.

As can be seen from these examples, register (what Gee calls 'social languages') and other interpersonal aspects of texts work to portray the authors of the texts as certain kinds of people and also construct readers of the texts as certain kinds of people. Another way to say this is that texts make available certain 'reading positions' (Hodge and Kress 1988) that situate readers in relation to the authors of the text, the topic that the text deals with and other people or institutions relevant to the topic. The extent to which readers are able and willing to occupy these 'reading positions' helps to determine the kind of ideological effect the texts will have.

The ideological effects of texts

While the kind of textual analysis illustrated here can tell us something about the versions of reality that texts construct and about the kinds of reading positions they make available, it is impossible to say for certain just by analysing texts what their actual effect will be on readers. Some pregnant women, for example, might respond more readily to the plain familiar language and the personal approach in example 1 above. Others might be more persuaded by the authoritative voice of example 2.

To really understand how people actually interpret texts or, for that matter, how ideologies end up finding their way into texts in the first place, it is necessary to go beyond texts themselves and analyse both *discourse practices*, the practices authors engage in when creating texts and the practices readers engage in when interpreting them, and *social practices*, the activities, norms and social relationships that make up readers' social worlds.

The more we know about the negotiations that went on between big tobacco companies and politicians in the United States in the late 1960s, for example, the better we can understand why early cigarette warnings were worded the way they were; and the more we understand readers' experiences of and knowledge about smoking and the status of smoking in their circle of acquaintances, the better we will be able to understand the effects warnings on cigarette packets might have on their behaviour. For this reason, people who are interested in studying ideology in discourse, known as *critical discourse analysts*, are increasingly supplementing textual analysis with more ethnographic research techniques such as interviews, observations and historical research.

👁 **Find more examples of ideology in texts online.**

THE TEXTURE OF TALK   B5

In the analysis of how people make sense of written texts (see A2 and B2), I introduced the concept of *texture*. *Texture*, I said, basically comes from two things: the ways different parts of a text are related to one another, and the various expectations that people have about texts. Making sense of conversations also involves these two aspects of communication: the structure and patterning of the communication and the broader expectations about meaning and human behaviour that participants bring to it. Generally speaking, *conversation analysis* focuses more on the first aspect, and *pragmatics* focuses more on the second.

The basis of *pragmatics* is the idea that people enter into conversations with the assumption that the people they are conversing with will behave in a logical way. The philosopher Herbert Paul Grice called this assumption the *cooperative principle*. When people engage in conversation, he said, they do so with the idea that people will:

Make (their) conversational contribution such as is required, at the stage at which it occurs, by the accepted purpose or direction of the talk exchange in which you are engaged.

(Grice 1975: 45)

What he meant by this was that when people talk with each other they generally cooperate in making their utterances understandable by conforming to what they believe to be the other person's expectations about how people usually behave in conversation. Most people, he said, have four main expectations about conversational behaviour:

1   that what people say will be true (the maxim of quality);
2   that what people say will be relevant to the topic under discussion (the maxim of relevance);
3   that people will try to make what they mean clear and unambiguous (the maxim of manner);
4   that people will say as much as they need to say to express their meaning and not say more than they need to say (the maxim of quantity).

Grice called these four expectations *maxims*. Maxims are not rules that must be followed; rather, they are general statements of principle about how things should be done. In actual conversations, however, people often violate or 'flout' these maxims: they say things that are not true; they make seemingly irrelevant statements; they are not always clear about what they mean; and they sometimes say more than they need to or not enough to fully express their meaning. The point that Grice was making was not that people always follow or even that they 'should' follow these maxims, but that when they *do not* follow them, they usually do so for a reason: the very fact that they have flouted a maxim itself *creates meaning*, a special type of meaning known as **implicature**, which involves implying or suggesting something without having to directly express it. When people try to make sense of what others have said, they do so against the background of these default expectations. When speakers do not behave as expected, listeners logically conclude that they are trying to imply something indirectly and try to work out what it is.

If your friend asks you if you think her new boyfriend is good looking, but you do not think he is, you might say something like, 'He has a lovely personality,' violating the maxim of relevance (her question was about his appearance, not his personality), or you might say something rather vague which communicates that you do not think he is very good looking but which avoids saying this explicitly, violating the maxim of manner.

The obvious question is, why do people do this? Why don't they simply communicate what they mean directly? One reason is that implicature allows us to manage the interpersonal aspect of communication. We might, for example, use implicature to be more polite or avoid hurting someone's feelings. We might also use implicature to avoid making ourselves too accountable for what we have said – in other words, to say something without 'really saying' it.

Of course, the fact that someone says something that is not true or is not entirely clear does not necessarily mean they are creating implicature. Sometimes people simply lie. You might, for example, tell your friend that you think her boyfriend is very handsome. In this case, you have not created any indirect meaning. Your meaning is very direct. It is just not true. Another example can be seen in the often-quoted exchange below from *The Pink Panther Strikes Again* (1976 United Artists):

A: Does your dog bite?
B: No.
A: [Bends down to stroke it and gets bitten] Ow! I thought you said your dog did not bite.
B: That is not my dog.

Here A has violated the maxim of quantity by saying too little, but, in doing so, he has *not* created implicature. He has simply said too little. And so for the flouting of a maxim to be meaningful, it must be done within the overall framework of the cooperative principle. The person flouting a maxim must expect that the other person will realise that they are flouting the maxim and that the meaning created by this is not too difficult to figure out.

How we do things with words

Another important aspect of pragmatics concerns how people accomplish various social actions when they talk, such as requesting, promising and threatening. The philosopher John Austin pointed out that certain utterances, when they are spoken, have the effect of actually performing some action in the physical world. When the officiant at a wedding ceremony, for example, says, 'I now pronounce you husband and wife,' it is by this *pronouncement* that the couple becomes married, or when a judge says, 'I sentence you to five years in prison,' it is by this utterance that the person to whom this is uttered is *sentenced*. Austin called these kinds of utterances **performatives**.

While Austin's insight might seem rather obvious now, it was quite revolutionary at the time he was writing, when most philosophers of language were mainly focused on analysing sentences in terms of whether or not they were 'true'. Austin pointed out that, for many utterances, their 'truth value' is not as important as whether or not they are able to perform the action they are intended to perform.

The more Austin thought about this idea of performatives, the more he realised that many utterances – not just those containing phrases such as 'I pronounce . . .' and 'I declare . . .' and 'I command . . .' – have a performative function. If somebody says to you, 'Cigarette smoking is dangerous to your health,' for example, he or she is usually not just making a statement. He or she is also *doing* something, that is, *warning* you not to smoke.

Austin called these utterances that perform actions **speech acts**. The important thing about these kinds of utterances, he said, is not so much their 'meaning' as their 'force', their ability to perform actions. All speech acts have three kinds of force: **locutionary force**, the force of what the words actually mean, **illocutionary force**, the force of the action the words are intended to perform, and **perlocutionary force**, the force of the actual effect of the words on listeners.

One of the problems with analysing speech acts is that, for many of the same reasons speakers express meanings indirectly by flouting conversational maxims, they also express speech acts indirectly. In other words, the *locutionary force* of their speech act (the meaning of the words) might be very different from the *illocutionary force* (what they are actually doing with their words). We have already discussed a number of examples of this, such as the question 'Do you have a pen?' uttered to perform the act of requesting (see A1).

And so the problem is, how do we figure out what people are trying to *do* with their words? For Austin, the main way we do this is by logically analysing the conditions under which a particular utterance is produced. He called the ability of an utterance to perform a particular action the 'felicity' (or 'happiness') of the utterance, and in order for speech acts to be 'happy', certain kinds of conditions must be met, which Austin called **felicity conditions**.

Some of these conditions relate to what is said. For some speech acts to be felicitous, for example, they must be uttered in a certain conventional way. The officiant at a wedding must say something very close to 'I now pronounce you husband and wife' in order for this to be a pronouncement of marriage. Some of the conditions have to do with who utters the speech act – the kind of authority or identity they have. Only someone specially empowered to do so, for instance, is able to perform marriages. If a random person walked up to you and your companion on the street and said, 'I now pronounce you husband and wife,' this would not be considered a felicitous pronouncement of marriage. Some of these conditions concern the person or people to whom the utterance is addressed. They must generally be able to decipher the speech act and comply with it. People under a certain age, for example, cannot get married, and so the pronouncement of marriage given above would not succeed as a speech act. Similarly, if the two people to whom this pronouncement is uttered are not willing to get married, the pronouncement would also lack felicity. Finally, some of these conditions may have to do with the time or place the utterance is issued. Captains of ships, for example, are only empowered to make pronouncements of marriage aboard their ships.

And so, according to Austin and his followers, the main way we figure out what people are trying to do when they speak to us is by trying to match the conditions in which an utterance is made to the conditions necessary for particular kinds of speech acts. So, when somebody comes up to me in a bar and says, 'Hey mate, I suggest you leave my girlfriend alone,' I use my logic to try to figure out what he is doing and what he is trying to get me to do. At first I might think that he is making a suggestion to me. But, when I consider the conditions of the situation, I realise that this utterance does not fulfil the necessary conditions of a suggestion, one of which is that whether or not I follow the suggestion is optional. I can tell quite clearly from the expression on this fellow's face that what he is 'suggesting' is not optional. I also realise that there will probably be unpleasant consequences for me should I fail to comply. Given these conditions, I can only conclude that what he is doing with his words is not making a suggestion but issuing a threat.

The important thing about this example is that I must use both of the tools introduced above. I must make use of the cooperative principle to realise that he is flouting the maxim of quality (he is not making a suggestion) and that there must be some reason for this, and I must be able to analyse the conditions in which this utterance is made to figure out what the speaker is actually trying to do.

Sense and sequencing: conversation analysis

Whereas pragmatics begins with the assumption that conversations are logical, *conversation analysis* begins with the assumption that they are *orderly*. What orderly means is that they follow a certain predictable pattern, with some kinds of utterances necessarily coming before or following other kinds of utterances.

Conversation analysts also see utterances as *actions*. Where they differ is in their ideas about how we interpret these actions – what gives 'force' to our words. Whereas followers of Austin consider the speaker's intentions and the conditions under which the words are uttered to be the most important things, conversation analysts consider the utterance that occurred *prior* to the utterance in question, and the one that occurs *afterwards* to be more important. In other words, they believe we interpret utterances chiefly based on how they 'fit' sequentially with other utterances in a conversation.

The core of conversation analysis, then, is the exploration of the sequential structure of conversation. According to Schegloff and Sacks (1973), social interaction is often arranged in pairs of utterances – what one person says basically determines what the next person can say. They call these sequences of 'paired actions' **adjacency pairs**. Examples of common adjacency pairs are 'question/answer', 'invitation/acceptance' and 'greeting/greeting'.

The most important thing about the two utterances that make up an adjacency pair is that they have a relationship of **conditional relevance**. In other words, one utterance is dependent on (*conditioned by*) the other utterance. The first utterance determines what the second utterance can be (a question, for example, should be followed by an answer, and a greeting should be followed by a greeting). In the same way, the second utterance also determines what the first utterance has been understood to be. If I have given you an answer, this provides evidence that I have taken your preceding utterance to be a question. This is a big difference between conversation analysis and the speech act theory of Austin. For speech act theory, the conditions for whether or not an utterance constitutes a particular speech act include things such as the intentions and identities of the speakers and the context of the situation. For conversation analysts, the conditions that determine how an utterance should be interpreted must exist *within the conversation itself*.

At the same time, conversation analysis also focuses on how speakers make use of the default expectations people bring to conversations in order to make meaning. The main difference is that important expectations are not so much about the *content* of utterances (whether or not, for example, they are 'true' or 'clear'), but rather about the *structure* of conversation, and particularly the ways that utterances should 'fit' with previous utterances. The idea behind adjacency pairs is that when one person says something, he or she creates a 'slot' for the next person to 'fill in' in a particular way. If they fill it in in the expected way, this is called a **preferred response**. If they do not fill in this slot in the expected way, their interlocutor 'hears' the preferred response as being **officially absent**. As Schegloff (1968: 1083) put it:

> Given the first, the second is expectable. Upon its occurrence, it can be seen to be the second item to the first. Upon its non-occurrence, it can be seen to be officially absent.

Take for example the following exchange between a woman and her boyfriend:

> *A*:   I love you.
> *B*:   Thank you.

The reason this exchange seems odd to us, and undoubtedly seems odd to A, is that the preferred response to an expression of love is a reciprocal expression of love. When this response is not given, it creates *implicature*. Thus, the most important thing about B's response is not the meaning that he expresses (gratitude), but the meaning that is *absent* from the utterance.

All first utterances in adjacency pairs are said to have a 'preferred' second utterance. For example, the preferred response to an invitation is an acceptance. The preferred response to a greeting is a greeting. What makes a preferred response preferred is not that the person who offered the first utterance would 'prefer' this response (the preferred response for an accusation, for example, is a denial), but rather that this is the response which usually requires the least additional conversational work. So the preferred response is the most *efficient* response. When we issue **dispreferred responses**, we often have to add something to them in order to avoid producing unintended implicature. For example, if you ask me to come to your party and I accept your invitation, all I have to do is say 'Sure!' But if I want to refuse the invitation, I cannot just say 'No!' If I do, I create the implicature that I do not much like you or care about your feelings. If I want to avoid communicating this, I have to supplement it with other things such as an apology ('I'm really sorry . . .') and an excuse or account of why I cannot come to your party ('I have to do my discourse analysis homework').

You can divide almost any conversation into a series of adjacency pairs. Sometimes, though, adjacency pairs can be quite complicated, with pairs of utterances overlapping or being embedded in other pairs of utterances. Nevertheless, for conversation analysts, it is this underlying 'pair wise organisation' of utterances that helps us to make sense of our conversations and use them to accomplish actions in an orderly way.

There is, of course, a lot more to both pragmatics and conversation analysis than has been covered in this brief summary. Pragmatics, for example, has much more to say about the various cognitive models that people bring to interaction, and conversation analysis has much to say about how people manage things such as turn-taking, topic negotiation, openings and closings, and repair in conversations. What we have focused on here is primarily how each of these approaches addresses the problem of ambiguity in spoken discourse – the problem that people do not always say what they mean or mean what they say.

👁 **Find more examples of the texture of talk online.**

NEGOTIATING RELATIONSHIPS AND ACTIVITIES

Power and politeness

Whenever we interact with others we always communicate something about our relationship with them. We do this by using various discursive strategies, which, as I said in unit A6, we can divide into two categories: *involvement strategies* and *independence strategies*. *Involvement strategies* are strategies people use to communicate friendliness or solidarity, and *independence strategies* are strategies people use to communicate respect or deference.

In many cases, both parties in an interaction share a fairly clear idea about how close they are and whether one has more power than the other, but in other cases, participants in interaction need to negotiate their relationship. Such negotiations are common, for example, as people move from more distant to closer relationships, or when one person wishes to challenge another person's assertion of power or dominance.

Regardless of whether or not a relationship is seen as 'negotiable', we always approach interactions with certain sets of expectations about how independence and involvement strategies will be used to communicate information about power and intimacy. We call these expectations **face systems**. Although expectations about when *independence* and *involvement strategies* are appropriate and what they mean vary across cultures and groups, most people enter interaction with three basic ideas: 1) in interactions where the parties are socially distant but relatively equal, both parties are likely to use independence strategies (**deference face system**); 2) in interactions where people are close and relatively equal, they are likely to use involvement strategies (**solidarity face system**); and 3) in interactions in which one person has more power than the other (regardless of their social distance), the more powerful one is more likely to use involvement strategies and the less powerful one is more likely to use independence strategies (**hierarchical face system**).

Like the conversational maxims we discussed in the last section, these 'systems' should not be treated as 'rules', but rather as broad sets of expectations people draw on to decide how to act towards other people and how to interpret others' behaviour towards them. Since power and distance are relative rather than absolute, and because interaction often involves the sometimes subtle use of power and distance, people usually employ both independence and involvement strategies, mixing them tactically depending on the situation and what they are trying to accomplish.

An example of the way participants strategically mix independence and involvement strategies can be seen in the following conversation between a senior engineer (Martin) and his subordinate (Ollie) reported in Ladegaard (2011):

Martin:	Happy birthday or (0.2) whatever it is (laughing)
Ollie:	thank you (0.2) it's actually a while ago
Martin:	okay eh: Ollie//
Ollie:	//there's Danish pastry over there if you're interested (0.2)

Martin: thanks ah: (0.6) (talks about tape recorder)
Martin: okay well to cut a long story short Sam called (0.2) and I'm not sure how busy you are or what you're doing right now (0.4)
Ollie: ah: we're just about to launch the [name] project and ah:
Martin: okay
Ollie: so this is where we are [xxx] quite busy (0.5) but Sam called you said
Martin: yes (0.2)
Ollie: and he? (0.3)
Martin: he needs some help here and now (0.2) he needs someone to calculate the price of rubber bands (0.3) for the [name] project in India
Ollie: okay
Martin: they expect the customer to sign today (1.3)
Ollie: okay

(Ladegaard 2011: 14–15)

In this example, Martin, the more powerful participant, begins using involvement strategies, wishing Ollie happy birthday (although it is not his birthday) and laughing. Ollie, on the other hand, though friendly, uses more independence strategies, accepting the inappropriate birthday wish and then using words such as 'actually' and 'a while' to soften his revelation that it is not his birthday, and then offering Martin some pastry in a way which is designed not to impose on him ('. . . if you're interested'). Were Martin and Ollie equals and friends, the inappropriate birthday wishes might have been answered in a more direct way, such as, 'What are you talking about? My birthday was ages ago!', and the offer of pastry might have been more insistent (Have some Danish!). In other words, the mixture of involvement and independence strategies in the beginning of the conversation are what one might expect within a hierarchical face system.

What happens next in the conversation, however, is rather interesting. Martin, the more powerful person, changes to independence strategies, asking Ollie how busy he is and making it clear that he does not wish to impose on him. In fact, he acts so reluctant to make the request that Ollie practically has to drag it out of him ('but Sam called you said . . . and he?'). This, in fact, is the opposite of what one might expect in a hierarchical relationship. Of course, this shift in politeness strategies, with the more powerful participant using independence strategies and the less powerful one showing more involvement does not really reflect a shift in power. Rather, it is a clever strategy Martin has used to make it more difficult for Ollie to refuse the request by putting him in the position of soliciting it.

The point of this analysis is that, even though our expectations about face systems form the background to how we communicate about relationships, people often strategically confound these expectations to their own advantage.

One further factor that determines which strategy a person will use to communicate his or her relationship with another person is the topic of the conversation he or she is engaged in. In cases in which the topic of the conversation is serious or potentially embarrassing for either party, or in which the weight of imposition is seen to be great, independence strategies will be more common, whereas in situations where the topic is less serious, the outcome more predictable and the weight of imposition seen to be relatively small, involvement strategies are more common.

As can be seen in the example above, rather than as simple reflections of *a priori* relationships of power and distance or the 'weightiness' of a particular topic, face strategies can be regarded as *resources* that people use to negotiate social distance, enact power relationships, and sometimes manipulate others into doing things which they may not normally be inclined to do. A person might use involvement strategies with another not *because* they are close, but because he or she wants to *create* or strengthen the impression that there is a power difference. Similarly, a person might use independence strategies not to create a sense of distance from the person they are interacting with, but rather to endow the topic under discussion with a certain 'weightiness'. In other words, face strategies are not just reflections of the expectations about relationships that people bring to interactions but *resources* they make use of to manage and sometimes change those relationships on a moment-by-moment basis.

Framing and contextualisation cues

As we have seen above, conversational strategies such as involvement and independence are not just ways that we communicate and manage our relationships with other people, but also ways that we communicate something about what we are doing (the degree, for example, to which we think we are imposing on other people). We also have other ways of signalling to people what we think we are doing in an interaction, whether we, for example, are arguing, joking, commiserating or making small talk. Whenever we speak, in fact, we communicate not just the message contained in (or implied by) our words, but also information about what we think we are doing and, therefore, how our words should be interpreted. We call the signals we use to communicate this information **contextualisation cues**.

In unit A6 I said that there are basically two kinds of *frames*: broader *primary frameworks* which consist of the relatively stable sets of expectations we bring to particular situations (such as lectures or medical consultations), and smaller, more dynamic *interactive frames*, which consist of our negotiated ideas about what we are doing moment by moment in a conversation, ideas which often change rapidly in the course of an interaction. Although *contextualisation cues* are often important in signalling *primary frameworks*, they are particularly important in the role they play in helping us to manage and negotiate *interactive frames*.

Sometimes contextualisation cues are verbal, that is, we signal what we are doing through our choice of topic, vocabulary, grammar or even the language that we use. For example, in her analysis of the talk of teachers in bilingual classrooms, Angel Lin (1996) has pointed out that when English teachers in Hong Kong are focusing on teaching, they tend to use English, but when they are engaged in reprimanding their students, they tend to switch to Cantonese. Sometimes these verbal cues involve adopting a particular register or social language (see A4 and B4) or certain genres (see A3 and B3) associated with particular kinds of activities. A doctor, for example, might begin a consultation with a period of small talk in which the language might be extremely informal and the topic might range from the weather to a local sports team before he or she 'shifts gears' and starts 'talking like a doctor'.

One of the most obvious ways we signal shifts in frames verbally is through what are known as **discourse markers**. These are words or phrases that often rather explicitly mark the end of one activity and the beginning of another. A lecturer, for example, might move from the pre-lecture chatting and milling around frame to the formal lecture frame with words such as '*Okay*, let's get started . . .'. Similarly, the doctor might move from small talk to the more formal medical examination by saying something such as '*So*, how are you feeling?' Discourse markers typically consist of words such as *okay, so, well* and *anyway,* as well as more formal connectors such as *first, next* and *however.* It is important to remember that discourse markers do not *always* signal a shift in frame – sometimes they signal other things, such as the relationship between one idea and another (see B2).

These verbal strategies are not the only ways, or even the most common ways, people signal what they are doing when they talk. *Contextualisation cues* also include *non-verbal* signals delivered through things such as gestures, facial expressions, gaze, our use of space and *paralinguistic* signals delivered through alterations in the pitch, speed, rhythm or intonation of our voices. For this reason, people who study frames and contextualisation cues often pay a lot of attention to marking things such as stress, intonation and pausing and even facial expressions, gestures and other movements when they produce transcripts of the conversations they are studying.

These non-verbal and paralinguistic contextualisation cues are sometimes much more subtle than verbal strategies and so more easily misunderstood. The way they are used and interpreted might also vary considerably from group to group or even person to person. In one of his most famous studies, Gumperz (1982a: 173–174) found a mismatch between the way south Asian servers in a staff canteen in a British airport used intonation as a contextualisation cue and the ways their British customers interpreted it. The south Asian servers used falling intonation when asking customers if they wanted gravy on their meat (consistent with the conventions of their variety of English), but the British customers, expecting the rising intonation they associated with a polite offer, interpreted the servers' behaviour as rude. What this example tells us is that contextualisation cues do not in themselves contain information about what we think we are doing – rather, they *activate* culturally conditioned assumptions about context, interactional goals and interpersonal relationships that might be different for different people.

As we said above, interactive frames are not static, but can change rapidly in the course of an interaction. They are also, as their name implies, *interactive* – that is, they are always a matter of negotiation between participants in the conversation, and the way they are used and interpreted often has a great deal to do with things that happened previously in the conversation and with the history of the relationship between those involved.

Sometimes participants in an interaction will experience disagreement regarding 'what's going on'. The way one person frames the conversation, for example, may be at odds with the other person's wishes, expectations or interpretation of the situation. In some cases, they may simply accept the framing that has been imposed by the other person, or they may contest or resist it by either attempting to reframe the conversation using their own contextualisation cues or by breaking the frame altogether and engaging in a 'meta-conversation' about 'what's going on'.

The film *When Harry Met Sally* (1988 Castle Rock Pictures) contains a number of good examples of characters competitively negotiating frames in interaction. In the following example, Harry, who is going out with Sally's best friend, tells Sally that he thinks she is attractive, and what ensues is a negotiation about what such a statement means based on what he was 'doing' when he said it:

HARRY: You're a very attractive person.

SALLY: Oh, thank you.

HARRY: Amanda never said you were so attractive.

SALLY: Maybe she doesn't think I'm attractive.

HARRY: It's not a matter of opinion. Empirically you are attractive.

SALLY: Harry, Amanda is my friend.

HARRY: So?

SALLY: So you're going with her.

HARRY: So?

SALLY: So you're coming on to me.

HARRY: No I wasn't.

HARRY (continuing): What? Can't a man say a woman is attractive without it being a come-on?

HARRY (continuing): All right. Let's just say for the sake of argument it was a come-on. Okay. What do you want me to do? I take it back. All right, I take it back.

SALLY: You can't take it back.

HARRY: Why not?

SALLY: It's already out there.
(An awkward pause)

HARRY: Ohm jeez. What are we supposed to do now? Call the cops? It's already out there.

SALLY: Just let it lie, okay?

HARRY: Right, right. Let it lie. That's my policy. Let it lie . . . So, you want to spend the night in the motel?

HARRY (continuing): See what I did? I didn't let it lie.

SALLY: Harry ——

HARRY: I said I would and then I didn't ——

SALLY: Harry ——

HARRY: I went the other way ——

SALLY: Harry ——

HARRY: Yes?

SALLY: We are just going to be friends, okay?

HARRY: Yeah. Great. Friends. Best thing.

In this example, Harry tries to frame his initial compliment as an 'objective observation' using formal language such as 'empirically'. Sally, however, labels what he is doing as a 'come-on', a label which he first resists with the question, 'Can't a man say a woman is attractive without it being a come-on?', framing the accusation as unreasonable and possibly sexist. He then half accepts her framing and offers to 'take it back'. This acceptance is only partial because he frames it as 'hypothetical' ('Let's just say for the sake of argument it was a come-on . . .'). Sally, however, does not accept his retraction, framing a 'come-on' as an irreparable breech in decorum, which Harry responds to by again shifting frames from conciliation to mocking ('What are we supposed to do now? Call the cops?'). What happens after this, however, is particularly interesting. After agreeing to 'let it lie', that is, abandon this particular negotiation about framing, Harry then issues what is unambiguously a 'come-on', and then deflects her objections by again engaging in meta-conversation about his own framing ('See what I did? I didn't let it lie . . . I said I would and then I didn't . . . I went the other way . . .').

Part of the humour in this scene lies in the fact that it foregrounds the process of framing itself, a process which is usually left tacit in conversations. It also shows how complex and contentious negotiations of framing can be, with parties not only shifting frames, breaking frames and attempting to reframe their utterances and those of others, but also superimposing frames on top of other frames in order to create strategic ambiguity (as when Harry imposes a 'hypothetical' frame onto his admission of guilt).

👁 **Find more examples of how people use face strategies and framing strategies online.**

THE SPEAKING MODEL

Speech acts, speech events and speech situations

The main unit of analysis for the ethnography of speaking is the *speech event*, which can be defined as a communicative activity that has a clear beginning and a clear ending and in which people's shared understandings of the relevance of various contextual features remain fairly constant throughout the event. Examples of speech events are such things as religious ceremonies, lessons, debates and conversations. Speech events occur within broader speech situations and are made up of smaller *speech acts* of the type we have already discussed (including such things as greeting, questioning, promising and insulting, see B5). For example, a university lecture can be considered a *speech event* which occurs within the *speech situation* of a school day and is made up of smaller *speech acts* such as asking and answering questions, giving explanations and illustrations of certain concepts, and even joking or threatening. Similarly, the *speech event* of a conversation may occur within the larger *speech situation* of a party and may include smaller *speech acts* such as joking. Notice that the same speech act, joking for example, can take place in many different kinds of speech events, and that different speech events, conversations for example, can occur in many different kinds of speech situations.

What distinguishes a *speech event* from a *speech situation* is not just its size and the fact that speech events tend to have clearer boundaries. The main distinction is *coherence* (see B2): participants tend to approach speech events with consistent sets of expectations that remain the same throughout the speech event, whereas participants' expectations about the relevant features of context may undergo dramatic changes throughout a speech situation: students eating lunch at the university canteen during a school day, for example, are likely to pay attention to different sorts of things than they do in a lecture during the same day. The way to distinguish between a speech situation and a speech event, then, is to ask if the same rules of SPEAKING apply throughout the phenomenon. If so, it can be regarded as a speech event.

SPEAKING

One potentially confusing aspect of the ethnography of speaking is that it does not, as its name implies, focus so much on rules and expectations about *speaking* so much as rules and expectations about the *circumstances* in which certain kinds of speaking takes place (or, does not take place). In fact, one of the most famous studies using this approach, Keith Basso's examination of silence among the Western Apache in the United States (Basso 1970), explored the conditions under which, for members of this speech community, *not speaking* is considered the most appropriate behaviour.

Ron and Suzanne Scollon have used the term 'the Grammar of Context' to refer to a model very much like Hymes's speaking model (Scollon *et al.* 2012). Their reasons for comparing the rules and expectations associated with context to the kinds of rules and expectations associated with the grammar of a language are twofold: first, to highlight that the same difference between competence and performance which we see in grammar also occurs in rules and expectations associated with context: not everyone performs in particular speech events exactly in accordance with how people in their speech community (including themselves) think they should; and second, to introduce the notion of **markedness** into the analysis of context.

The idea of 'unmarked' (the usual or normal way of saying or doing something) versus 'marked' (an unusual or deviant way of saying or doing something) was introduced into structural linguistics by the Prague School of linguists, which included such figures as Roman Jakobson (see Jakobson 1990: 134–40). Although the concept is quite complex, the general idea is that when people deviate from the default or expected way of using language, the result is often the expression of some special, more precise or additional meaning. This is an idea we have already encountered in our discussion of the *cooperative principle*. When it is applied to 'context', it reminds us that communicative competence does not refer to a set of 'rules' that must be followed, but rather to a set of expectations that experienced speakers can sometimes manipulate in order to strategically manage the meanings of speech acts, the relationships among participants or the outcomes of the speech event.

The components of the SPEAKING model devised by Hymes, therefore, are not meant to provide an objective list of those elements of context which need to be taken into account by the analyst, but rather a set of guidelines an analyst can use in attempting to find out what aspects of context are important and relevant *from the point of view of participants*. In other words, in any given speech event, different elements will be afforded different weight by participants, and some might be regarded as totally unimportant.

The first component in the model is **setting**, which refers to the time and place of the speech event as well as any other physical circumstances. Along with the physical aspects of setting, Hymes included what he called the 'psychological setting' or the 'cultural definition' of a scene. The unmarked setting for a particular speech event, for example, might be in a church. A church has particular physical characteristics, but it is also likely to have certain associations for people in a particular culture so that when they enter a church they are predisposed to speak or behave in certain ways. Thus, the component of setting can have an effect on other components such as *key* and *instrumentalities* (see below).

The second component in the SPEAKING model is **participants**. Most of the approaches to spoken discourse we have looked at so far, including conversation analysis and pragmatics, begin with the assumption of an essentially didactic model of communication in which the participants are the speaker and the hearer. Ethnographic work, however, indicates that many if not most speech events involve many kinds of participants, not just speakers and hearers, but also participants such as audiences and bystanders. Furthermore, groups differ in their ideas of which participants in speech events are considered legitimate or relevant (for example, maids, pets, supernatural beings). Besides identifying the relevant participants, the different kinds of identities, roles and rights different participants have are also important. These aspects, of course, will depend on things such as the *genre* of the speech event and may change over the course of the speech event in accordance with a particular *act sequence* (see below).

The third component of the model is **ends**, which refers to the purpose, goals and outcomes of the event, which, of course, may be different for different participants (the goals of a teacher, for example, are not always the same as the goals of his or her students), and the fourth component is **act sequence**, the form the event takes as it unfolds, including the order of different speech acts and other behaviours. Both of these components are intimately connected not just with expectations about participant roles, but also with the *genre* of the speech event.

The fifth component in the model is **key**, by which is meant the overall 'tone' or mood of the speech event. Key is important because it provides an attitudinal context for speech acts, sometimes dramatically altering their meaning (as with sarcasm). At the same time, key is often signalled in very subtle ways that are sometimes outside the purview of most linguistic analysis. We have already explored some of these signals in our discussion of *contextualisation cues* in B6.

The sixth component is **instrumentalities**, meaning the 'message form' – the means or media through which meaning is made. Speech, for example, might be spoken, sung, chanted or shouted, and it may be amplified through microphones, broadcast through electronic media, or written down and passed back and forth between participants. Typically, speech events include complex combinations of instrumentalities that interact with one another and with the other components in the model. In the next unit on mediated discourse analysis we will explore in more detail the effect different instrumentalities can have on speech acts and speech events.

The seventh component is **norms**, which can be divided into **norms of interaction** and **norms of interpretation**. These are the common sets of understandings that participants bring to events about what is appropriate behaviour and how different actions and utterances ought to be understood. The important thing about norms is that they may be different for different participants (a waiter versus a customer, for example) and that the setting of norms is often a matter of power and ideology (see A4).

Finally, the eighth component is **genre**, or the 'type' of speech event. We have already dealt at length with the concept of genre (see A3, B3) and, although Hymes's understanding of genre is slightly different from that of genre analysts like Swales and Bhatia, much of what was said before about community expectations, form and communicative purpose applies here. The most important aspect of this component is the notion that certain speech events are *recognisable* by members of a speech community as being of a certain type, and as soon as they are 'labelled' as such, many of the other components of the model such as ends, act sequence, participant roles and key are taken as givens.

It should be clear from this brief rundown of the components of the SPEAKING model that none of them can really be considered alone: each component interacts with other components in multiple ways. The most important job of an analyst using this model, then, is not just to determine the kinds of knowledge about the different components members of speech communities need to successfully participate in a given speech event, but also to determine how the different components are linked together in particular ways for different speech events. For it is in these *linkages*, the ways, for example, different kinds of participants are associated with different genres, or different settings are seen as suitable for different purposes, or different forms of discourse or media are associated with different keys, that the analyst can begin to get an understanding of deeper *cultural assumptions* about people, places, values, power and communication itself that exist in a particular speech community.

👁 **Find examples of how the SPEAKING model can be applied to different speech events online.**

MEDIATION   **B8**

Cultural tools

The starting point for mediated discourse analysis is the concept of *mediation*. The traditional definition of mediation is the passing of a message through some *medium*, which is placed between two or more people who are communicating. When we think of *media*, we usually think of things such as newspapers, television and computers. Lots of people have pointed out that when messages pass through media, they change fundamentally. Different kinds of media favour different kinds of meanings. The kinds of meaning people can make in a newspaper article, for example, are different from those they can make in a television broadcast. This fact led the media scholar Marshall McLuhan (1964/2001) to make the famous pronouncement: 'the medium *is* the message'.

Mediated discourse analysis is also interested in how different media such as televisions and computers affect the way people use discourse, but it takes a rather broader view of media and mediation. This view comes from the work of the Russian psychologist Lev Vygotsky. Vygotsky (1981) had the idea that *all* actions that people take in the world are somehow mediated through what he called *cultural tools*. *Cultural tools* can include technological tools such as televisions, computers and megaphones, but also include more abstract tools such as languages, counting systems, diagrams and mental schema. Anything an individual uses to take action in the world can be considered a cultural tool.

The important thing about cultural tools is that they make it easier to perform some kinds of actions and communicate some kinds of meanings, and more difficult to take other kinds of actions and communicate other kinds of meanings. In other words, all tools come with certain **affordances** and **constraints**. Writing a letter or an email, for example, allows us to do things that we cannot do when we are producing spoken discourse in the context of a conversation, things such as going back and deleting or revising things we have written before. But it is more difficult to do other things such as gauge the reaction of other people to what we are writing as we are writing it (as we can do with spoken language in face-to-face conversations). A microphone makes it easier to talk to a large group of people, but more difficult to say something private to a person standing next to you (as some politicians have rather painfully learned). Most instant messaging programs make it easy to have a real-time conversation, but more difficult to interrupt one's conversational partner in the middle of an utterance the way we can do in face-to-face conversations.

What this idea of *affordances* and *constraints* means for discourse analysis is that the kinds of discourse and other tools we have available to us affect the kinds of actions that we can take. In many situations, for example, such as ordering lunch in a restaurant in a remote area of China, access to the 'tool' of the Chinese language will allow us to do different things than we could do with the tool of English. Different modes and media also allow us to do different things: we can perform different actions with pictures and gestures than we can with words (see A9, B9), and we can do different things with mobile telephones than we can with landlines. Even genres and social languages have affordances and constraints. A résumé, for example, might be effective for getting a job, but less effective for getting a date with a man or a woman whom we fancy. Even in the context of getting a job, the genre may make it easy to communicate things about formal education, credentials and work experience, but more difficult to communicate things about more informal learning and non-work experience.

And so, when we perform mediated discourse analysis, we first identify the *actions* that are important to a particular social actor in a particular situation and then attempt to determine how the *cultural tools* (such as languages and other modes, media, genres and social languages) contribute to making these actions possible and making other kinds of actions impossible or more difficult. Of course, we also have to recognise that many of the cultural tools we use to perform actions are *not* discursive. If you want to put together a piece of furniture you have bought at Ikea, while some discourse such as the instructions for assembly might be very important, if you lack access to technological tools such as a hammer and a screwdriver, no amount of discourse can make it possible for you to perform the actions you need to perform.

This simple idea that having access to different kinds of tools makes it easier or more difficult to perform social actions has important implications. Earlier, for example, we discussed how people sometimes try to use discourse to advance certain ideologies or versions of reality in order to try to affect what people think. Mediated discourse analysis highlights the fact that discourse does not just have a role in affecting what we think, but also, in a very practical way, in affecting what we can do. If we do not have the proper tools available to us, there are certain things that we simply cannot do. And so people who have access to particular tools (such as languages, genres, electronic media) can often exert certain power over people who do not in very concrete ways. If we also consider that our social identities are created through the actions that we can take, we come to the conclusion that the tools we have available to us and how we use them help to determine not just what we can do, but who we can be.

At the same time, human beings are extremely creative in their use of tools. If I do not have a screwdriver to put together my Ikea table, I might try using a butter knife. If the genre of the résumé does not allow me to showcase my talents, I might try to bend that genre or blend it with another genre. In fact, one important focus of mediated discourse analysis is in exploring the *tension* that exists between the affordances and constraints built in to different cultural tools and the ways people creatively *appropriate* and *adapt* those tools into different situations to achieve different goals.

One example of the way technological tools can affect the kinds of things we can do when we communicate, and the creative ways people adapt to these affordances and constraints, can be seen in the way people use online personal ads and dating sites. In B3 we considered print-based personal ads as a kind of *genre* and discussed how, by mastering the structure of the genre, people claim membership in different discourse communities. Nowadays, however, most people rely on electronic personal ads (or 'profiles') rather than print-based ones. These new online 'profiles' introduce a new set of affordances and constraints for users. In older, print-based ads, for example, users had much more control over self-presentation, which was performed entirely through text.

While such ads often invited the later exchange of pictures, users had a way of vetting potential prospects before sending a picture, thereby maintaining some degree of privacy. On online dating sites, where the inclusion of a picture is expected up front, users relinquish their control over physical self-description and risk disclosing their identities to unintended parties (such as employers, co-workers or family members). In other words, the inclusion of pictures in profiles introduces both *affordances* (it allows for a fuller and more accurate presentation of self) and *constraints* (it makes it more difficult for the owners of profiles to control information about themselves). In my own study of online gay dating sites (Jones 2009a), I discovered how users creatively deal with this challenge by posting pictures designed to strategically obscure their identities or by posting pictures of celebrities, cartoon characters or even inanimate objects which reveal something about their personalities or interests without giving away their identities. There are two important points to take from this example. The first is that every new *affordance* in a cultural tool also brings along with it some new *constraint*, and second, experienced users of tools, like experienced users of genres (see B3), often find ways to creatively adapt to the affordances and constraints of the tools they are using.

Context revisited: sites of engagement

Mediated discourse analysts call the situations into which tools are appropriated **sites of engagement**. Sites of engagement are moments when different kinds of social actors, different kinds of cultural tools and different kinds of social relationships come together to make certain actions possible.

Previously we have explored the importance of 'context' in the production of meaning (see A7, A8). The problem with the idea of 'context' from the point of view of mediated discourse analysis is that it takes 'texts' as its reference point. The concept of *sites of engagement* takes social actions as its reference point. Instead of making an artificial distinction between discourse and everything else, it considers all cultural tools (texts, furniture, objects, machines) that are available to social actors at a particular time in a particular place and explores how they contribute to making possible certain kinds of actions.

Ron and Suzanne Wong Scollon (2004) say that all social actions occur at the *nexus* or 'coming together' of three crucial elements: 1) the discursive resources and other cultural tools that people have available for action (which they call **discourses in place**); 2) the social relationships among the people involved (which they call the **interaction order**); and 3) the knowledge, abilities and experiences of the individual social actor (which they call the **historical body**).

To illustrate how these three elements come together to form the *site of engagement* of a social action we can take the example of crossing a busy city street (see Figure B8.1). There is normally a lot of discourse available to people in this situation. There are things such as street signs, traffic signals and zebra stripes painted on the pavement to assist pedestrians in crossing the street; there is also a lot of discourse such as shop signs and advertisements that might actually interfere with the action of successfully crossing the street. And so one of the most important things for people engaged in performing this action is determining which discourse to attend to and which discourse to ignore.

The second element is the interaction order, the relationships people have with the people with whom they are crossing the street. If we are crossing the street alone, for example, we might take extra care in checking for oncoming traffic, whereas if we are part of a large crowd of people, we might pay more attention to the actions of other pedestrians to decide when to cross simply by following them. If we are with someone else, we might find we need to distribute our attention between the action of crossing the street and some other action such as carrying on a conversation or making sure our companion (if they are, for instance, a small child) gets across the street safely.

Finally, the action of crossing the street depends on people's knowledge and experience of crossing city streets, the habits and mental models they have built up around this social practice, which the Scollons refer to as the historical body. Most of the time we do things such as crossing the street in a rather automatic way. When we find ourselves in unfamiliar situations, however, our habitual ways of doing things sometimes do not work so well. Most of us have found ourselves having some difficulty crossing streets in cities where conventions about which discourses in place pedestrians ought to attend to or what kind of behaviour is expected from drivers are different from those in the city in which we live.

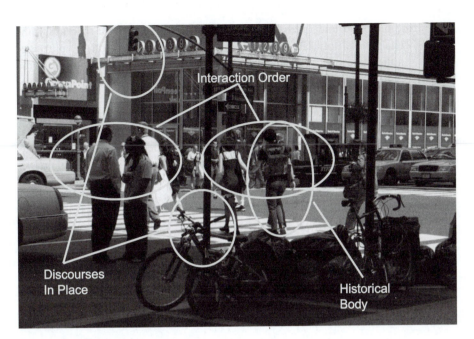

Figure B8.1 Crossing the street

And so the main differences between the ideas of 'site of engagement' and 'context' are, first, that while 'contexts' take 'texts' as their points of reference, sites of engagement take *actions* as their points of reference, and second, that while contexts are usually considered to be external to the social actor, sites of engagement are a matter of the *interaction* among the texts and other cultural tools available in a social situation, the people that are present and the habits, expectations and goals of those people.

👁 **Find more examples of mediated discourse analysis online.**

MODES, MEANING AND ACTION   **B9**

As discussed in unit A9, *multimodal discourse analysis*, the analysis of how multiple modes of communication interact when we communicate, can be divided into two broad approaches, one which focuses on 'texts' (such as magazines and web pages) and the other which focuses on 'real time' interactions. One important concept that is common to both of these approaches is the idea that different modes have different *affordances* and *constraints*. Different modes have different sets of 'meaning potential' and allow us to take different kinds of actions.

In written text and spoken language, for example, we must present information in a sequential way governed by the logic of time. Thus, an author or speaker can manipulate the order and speed at which information is given out, perhaps with-holding certain facts until later in the text or conversation for strategic purposes. Images, on the other hand, are governed by the logic of space. The producer of the image presents all of the elements in the image all at once and has limited control over the order in which viewers look at those elements. Similarly, images allow for the communication of very fine gradations of meaning when it comes to things such as shape and colour – the exact shade of pink in someone's cheeks, for example – whereas language forces us to represent things in terms of *types* – the word 'pink', for example, cannot represent an exact colour, but only a range of colours within a particular class.

The fact that different modes make some kinds of meaning more possible and others less possible is one of the reasons why people strategically mix different modes when they are communicating, so that the constraints of one mode are balanced out by the affordances of others. While there are some things that 'just cannot be expressed in words', it might be possible to express them with a carefully timed facial expression or a carefully placed image.

Communicative functions of modes

In A4 I introduced Halliday's idea that language has three basic functions: it is used to represent our experience of the world; it is used to communicate something about the relationship between us and the people with whom we are communicating; and it is used to organise ideas, representations and other kinds of information in ways that people can make sense of. Halliday calls these three functions the *ideational function*, the *interpersonal function* and the *textual function*. Although these three functions were originally conceived of as a model for understanding language, Kress and van Leeuwen insist that they provide a useful starting point for studying all modes. In their book *Reading Images: The grammar of visual design*, they explore how images also fulfil these three functions, but do so in a rather different way than language (see D9).

Ideational function

As noted in A4, the ideational function of language is accomplished through the linking together of *participants* (typically nouns) with *processes* (typically verbs), creating what Gee (2010) calls 'whos doing whats'. In images, on the other hand, participants are generally portrayed as *figures*, and the processes that join them together are portrayed visually.

Images can be **narrative**, representing figures engaged in actions or events, **classificatory**, representing figures in ways in which they are related to one another in terms of similarities and differences or as representatives of 'types', or **analytical**, representing figures in ways in which parts are related to wholes.

In narrative images, *action processes* are usually represented by what Kress and van Leeuwen call **vectors**, compositional elements that indicate the directionality of an action. In Figure B9.1, for example, the arm of the boxer on the left extending right-ward towards the head of the other boxer portrays the process of 'hitting'. There are also other processes portrayed. For example, the upward gazes of the figures in the background create vectors connecting the spectators with the fighters.

Figure B9.1 Warriors (photo credit Claudio Gennari)

Like this image, many images actually represent multiple processes simultaneously. Figure B9.2, for example, also involves action processes, the face on the left (representing a library user) joined to the different kinds of resources he or she 'consumes, uses, evaluates, creates, combines, and shares'. This image, however, is more abstract, and so the vectors are represented as labelled arrows rather than visual representations of these actions. At the same time, the image also contains classificatory relationships – the objects portrayed under the headings 'Information Literacy', 'Media Literacy' and 'Digital Literacy' representing distinct classes of things – and analytical relationships – the smaller faces in the lower right corner, for example, portrayed as parts of a larger social network.

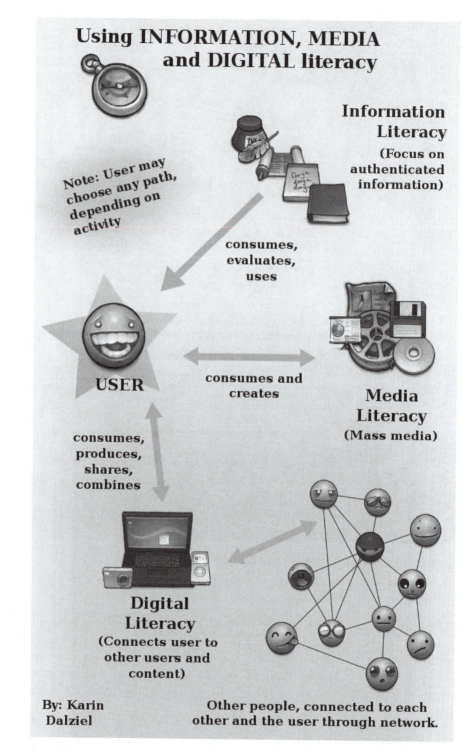

Figure B9.2 Using information, media and digital literacy (credit Karin Dalziel)

Interpersonal function

Another important function of any mode is to create and maintain some kind of relationship between the producer of the message and its recipient. As discussed in units A4 and B4, in language these relationships are usually created through the language's system of modality, as well as through the use of different *social languages* or *registers*.

In images, viewers are placed into relationships with the figures in the image and, by extension, the producers of the image, through devices such as perspective and gaze. The image of the child in Figure B9.3 illustrates both of these devices. The camera angle positions the viewer above the child rather than on the same level, creating the perspective of an adult, and the child's direct gaze into the camera creates a sense of intimacy with the viewer, though the expression on the child's face does denote some degree of uncertainty. Another important device for expressing the relationship between the viewer and the figures in an image is how close or far away they appear. Long shots tend to create a more impersonal relationship, whereas close-ups tend to create a feeling of psychological closeness along with physical closeness.

Figure B9.3 Child (photo credit Denis Mihailov)

'Modality' in images is partially realised by how 'realistic' the image seems to the viewer. Photographs, for example, generally attest more strongly to the 'truth' of a representation than drawings or paintings. However, this is not always the case. Scientific diagrams and sketches, for example, are often regarded as having even more 'authority' than photographs, and black and white photographs like those often found in newspapers are often regarded as more 'realistic' than highly saturated colour images in magazine advertisements.

Textual function

As I said above, while texts are organised in a linear fashion based on sequentiality, images are organised spatially. Figures in an image, for example, can be placed in the centre or periphery of the image, on the top or the bottom, the left or the right, and in the foreground or in the background. Although producers of images have much less control than producers of written texts over how viewers 'read' the image, they can create pathways for the viewer's gaze by, for example, placing different figures in different places within the frame and making some more prominent and others less prominent.

One obvious way to do this is by creating a distinction between foreground and background, the figures which seem closer to the viewer generally commanding more prominence. Another way is to place one or more figures in the centre of the image and others on the margins. Many images make use of the centre/margin distinction to present one figure or piece of information as the centre or 'nucleus' of the image and the marginal figures as somehow dependent upon or subservient to the central figure (Kress and van Leeuwen 2006).

Two other important distinctions in the composition of images, according to Kress and van Leeuwen (2006), are the distinction between the left side and the right side of the image, and the distinction between the upper part and the lower part. Taking as their starting point Halliday's idea that in language, 'given' information (information that the reader or hearer is already familiar with) tends to appear at the beginning of clauses, and new information tends to appear closer to the end of clauses, they posit that, similarly, the left side of an image is more likely to contain 'given' information and the right side to contain 'new' information. This is based on the assumption that people tend to 'read' images in the same way they read texts, starting at the left and moving towards the right. This, of course, may be different for people from speech communities that are accustomed to reading text from right to left or from top to bottom.

The distinction between the upper part of an image and the lower part is related to the strong metaphorical connotations of 'up' and 'down' in many cultures (Lakoff and Johnson 1980). According to Kress and van Leeuwen, the top part of the image is often used for more 'ideal', generalised or abstract information, and the bottom for 'real', specific and concrete information. They give as an example advertisements in which the upper section usually shows 'the "promise of the product", the status of glamour it can bestow on its users' and the lower section tends to provide factual information such as where the product can be obtained (2006: 186).

Both of these principles can be seen in Figure B9.4. In order to make sense of the 'narrative' of HIV transmission that the text tells, one must begin at the far left of the advertisement and move to the far right. The figures of the man and the woman on the left of the image constitute 'given' information, while the virus on the right of the image constitutes the 'new' information. There is also a clear demarcation between the upper half of the text and the lower half. While the upper half does not portray the positive 'promise' of a particular product as many advertisements do, it does represent a kind of idealised hypothetical situation which the viewer is invited to imagine. Rather than a 'promise', however, it is something more akin to a 'threat'. And the lower half of the image, rather than giving information about where the product portrayed in the upper half can be obtained, it gives information on how this hypothetical situation can be *avoided*, along with specific information about such things as the name of the organisation that produced the ad and the condom company that sponsored it.

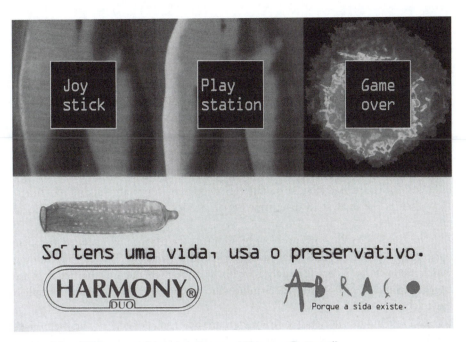

Figure B9.4 AIDS prevention advertisement (Abraco, Portugal)

This text also illustrates how images and words often work together. The words 'Joy Stick', 'Play Station' and 'Game Over' tell the viewer how the images are to be interpreted, and the slogan in the lower half of the text ('You only have one life: use a condom'), explains the image of the condom above it. Finally, this text shows how multimodality can be effective in getting viewers to make connections between different 'Discourses'. While the images belong to the 'Discourse of biomedicine', the words invite the viewer to interpret these images within the framework of the 'Discourse of video games'.

Multimodality in interaction

Modes in face-to-face interaction such as gaze and gesture also fulfil these three functions. The mode of gaze, for example, has an obvious *interpersonal* function, creating a relationship between the gazer and whomever or whatever is the object of the gaze. It also carries *ideational* meaning, conveying that the gazer is looking at, watching or paying attention to something. Finally, gaze is often an important *textual* resource, helping people to manage things such as turn-taking in conversations.

While the 'inter-modal' relationships (the ways multiple modes work together) in static texts such as the advertisement analysed above can be complicated, they can be even more complicated in dynamic interactions. One of the problems with analysing real-time, face-to-face interactions is that participants have so many modes available to them to make meaning. There are what Norris (2004) calls 'embodied' modes such as gaze, gesture, posture, head movement, proxemics (the distance one maintains from his or her interlocutor), spoken language and prosody (features of stress and intonation in a person's voice). And there are also 'disembodied' modes such as written texts, images, signs, clothing, the layout of furniture and the architectural arrangement of rooms and other spaces in which the interaction takes place. All of these different modes organise meaning differently. Some, such as spoken language and gaze, tend to operate *sequentially*, while others, such as gesture and prosody, tend to operate *globally*, often helping to create the context in which other modes such as spoken language are to be interpreted (see section B6). Not all of these modes are of equal importance to participants at any given moment in the interaction. In fact, different modes are likely to take on different degrees of importance at different times. How then is the analyst to determine which modes to focus on in a multimodal analysis?

Norris (2004) solves this problem by adopting the practice of *mediated discourse analysis* (see A8 and B8) and taking *action* as her unit of analysis. Thus, in determining which modes to focus on, the analyst begins by asking what actions participants are engaged in and then attempts to determine which modes are being used to accomplish these actions.

As I said in unit A8, actions are always made up of smaller actions and themselves contribute to making up larger actions. Norris divides actions into three types: *lower-level actions*, the smallest pragmatic meaning units of communicative modes (including things such as gestures, postural shifts, gaze shifts and tone units), *higher-level actions* (such as 'having a cup of coffee'), and *frozen actions* (previously performed actions that are instantiated in material modes – a half-eaten plate of food, for example, or an unmade bed).

One of the goals of multimodal interaction analysis, then, is to understand how participants in interaction work cooperatively to weave together lower-level actions such as gestures, glances and head and body movements into higher-level actions and, in doing so, help to create and reinforce social practices, social relationships and social identities (see C9).

👁 **Find more examples of the communicative functions of images and other modes online.**

B10   PROCEDURES FOR CORPUS-ASSISTED DISCOURSE ANALYSIS

Conducting a corpus-assisted discourse analysis requires a number of steps, which include building a corpus, cleaning and tagging the corpus, analysing the corpus with computer tools using a number of procedures and, finally, interpreting the data. These last two steps tend to be cyclical and recursive. That is, usually the results of several procedures need to be combined when we are interpreting the data, and often our interpretations lead us to re-performing these procedures or performing other procedures.

The first step in building a corpus is deciding what kinds of texts you want to include in it and making sure that you can include a representative sample of those kinds of texts. For very specialised corpora, such as the works of a particular author, this is easy since there are a limited number of texts and you can simply include them all. This is more difficult the less specific the corpus is. For example, if you want to build a corpus of business letters, you need to decide what kind of letters (sales letters, complaint letters, etc.) you want to include and what kinds of company these letters will come from. You might choose texts based on some predetermined criteria such as topic or the inclusion of some keyword. Baker and McEnery, in their study reprinted in section D10, for example, chose the texts for their corpus on the basis of whether or not they contained the words 'refugee' or 'refugees' or the phrases 'asylum seeker' or 'asylum seekers'.

Another important decision is how many texts you are going to include in your corpus. Generally, with corpus-assisted analysis, the bigger the corpus the easier it will be for you to make generalisations from your results. However, it is also possible to have very small corpora.

You will probably also need a **reference corpus**. A reference corpus is another corpus that you will compare your primary corpus with. It is usually made up of a broader spectrum of texts or conversations than the corpus you are analysing.

You might, for example, use one of the large corpora such as the British National Corpus, or you might choose another specialised corpus with a broader sample of texts.

Nowadays it is actually quite easy to build a corpus since so many texts are already in electronic format on the Internet. But it is important that you go through these texts carefully and take out any HTML code or formatting that might have been attached to them, which might interfere with your analysis. You also might want to attach new code to certain parts of the text or to certain words to aid your analysis. This latter process is called 'tagging'. Analysts, for example, sometimes insert code to indicate different parts of a text (such as introduction, body and conclusion), and others tag individual words based on their grammatical function so they can detect grammatical patterns in their analysis along with lexical patterns. It is important that each text in your corpus is saved in a separate text file.

The analysis of the corpus is carried out with a computer program, and there are a number of such programs available from the Internet. The most widely used commercial program is called WordSmith Tools (http://www.lexically.net/word-smith/index.html), but there is also a very good free program available called AntConc, developed by Laurence Anthony, which works on both Windows and Macintosh operating systems (http://www.antlab.sci.waseda.ac.jp/ antconc_index.html). In the explanations and examples below I will describe how to perform the relevant procedures using AntConc.

After your corpus has been 'cleaned' and 'tagged', you need to import it in the form of text files into your analysis program. In AntConc this is done by using the commands File < Open File(s) (or Ctrl F). You may choose as many files as you wish. If you would like to open a directory of files, choose Open Dir (or Ctrl D).

While there are a whole host of different operations that can be performed on corpora using this software, the six most basic procedures useful for discourse analysis are as follows:

1 generating word frequency lists;
2 calculating type token ratio;
3 analysing concordances;
4 analysing collocation;
5 analysing keywords;
6 creating dispersion plots.

Most of these procedures can be performed on their own, but it is usually a good idea to perform them together with the other procedures since the results from one procedure can often inform your interpretation of the results from the others.

Word frequency and type token ratio

One of the most basic pieces of information you can get from a computer-aided analysis of your corpus is information about the frequency with which different words occur. In AntConc a **word frequency** list for a corpus can be generated by clicking on the Word List tab and then clicking the Start button. Unless you have a good reason to treat words in different cases (e.g. 'refugee' versus 'Refugee') as separate words, you should tick 'Treat all data as lower case' in the Display Options. Words in frequency lists can be sorted by rank, frequency or word, so an analyst can easily determine not just the most or least frequently occurring words, but also check the frequency of specific words.

After a word list is generated, the information necessary to calculate **type token ratio** appears at the top of the AntConc window. Type token ratio is basically a measure of how many different kinds of words occur in the text in relation to the total number of words, and so can give some indication of the lexical complexity of texts in a corpus. It is calculated by dividing the number of types by the number of tokens. A low type token ratio generally indicates a relatively narrow range of subjects, a lack of lexical variety or frequent repetition. A high type token ratio indicates a wider range of subjects, greater lexical variation and/or less frequent repetition. In the British National Corpus, the type token ratio for the corpus of written texts is 45.53, whereas the type token ratio for the corpus of spoken texts is 32.96. This confirms a number of things we already know about the differences between speech and writing, in particular that writing tends to involve a much more varied and complex vocabulary, and that speech tends to involve frequent repetition.

Usually the most frequent words in any text are **function words** (articles, prepositions, pronouns and other grammatical words) such as 'the' and 'a'. While looking at function words can be useful in helping you to understand grammatical patterns, style and register in the corpus, **content words** such as nouns, verbs and adjectives are usually more relevant to finding evidence of 'Discourses'.

Concordances

Concordances show words in the context of the sentences or utterances in which they were used. Usually we use frequency lists to give us an idea of what some of the important words in a corpus might be, and then we do a concordance of those words in order to find out more information about them. Concordances can be sorted alphabetically based on the words either to the right or left of the word that you searched for, and playing around with this sorting system is often a good way to spot patterns in word usage. For example, in Baker and McEnery's study reprinted in section D10, the alphabetical sorting of words directly to the left and right of the target word ('refugee') helped reveal that refugees were commonly described in newspaper articles in terms of quantification (using numerals or terms such as 'tens of thousands of' and 'more and more').

In AntConc concordances are created by typing a word or phrase into the Search Term box, generating a list of instances in which this word appears in the corpus listed in their immediate contexts. The search word appears in the concordance in the centre of the page highlighted in blue, with what occurs before and after appearing to the left and the right of the word. The Kwic Sort dialogue can be used to sort the concordance alphabetically based on the word one, two, three, etc. places to the left or the right of the search term.

Collocation analysis

Collocation has to do with the fact that certain words tend to appear together. Often words take on a negative or positive meaning based on the kinds of words they are most often grouped with. As Firth (1957) put it, 'You shall know a lot about a word from the company it keeps.' For example, the verb 'commit' is nearly always associated with negative words such as 'crime'. We don't 'commit' good deeds, we 'perform' them. Thus we find phrases such as 'commit random acts of kindness' humorous.

Analysing the kinds of words that appear together with other words is an especially useful way to understand the 'Discourses' that are expressed in a corpus because they can reveal patterns of association between different kinds of words or concepts. In their study of the portrayal of refugees in the British press, for example, Baker and McEnery note not just that the word 'stream' is used frequently in their corpus to describe the movement of refugees, but that in the British National Corpus this word frequently collocates with the words 'tears', 'blood', 'sweat', 'water' and 'rain', giving it a generally negative connotation. Baker (2006) refers to the situation where patterns can be found between words and various sets of related words in ways that suggest a 'Discourse' as **discourse prosody**. Others (see for example Sinclair 1991) refer to this as **semantic prosody**.

In order to perform a collocation analysis with AntConc, click the Collocate tab and enter your chosen search term. You will also need to determine the **span** to the left or right of the search term within which you want to check for collocates. This can be set from any number of words to the left of the search term to any number of words to the right of the search term using the Window Span dialogue. The result will be a list of collocates, their rank, overall frequency and the frequency with which they occur to the left of the search term and to the right of the search term.

Keyword analysis

Word frequency lists can only tell you how frequently certain words occur in the corpus. Some words, however, such as articles, occur frequently in nearly every text or conversation. The frequency with which a word occurs in a corpus is not in itself necessarily meaningful. What is more important is whether or not a word occurs more or less frequently than 'normal'. This is what **keyword analysis** is designed to determine.

The difference between keywords and frequent words is that keywords are words that appear with a greater frequency in the corpus that you are studying than they do in a 'reference corpus'. Reference corpora usually consist of a broader sampling of texts or conversations. Many people, for example, use large publically available corpora such as the British National Corpus.

In order to generate a list of keywords for your corpus with AntConc, it is first necessary to load your reference corpus. This is done using the Keyword List preferences (Tool Preferences < Keyword List). The reference corpus can be loaded either as a list of files or as a directory. Once it is loaded, the keyword list is generated by choosing the Keyword List tab and clicking Start. The result will be a list of keywords, their rank, frequency and a number measuring their **keyness**. The *keyness* value indicates the degree to which the word occurs more frequently than expected in your primary corpus (taking the reference corpus as representing a 'normal' pattern of frequency). Some programs also allow you to calculate **negative keyness**, that is, to determine which words occur *less* frequently than expected.

Dispersion plots

Dispersion plots, referred to in AntConc as 'concordance plots', can give you information about where words occur in texts. This can be particularly useful if an analyst is interested in the structure of texts or conversations. A genre analyst, for example, might be interested in the kinds of words or phrases that occur in a section of a text associated with a particular move, or a conversation analyst might want to explore the kinds of words that occur in different parts of a conversation, such as the opening or the closing.

In AntConc, concordance plots are generated by clicking the Concordance Plot tab, typing in a search term and clicking Start. The result is a series of bars, each representing a text in the corpus with lines representing where the search term has appeared. Figure B10.1 shows the dispersion plots generated by searching for the word 'love' in a corpus of Lady Gaga songs.

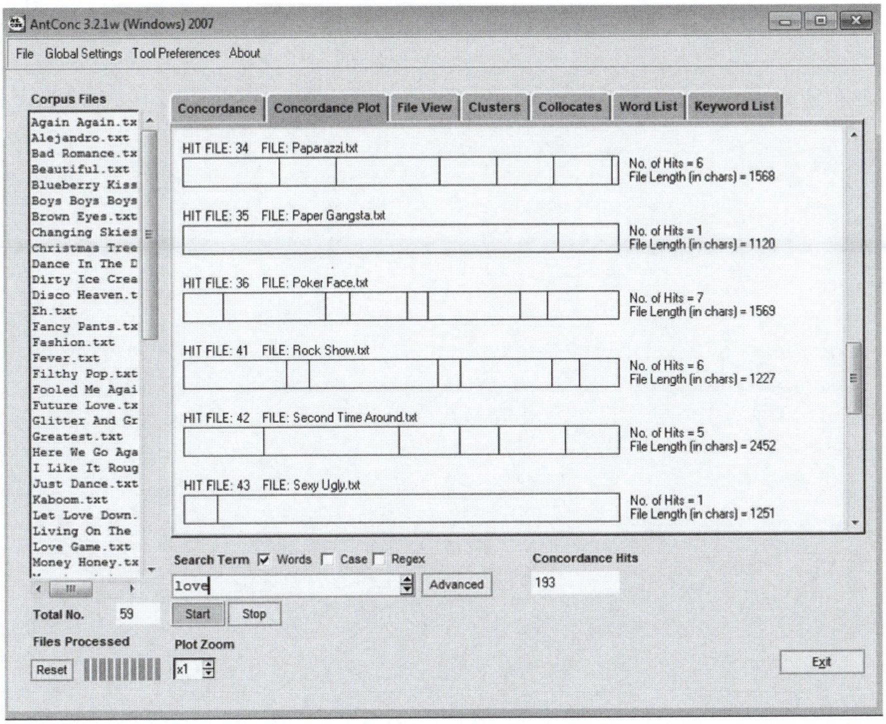

Figure B10.1 Concordance plot for 'love' in Lady Gaga songs

👁 **Find examples of these and other procedures for corpus analysis online.**

Section C

EXPLORATION
ANALYSING DISCOURSE

C1 DOING DISCOURSE ANALYSIS: FIRST STEPS

As discussed in unit B1, there are basically three different ways of looking at discourse: discourse as language beyond the clause; discourse as language in use; and discourse as social practice. Each of the three different ways of looking at discourse can lead us to ask different kinds of questions about the texts and interactions that we encounter in our everyday lives. A view that sees discourse as language above the level of the clause or the sentence leads us to ask: What makes this text or conversation a *text* or *conversation* rather than just a random collection of sentences or utterances? What holds it together so that people can make sense of it? A view that sees discourse as language in use leads us to ask: What are people trying to do with this text and how do we know? Finally, a view that sees discourse as a matter of social practice and ideology leads us to ask: What kinds of people are the authors of this text or the participants in this conversation trying to show themselves to be, and what kinds of beliefs or values are they promoting?

Consider, for example, the text that is printed on the cardboard sleeve that comes wrapped around a cup of coffee that you buy at Starbucks (Text C1.1) and try to answer these three questions.

Text C1.1: Text from Starbucks cardboard sleeve

Starbucks is committed to reducing our environmental impact through increased use of post-consumer recycled materials. Help us help the planet.

‾‾‾‾‾

First-ever 10% post-consumer fiber cup 60% post-consumer fiber sleeve

‾‾‾‾‾

Intended for single use only.
© 2005 Starbucks Coffee Company All rights reserved
US Patent no. 5.205.47S and no. 6.863.644 and related foreign patents pending
www.starbucks.com/wayiseeit

Although this text seems to be rather straightforward and in some ways trivial, if we apply the three perspectives on discourse that were discussed in B1, we can start to see how complex it really is, and how it relates to all sorts of non-trivial aspects of our daily lives.

We might start by looking at how this text is put together in a formal way. First of all, we would notice that there are three different sections, and so can ask ourselves how we interpret these three sections as going together, and how we interpret the separate sentences in each section as relating to one another.

One way we are able to make sense of this text is because of certain grammatical features in it. For example, we know that the pronoun 'us' in the second sentence refers to the name Starbucks in the first sentence, and this helps us to link these two sentences together. Also, the sentence in the second section ('First-ever 10% post-consumer fiber cup 60% post-consumer fiber sleeve') and the first sentence in the third section ('Intended for single use only') are incomplete. What they really mean is '*This cup and sleeve are the* first-ever 10% post-consumer fiber cup *and* 60% post-consumer fiber sleeve' and '*This cup and sleeve are* intended for single use only.' Since the same bit is left out of both of these sentences, this helps us to relate the two sentences together.

But another way we make sense of this text comes from our expectations about how texts like this are put together. We have seen thousands of similar kinds of texts (such as product labels) in our lives, and so we know that what the product manufacturers are trying to emphasise is usually placed in a more prominent position (such as the top) and that 'legal' or 'technical' information (e.g. stuff about patent, copyright, warnings, etc.) is usually put at the bottom in smaller lettering. This makes us pay less attention to it, although sometimes this information is really the most important information in the text.

After considering the formal features of the text, we might then go on to consider what exactly the authors of this text are trying to do. We would see that they are actually trying to do a number of things. For example, in the first section, there are two kinds of things they are doing: one is informing us ('Starbucks is committed to reducing our environmental impact . . .') and the second is telling us to do something through an imperative sentence ('Help us help the planet'). Such actions are sometimes not altogether straightforward. For example, when Starbucks asks you to 'help us help the planet' what they are also doing is asking you to help them make more money by buying more coffee.

The third section of the text also contains some rather 'indirect' actions. By giving the patent number of the sleeve, for example, Starbucks is not just informing us, but is also *warning* us that the design for this sleeve belongs to them and we cannot use it. Finally, by giving us their website URL, they are not just informing us, but also *inviting* us to visit this website.

All in all, what the company is doing with this text is rather complex and sometimes indirect. They are not just trying to tell us about this sleeve or about their company policies; they are also trying to portray themselves as a 'good company' in order to make us want to buy more coffee from them.

If we then consider this text from the perspective of discourse as social practice, we might notice that there are several different ('capital D') 'Discourses' mixed together. There is the 'Discourse of environmentalism' in the first section, the 'Discourse of science' in the second section (signalled by numbers such as 10% and 60% and technical terms such as 'post-consumer fiber') and the 'Discourse of law' in the last section (signalled by legal terms such as 'All rights reserved'). By using these three Discourses, the company is trying to show you that they are a certain kind of company with certain kinds of values and certain kinds of power: first, that they are a 'green' and 'socially responsible' company; second, that they are a 'modern' and 'scientific' company that is on the cutting edge of innovation; and third, that they are a powerful company that is able to hire lawyers to sue you if you infringe on their patent or copyright.

This way of looking at this text and texts like it can be useful because it not only helps us to interpret the meanings the authors are trying to express and the actions they are trying to perform with the text, but also how the authors are trying to manipulate us into thinking certain things or feeling certain emotions about Starbucks or performing certain actions ourselves such as ordering a second cappuccino.

And so one 'way in' to discourse analysis is to consider a text or a conversation from the three perspectives on discourse we described in section B1. In the following sections, you will practise applying analytical tools and methods that grow out of these three perspectives on discourse.

Activity ✪

Another 'way in' to discourse analysis might be to apply the four principles of discourse discussed in unit A1 to a particular text or interaction.

1 the ambiguity of language
2 language in the world
3 language and social identity
4 language and other modes.

These principles also lead us to ask specific kinds of questions about a text or interaction.

Look, for example, at the interaction below taken from my Facebook 'News Feed' (Figure C1.1). The first thing you need to know, if you do not know this already, is that people who use Facebook often take various 'quizzes' or surveys which purport to tell them something about their personalities or their hidden desires. Friends sometimes pass these surveys around among themselves as a way to share things that are of interest to them and build a feeling of closeness.

The second thing you need to know is that Emily Jane Wheeler is my niece and when she took this quiz she was 13 years old. Cheri Jones Wheeler is her mother and my sister.

In order to apply the principles we discussed in section A1 to this text, we might ask the following four sets of questions:

1 How is the language in this interaction ambiguous? What do the people need to know in order to interpret one another's utterances correctly? Are there any hidden or 'veiled' meanings expressed?
2 How is meaning *situated*? How much does the meaning of these utterances depend on where they appear and who says them and what they are trying to do with these utterances?
3 How do people use language to express something about who they are (including the 'kinds of people' they are and what kinds of relationships they have with the other people in the interaction)?

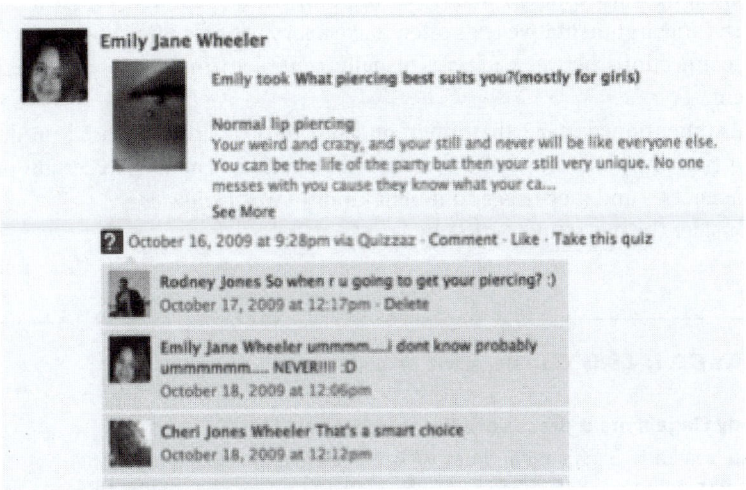

Emily Jane Wheeler

Emily took **What piercing best suits you?(mostly for girls)**

Normal lip piercing
Your weird and crazy, and your still and never will be like everyone else.
You can be the life of the party but then your still very unique. No one
messes with you cause they know what your ca...

See More

October 16, 2009 at 9:28pm via Quizzaz · Comment · Like · Take this quiz

Rodney Jones So when r u going to get your piercing? :)
October 17, 2009 at 12:17pm · Delete

**Emily Jane Wheeler ummmm.....i dont know probably
ummmmmm.... NEVER!!!! :D**
October 18, 2009 at 12:06pm

Cheri Jones Wheeler That's a smart choice
October 18, 2009 at 12:12pm

Figure C1.1 My Facebook News Feed

4   How are other modes (pictures, layout, emoticons) combined with
language to express meaning?

Discuss how posing these kinds of questions can help you to better understand this interaction and then use the two methods outlined in this section
(applying the 'three perspectives' and the 'four principles') to perform a
preliminary analysis on a piece of discourse from your own life.

Do more activities online.

ANALYSING TEXTURE

As I noted in unit B2, not only is *texture* (*cohesion* and *coherence*) necessary to turn a
collection of words or sentences into a *text*, but different kinds of texts – such as shopping lists, newspaper articles and 'before and after ads' – have specific kinds of texture
associated with them.

First, different kinds of texts tend to use different kinds of cohesive devices.
Descriptive texts which give information about people or things (scientific descriptions, encyclopaedia entries) often make heavy use of pronoun reference since
pronouns allow writers to refer to the person or thing being talked about without
repeating his, her or its name. Advertising texts, on the other hand, which describe
products, are more likely to use repetition, since there are benefits to repeating the
name of the product in this context. Legal texts also prefer repetition to reference

C2

since repeating a word rather than referring to it with a pronoun avoids ambiguity. Analytical and argumentative texts often make heavy use of *conjunction*, since making logical connections between ideas is usually central to the process of making an argument.

I also mentioned in B2 that different kinds of texts are also based on different kinds of *generic frameworks* – they present information or actions in certain predictable sequences – and they trigger different kinds of *word knowledge*.

Consider the newspaper article in Text C2.1.

Text C2.1: Lady Gaga's meat dress

Lady Gaga's meat dress voted most iconic outfit

Pop diva Lady Gaga's meat dress which raised eyebrows at the recent MTV Video Music Awards has topped the list of the most iconic outfits of 2010.

The eccentric 'Poker Face' hitmaker, who is known for her outrageous fashion sense, created ripples with her meaty outfit, which has swept a poll by website MyCelebrityFashion.com.

"What's everyone's big problem with my meat dress? Haven't they seen me wear leather? Next time, I'll wear a tofu dress and the soy milk police will come after me," said the 24-year-old singer who lashed at her critics for the controversy created by her meat ensemble.

http://timesofindia.indiatimes.com/world/uk/Lady-Gagas-meat-dress-voted-most-iconic-outfit/articleshow/7127426.cms

---

Perhaps the most obvious thing that makes the above text a text is that we immediately recognise it as a certain kind of text: a news article. This generic framework is triggered by a number of things. First and most obvious are the circumstances in which we are likely to encounter the text, in this case on the website of *The Times of India*. There are other features of the text as well that mark it as a newspaper article so that, even when it is transplanted into a different context (such as this book), we still recognise it as a news article. One of the most salient is the headline – a kind of title which summarises the main idea of the text in a kind of telegraphic language in which non-essential words such as articles and auxiliary verbs are left out.

Once the generic framework of a newspaper article is triggered, we expect the information in the text to be presented in a certain way. For example, we expect the first paragraph of the article to sum up the main points in the article, the second paragraph to give a more elaborated account of these main points, and subsequent paragraphs to present further details or the reactions of various people to the news. It is in part because newspaper articles are structured in this way that we are able to read them so efficiently.

Apart from its overall structure, this text is also held together by a number of cohesive devices that are also characteristic of news articles. It might be useful, however, to first consider the kinds of devices which are *not* used. There are no instances, for example, of *conjunction*. This is not unusual since news articles (as opposed to editorials or opinion pieces) are meant to report what has happened rather than to offer analysis or opinions. When news articles do use logical connectors, they are usually of the *additive* or *sequential* type.

There is also relatively little use of *reference* in the text. Although there are instances in which relative pronouns point back to their antecedents ('meat dress, *which* . . .', 'hitmaker, *who* is known . . .'), and also places where possessive pronouns are used ('*her* outrageous fashion sense', '*her* meaty outfit') and where the definite pronoun is used to refer back to a specific thing ('*The* eccentric "Poker Face" hitmaker'), there are no instances in which Lady Gaga is referred to as 'she' or the meat dress is referred to as 'it'. The exception to this relative paucity of pronouns is in a quote from Lady Gaga herself in the third paragraph in which she refers to herself using the pronouns 'I' and 'me' and her critics using the pronoun 'they'.

Rather than using pronouns, the author of this article chooses to refer back to previously mentioned people and objects by calling them different names. Lady Gaga, for example, becomes 'The eccentric "Poker Face" hitmaker', and 'meat dress' becomes 'meaty outfit' and 'meat ensemble'. Such rephrasing is not limited to people and objects, but is also used for actions, for example, 'raised eyebrows' becoming 'created ripples'.

There are many possible reasons for this, not least of which is the fact that phrases such as 'eccentric "Poker Face" hitmaker' are much more interesting than mere pronouns and so increase the entertainment value of the piece. A more important reason, however, given the purpose of a news article to convey information, is that such rephrasing allows the author not only to achieve cohesion but also to efficiently deliver to the reader additional information about the people and things under discussion. By calling Lady Gaga 'The eccentric "Poker Face" hitmaker', the author is able not just to refer back to Lady Gaga, but also to deliver additional information about her: that she is 'eccentric', that she has a number of hit songs and that the title of one of those songs is 'Poker Face'.

The reiteration of key people, objects and concepts in articles such as this using alternate words and phrases creates *lexical chains*, which not only serve to bind the sentences and paragraphs together but also reinforce the main messages of such articles. In the article above, there are four such chains: first is the one formed by words related to Lady Gaga ('pop diva', 'hitmaker', 'singer'); second, the one formed by words related to the 'meat dress' ('outfit', 'fashion', 'wear', 'dress', 'ensemble'); third, the one formed by words related to the winning of awards or 'elections' ('voted', 'iconic', 'Awards', 'sweeped (sic)', 'poll'); and, finally, the one formed by words having to do with shock or controversy ('raised eyebrows', 'eccentric', 'outrageous', 'created ripples', 'problem', 'come after', 'lashed', 'critics', and 'controversy'). These four lexical chains taken together serve to highlight the four main elements of the story: *Lady Gaga's meat dress*, which caused a *controversy* when she wore it, has been *voted* as most *iconic* fashion item by website MyCelebrityFashion.com.

Activity ✪

Now have a look at a text about the same topic which has a rather different purpose and, consequently, a rather different *texture*. The text below is from a blog by the animal rights group PETA (Text C2.2). Its purpose is not so much to give information about what Lady Gaga wore as it is to make an argument that her choice of dress was unethical.

Text C2.2: PETA webpage

Last night, Lady Gaga tried once again to shock the world, this time by wearing a "meat dress" during her acceptance of the Video of the Year award at MTV's Video Music Awards. Lately, Lady Gaga has been having a hard time keeping her act "over the top." Wearing a dress made out of cuts of dead cows is offensive enough to bring comment, but someone should whisper in her ear that there are more people who are upset by butchery than who are impressed by it—and that means a lot of young people will not be buying her records if she keeps this stuff up. On the other hand, maybe it was fake and she'll talk about that later. If not, what's next: the family cat made into a hat? Meat is the decomposing flesh of a tormented animal who didn't want to die, and after a few hours under the TV lights, it would smell like the rotting flesh it is and likely be crawling in maggots—not too attractive, really. The stunt is bringing lots of people to PETA.org to download a copy of our vegetarian/vegan starter kit, so I guess we should be glad.

http://www.peta.org/b/thepetafiles/archive/2010/09/13/Lady-Gagas-Meat-Dress.aspx

---

Analyse the texture of the above text, noting how the strategies used to achieve *cohesion* and *coherence* are different from those used in the news article and discuss why you think these differences exist. You can use the following questions to guide your analysis:

❏ What are the most common cohesive devices used in the text? What kinds of relationships do these devices create among different parts of the text? Are these relationships clear and logical?

❏ What kind of overall structure does the text have? Is the order in which information is given in the text important? Do you have to use any previous knowledge about this kind of text or about the topic of the text to understand it?

 **Do more activities online.**

ANALYSING GENRES   C3

Analysing genres involves more than just analysing the structure of particular types of text. It involves understanding how these text types function in social groups, how they reinforce and reflect the concerns of and social relationships in these groups, and how they change over time as societies and the groups within them change. Therefore, analysing genres requires as much attention to social context as it does to texts.

Part of this context includes other genres that the genre under consideration is related to. Genres are related to other genres in a number of different ways. First, actions or 'communicative events' associated with genres are usually part of larger *chains* of events that involve different genres. The personal ads we looked at in unit B3, for example, might be followed by letters or emails, phone calls and dinner dates. And so, just as moves in a genre are often arranged in a kind of sequential structure, genres themselves are also often related to one another in sequential chains based on the ways they are employed by people as they work to achieve larger communicative purposes.

Genres are also related to other genres in non-sequential relationships that are called *networks*. A job application letter, for example, is related to the job ad that prompted it, the applicant's résumé which might accompany the letter, and any letters of reference former employers or teachers of the applicant might have written in support of the application. The letter is also related to the letters of all of the other applicants who are applying for the same job. Genres are said to be linked together in *networks* when they have some sort of *intertextual* relationship with one another, that is, when one genre makes reference to another genre or when the users of a genre need to make reference to another genre in order to realise the communicative purpose for which the genre is intended.

Genres can also be seen as existing in larger *genre ecologies* in which texts that are not directly related to one another in chains or networks can nevertheless affect one another in sometimes subtle and sometimes dramatic ways. Like natural ecologies, genre ecologies are not static: conditions change; old discourse communities dissolve and new ones form; and genres change and evolve as users creatively *bend* or *blend* them, or else become extinct if they can no longer fulfil the communicative goals of their users. Online personal ads, for example, are fast replacing print-based personal ads because they offer users more efficient ways to fulfil their communicative goals. Similarly, online news sources are giving rise to changes in print-based news magazines, many of which now contain shorter articles and more pictures in imitation of their online counterparts.

Genre analysis, therefore, must account not just for the way a particular genre is structured and its function in a particular discourse community, but also the dynamic nature of the genre, how it has and continues to evolve in response to changing social conditions, the relationships it has to other genres past and present, and the multiple functions it might serve in multiple discourse communities.

One particularly good example of the dynamic nature of genres and their adaptability to different discourse communities and different communicative purposes is the genre of the weblog, or blog. Technically a blog is simply a dynamic web page that is frequently updated with entries appearing in reverse chronological order. Since the introduction of blogs in the mid-1990s, however, they have developed certain conventionalised features: blog entries, for example, are typically short, written in an informal style, and often contain links to other blogs, web pages or online content such as videos. Blogs also often contain features such as opportunities for readers to comment, 'blogrolls' (a list of hyperlinks to related blogs) and 'perma-links' (hyperlinks that point to specific entries or forums contained in the blog's archives).

Like the personal advertisements analysed in the last section, the genre of the blog also contains many sub-genres used by different discourse communities for different communicative purposes. There are, for example, art blogs and photo blogs and video blogs and microblogs, just to mention a few varieties. Scholars of this genre, however, have identified two broad types of blog: the filter type and the diary type. These two types have different conventions associated with them and tend to serve different discourse communities.

Filter-type blogs are blogs whose main purpose is to deliver to readers news stories and links to other media which are 'filtered' based on readers' presumed membership in a particular discourse community (usually characterised by things such as political beliefs, lifestyle or profession). Figure C3.1 is an entry from one of these types of blogs called *The Daily Dish*, a political blog moderated by the commentator Andrew Sullivan from 2006 to 2011, which advocated socially progressive and fiscally conservative views.

This entry illustrates many of the moves typical of entries in filter-type blogs. They usually begin with a *title*, followed by information about when the entry was published (*Date/Time*) and who wrote it (*Author*). The body typically begins with an *introduction* to the material that will be linked to, quoted or embedded, as well as some kind of *comment* on the material. Introducing and commenting moves are sometimes realised separately, but sometimes, as in this example, they are realised together ('A powerful video of a man standing up for his mothers.') The most important move in entries in filter-type blogs is that of *pointing* readers to some news, information or media external to the blog itself. This is sometimes done with a hyperlink, sometimes with a quote from the original source, sometimes with some embedded media (such as a photograph or a video), and sometimes with a combination of these methods. All three methods are present in Figure C3.1. Some sort of *attribution* of the original source or author of the material is also usually included. Finally, such entries also commonly include tools at the end which give readers a chance to comment on the entry or to share it through email or social media such as Facebook.

As was noted above, the main communicative purpose of this type of blog entry is to 'filter' or select content from other websites that may be of interest to

"**Our Family Isn't So Different From Any Other Iowan Family**" ⟵——————— Title

02 FEB 2011 03:31 PM ⟵——————— Date/Time

by Patrick Appel ⟵——————— Author

A powerful video of man standing up for his mothers: ⟵——————— Introduction/Comment

⟵ Embedded Media

Maggie Koerth-Baker sets the scene: ⟵——————— Attribution

This week, the Iowa legislature took a step toward amending their state's constitution so that it ⟵——— Hyperlink
specifically bans marriage between two men or two women. Zach Wahls—a 19-year-old Iowa college ⟵——— Quote
student and the son of two mothers—is one of the many Iowans who thinks it's wrong to grant special
privileges to some families, and deny them to others, based solely on sexual orientation.

Permalink :: Sphere It! :: Share This ⟵——————— Interactive Tools

Figure C3.1 From *The Daily Dish*

readers of a particular blog. It is this process of selection, along with the perspective that the blogger takes on the selected content, that acts to define membership in the particular discourse community that the blog serves. By linking to this particular story, embedding this particular video, and referring to it as 'powerful' and to the speaker as 'a man standing up for his mothers', the author of this entry constructs the discourse community which this blog serves as made up of people who are likely to support marriage rights for same-sex couples. At the same time, readers of the blog who choose to 'share' this entry are also likely to share it with other like-minded people. For this reason, critics of filter-type blogs have pointed out that, rather than encouraging political debate, they tend to act as 'echo chambers' in which members of discourse communities simply communicate among themselves and reinforce one another's opinions.

⭐ **Activity**

Diary-type blogs tend to follow a slightly different structure and include different kinds of moves. The example in Figure C3.2 is from the blog of a young woman from Singapore attending Brown University in the United States.

brown university   1) _____

3:00 a.m. – 2008-08-31   2) _____

i've uploaded all my photos on facebook but   3) _____
for those who wanna listen to my commentary
then here goes =)

brown is fantastic. i'm not big on the   4) _____
socializing but there are people from allll over.
the campus is beautiful. food is not bad. i
skipped a good part of international
orientation to get stuff done and now i'm
ponning again and relaxing in my room =)

i stay in new pembroke #4 which is like in the   5) _____
middle with regards to rooming standards, not
the best, not the worse.
spent a bomb furnishing my room...actually i
think it was okay la, i spent like 120 USD on
everything excluding bedding though i paid for
it before i came. bought like...bed raisers, fan,
lamps, shoerack, hangers, a full length
mirror...and some other misc stuff.I AM NOT
SPENDING ANYMORE MONEY.i hope.

here's my room/bed   6) _____
BEFORE (its not like totally before but i
couldn't stand the bare bed so i put on the
sheets immeidately)

7) _____

Figure C3.2 From *Don't Make Me Mad* (Cheryn-ann Chew's blog)

❏   Identify the moves in this blog entry and label them in the spaces
    provided above.
❏   What do you think the overall communicative purpose of this blog is?
    How does each of the moves you identified contribute to the overall
    purpose?

❏ Do these moves generally occur in any particular order in such blogs? How does the order of moves contribute to the overall communicative purpose?

❏ How do you think blog entries of this type might be linked to other texts, either in genre chains or genre networks?

❏ How does this genre contribute to defining and maintaining a discourse community? Who do you think belongs to the community that reads this blog?

Find suggested answers to these questions online.

As you can see from your analysis above, blog entries often exist in complex intertextual relationships with other texts and other genres. They are sequentially linked in chains to previously posted entries and are often entrained to a sequence of external events, whether it is an unfolding news story or the unfolding personal life of the blogger. They form networks with other texts such as entries on other blogs, web pages, social media sites, stories in online newspapers and YouTube videos. They are also part of wider ecologies of texts and relationships within discourse communities and societies, often playing an important part in the management of social networks or in public debates about important events or political issues.

Blogs also have a complex evolutionary history and relationship with older genres. Although blogger Rebecca Blood (2000) insists that blogs are the Internet's first 'native genre', other scholars have pointed out their relationship to older genres. Diary-type blogs, for example, fulfil some of the communicative functions previously fulfilled by handwritten journals, travel logs, personal letters and personal web pages; and filter-type blogs draw on the traditions of press clipping services, news digests, edited anthologies, newspaper editorials and letters to the editor. Many scholars therefore consider blogs to be a hybrid genre, the result of a creative *blending* of multiple other genres made possible by new technology.

✪ Activity

Because of their short history and the multiple purposes to which they can be put, the conventions and constraints associated with blogs are difficult to pin down. Even the distinction between filter-type blogs and diary-type blogs discussed here is not hard and fast; many blog entries combine features of both types.

The advantage of analysing blogs is that they give us an opportunity to observe a newly emerging and dynamic genre, which has the potential to fulfil many different kinds of communicative purposes for many different kinds of discourse communities. In order to understand something about this variety, go to a blog directory such as Technorati.com (http://technorati.com/blogs/directory/) and compare entries from blogs from two different categories. The categories listed in Technorati include: entertainment, business, sports, politics, autos, technology, living, green and science.

Use the following questions to guide your analysis:

❏ What are the discourse communities these blogs serve? How do you know? In what ways do they fulfil Swales's defining characteristics of a discourse community (see D3) and in what ways do they deviate from these defining characteristics? How do the blogs you have chosen contribute to defining and maintaining these discourse communities?

❏ What are the communicative purposes of these blogs? How do they differ?

❏ How are the move structures of the two entries that you have chosen similar or different? Do they resemble diary-type blog entries or filter-type blog entries, or do they constitute a different type altogether? How do the moves and the ways they are structured contribute to the realisation of the overall communicative purposes of the two entries?

❏ How are the blog entries that you have chosen linked to other texts or genres in either genre chains or genre networks? How are they situated within larger textual ecologies? What other genres do they resemble?

Do more activities online.

C4 OTHER PEOPLE'S VOICES

Texts are always linked to, draw upon, respond to and anticipate other texts. And the ways authors position themselves and their texts in relation to other authors and other texts contributes significantly to the version of reality they end up portraying and the ideology they end up promoting.

There are many different ways authors might represent the words of other people in their texts. They might, for example, quote them verbatim using some kind of reporting verb such as 'said' or 'claimed'. Sometimes the effect of direct quotation can be to validate the words of the other person by implying that what they said or wrote is so important and profound that it is worth repeating word for word. Ironically, however, this technique can also have the opposite effect, creating a distance between the author and the words he or she is quoting and sometimes implying a certain scepticism towards those words – a way of saying, 'please note that these are not *my* words.' Often in cases of direct quotation, the reporting word that is used is important in indicating the author's attitude towards the words being quoted; it is quite a different thing to 'note' something, to 'claim' something or to 'admit' something.

Another way authors represent the words of other people is to paraphrase (or 'summarise') them. This, of course, gives author's much more flexibility in characterising these words in ways that support their point of view. Reporting words are also often important in paraphrases. In fact, sometimes words characterising what the other person seems to be doing with his or her words are used as a substitute for the utterance, as when 'He said, "I'm terribly sorry" ' is glossed as 'He apologised.'

Sometimes authors will employ a mixture of quotation and paraphrase, using quotation marks only for selected words or phrases. This is most often done when authors want to highlight particular parts of what has been said either to validate those words or to express scepticism about them. Quotes that are put around single words or phrases are sometimes called 'scare quotes' and are usually a way of saying things such as 'so called . . .' or 'as s/he put it . . .'.

By far the most common way to appropriate the words of others is by *not* attributing them to another person at all, but by simply asserting them as facts. Such practices have different implications in different contexts. In academic contexts, for example, they are often considered acts of plagiarism. In most other contexts, however, such practices are seen as signs that the author of the text has 'bought into' the ideas promoted by the other person. If a politician says in a speech, 'In order to be a secure nation, we must work for energy independence,' and then the next day a newspaper editorialist asserts, 'Energy independence is vital to our national security,' without citing the politician as the source of this idea, chances are that the politician would not accuse the newspaper of plagiarism, but rather praise it for the wisdom of its editorial staff.

Finally, often the words and ideas of other people are not directly asserted, but rather indirectly *presumed* in texts. Presuppositions are implicit assumptions about background beliefs that are presented as taken-for-granted facts. They are among the main devices authors use to promote their ideological positions. They are particularly effective in influencing people because they portray ideas as established truths and pre-empt opportunities to question or debate them.

Both assertions and presuppositions make the words and ideas represented more difficult to evaluate because the sources of those words and ideas are invisible. Like paraphrase, both also open up lots of possibilities for authors to change, alter, exaggerate, underplay or otherwise distort the words and ideas of others. On the other hand, assertion and presupposition also make the relationship between the author and the person whose words he or she is borrowing more ambiguous. The discourse analyst can never be certain of how conscious authors are of the source of these ideas in the discourse of others or certain of who these others are.

Table C4.1 gives examples of these different forms of discourse representation.

Table C4.1 Different forms of discourse representation

Direct quotation	The councilwoman said, 'because of unforeseen circumstances, we will be revising the planned completion date of the project.'
Paraphrase	The councilwoman said that the project would be delayed.
Selective quotation	The councilwoman admitted that the completion date of the project would have to be 'revised'.
Assertion	The project is experiencing severe delays.
Presupposition	Unreasonable delays have plagued the project.

C4

Whose islands are these?

As an example of the way authors represent the words, actions and ideas of other people and how these representations promote certain versions of reality, consider the newspaper article below published on the CNN website in 2009 (Text C4.1). The article concerns a dispute between China and Japan over the sovereignty of a small group of islands in the South China Sea – known by the Chinese as the Diaoyu Islands and by the Japanese as the Senkaku Islands – and efforts by the US government to mediate in the dispute. Although many people consider news articles to be relatively 'objective' presentations of the facts of a particular event, the words reporters use to portray participants and processes, and the way they choose to represent what relevant parties say about the event, almost always promotes a particular ideological stance.

Text C4.1: CNN article

China shuns U.S. mediation in its island dispute with Japan
By the CNN Wire Staff
November 3, 2010 – Updated 0401 GMT (1201 HKT)

(CNN) – The United States can forget about hosting trilateral talks involving China and Japan over the disputed islands, Beijing said via state media Wednesday.

"The territorial dispute between China and Japan over the Diaoyu Islands is the business of the two nations only," Foreign Ministry spokesman Ma Zhaoxu said, according to the Xinhua news agency.

U.S. Secretary of State Hillary Clinton made the offer during discussions with Chinese Foreign Minister Yang Jiechi last week, Xinhua said.

Relations between Beijing and Tokyo have been strained by their growing dispute over the islands, which China calls the Diaoyu and Japan calls the Senkaku.

Japan in early September arrested a Chinese fishing crew off the islands, leading to a diplomatic battle.

In response, China made increasingly aggressive diplomatic threats. Beijing also halted ministerial-level talks with Tokyo, and both sides canceled trips to each other's nations.

Japan has since released the fishing crew, but Beijing has repeatedly said the islands belong to China.

Beijing also says most of the South China Sea belongs to China, disputing neighboring countries' claims. The clash over territorial waters and islands—and the natural resources that go with them—is a flashpoint in the Asia-Pacific region.

From: http://articles.cnn.com/2010-11-03/world/china.japan.disputed.islands_1_
island-dispute-diaoyu-islands-beijing-and-tokyo?_s=PM:WORLD

The first thing that we can notice about this version of the facts is the different kinds of processes the different parties are portrayed as engaging in. China (meaning the

Chinese government) is described as 'shunning mediation', 'making threats' and 'halting talks', whereas the US (in the person of the secretary of state) is described as 'making an offer' and wishing to 'host talks'. Clearly, the US side is portrayed as the more reasonable and conciliatory of the two parties. The portrayal of Japan is more neutral: although it is portrayed as 'arresting' a Chinese fishing crew, later it is portrayed as 'releasing' the crew.

Apart from the processes associated with the different actors, the ways the words of those actors are represented also reinforce the impression that China acted aggressively. In the first paragraph, the words of the Chinese Foreign Ministry spokesperson are paraphrased in a way that gives them an aggressive, argumentative tone: 'The United States can forget about hosting trilateral talks.' From the direct quotation that is given in the next paragraph, however, it is clear that this is not at all what the spokesperson said. The article does not quote nor give much detail about what the US Secretary of State said that led to this response other than characterising it as an 'offer'. Whether it was an offer, however, or something else, such as a 'threat' or a 'warning', is clearly open to interpretation given the Chinese response.

The final paragraphs of the article give background information about the situation in the form of multiple assertions and presuppositions whose sources the reader cannot be certain of. It is asserted, for example, that China has made 'increasingly aggressive diplomatic threats', although it is not clear why their actions have been characterised in such a way or by whom. In the last paragraph, the seemingly objective statement, 'the clash over the territorial waters and the islands – and the natural resources that go with them – is a flashpoint in the Asia-Pacific region', hides within it the presupposition that the motivation behind the disputes is primarily economic rather than a matter of patriotism or the historical legitimacy of the claims.

⭐ **Activity**

The article below (Text C4.2), published in the *China Daily*, gives a rather different version of events. Try to analyse it in the same way, noting how different participants and processes are characterised, how the words of different actors are represented and how these features in the text contribute to its ideological stance.

Text C4.2: China Daily article

China: Trilateral talks merely US wishful thinking
(Xinhua) Updated: 2010-11-02 14:54

BEIJING – Chinese Foreign Ministry Spokesman Ma Zhaoxu said Tuesday it is merely wishful thinking of the United States to propose hosting official talks between China, Japan and the US.

Ma made the remarks when asked to comment on a hearsay that the US side has told the Chinese side that it is willing to host trilateral talks between China, Japan and the United States to impel China and Japan to exchange views on a series of issues.

"I'd like to clarify the discussions between Chinese Foreign Minister Yang Jiechi and US Secretary of State Hillary Clinton in Hanoi last week," said Ma.

He said both sides discussed strengthening cooperation between China, Japan and the United States, so as to work together for the peace and development of the Asia-Pacific region.

He noted the US side proposed holding official trilateral talks between China, Japan and the United States.

"I'd like to stress that this is only the thinking of the US side," he said.

He said China is looking at making full use of all current dialogue and cooperation mechanisms in the Asia-Pacific region with the hope of making them more effective in promoting peace and development in the region.

"The Diaoyu Islands and their adjacent islets are an inalienable part of China's territory and the territorial dispute over the islands is an issue between China and Japan," said the spokesman.

"It is absolutely wrong for the United States to repeatedly claim the Diaoyu Islands fall within the scope of the US-Japan Treaty of Mutual Cooperation and Security. What the United States should do is to immediately correct its wrong position," Ma said.

"Chinese Foreign Minister Yang Jiechi and China's foreign ministry have made clear many times on various occasions China's solemn stance," he added.

After her meeting with Japanese Foreign Minister Seiji Maehara in Hawaii last Thursday, US Secretary of State Hillary Clinton claimed the Diaoyu Islands issue could invoke the US-Japan security treaty.

The Chinese government was strongly dissatisfied with her statement.

Ma said Friday that as a bilateral agreement reached during the Cold War, the US-Japan security treaty should not harm the interests of third parties, including China.

http://www.chinadaily.com.cn/china/2010-11/02/content_11491199.htm

Find a suggested analysis of this text online.

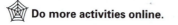 **Do more activities online.**

C5   ANALYSING SPEECH ACTS

In this unit we will consider how principles from pragmatics and conversation analysis can be applied to understanding how people make sense of potentially ambiguous contributions in social interaction. The two types of contribution we will focus on are apologies and threats. Apologies are potentially ambiguous because, although they are often accompanied by rather explicit language such as 'I'm sorry' or 'I apologise', this language, in the absence of other things such as an assumption of responsibility or a promise not to repeat the offending action, is sometimes not enough to make the apology felicitous. Furthermore, words such as 'I'm sorry' are sometimes used in cases where no apology is intended at all. Threats are potentially ambiguous because people often issue them in an indirect fashion in order to avoid legal or moral accountability, and because, in some situations, people might interpret utterances as threats, when they were not intended as such.

Interpreting apologies

Apologies are among the most studied kind of speech act. Despite this, because of the complexity and context-dependent nature of apologies, there is still considerable disagreement among scholars as to the conditions that must be present to make an apology felicitous. Part of the reason for this is that people themselves vary considerably in terms of what they require to be 'satisfied' by another's attempt at apologising in different situations. Consider the following conversation);

> A: You forgot!
> B: Yes. I *am* sorry.
> A: You're always doing it.
> B: I know.
>   (from Schegloff 1988)

As analysts looking at this conversation with no knowledge of the context in which it takes place, we must rely on the sequential placement of the utterances in order to make sense of what the speakers mean by their words. In particular, the phrase 'I *am* sorry' in B's utterance in the second line helps us to make sense of A's previous utterance ('You forgot') as a 'complaint' rather than as simply an assertion. At the very least, we can be sure that B has taken this utterance to be a complaint. Furthermore, coming as it does after a statement about his or her own behaviour (<u>You</u> forgot!), rather than a statement about something or somebody else (such as 'It's raining'), we are able to interpret B's statement 'I *am* sorry' as an apology rather than an expression of sympathy. Finally, we are able to interpret B's statement as an apology because A appears to interpret it in that way.

At the same time, however, A does not fully accept B's apology: rather than saying something such as, 'It's okay,' he or she makes yet another assertion ('You're always doing it'), which we also interpret as a complaint, or rather, an elaboration on the first complaint. This is not the preferred response to an apology (which is an acceptance of the apology) and thus leads B to infer that further work has to be performed on the apology front. Thus B's next contribution, 'I know,' is offered not as a simple statement of fact or agreement but as a further admission of guilt, an elaboration of the original apology.

The important thing to notice about this exchange is that the statement 'I *am* sorry' is apparently not sufficient to successfully perform the apology. In the first instance it is also accompanied by an acknowledgement of fault ('Yes'), but even this is not enough to elicit A's acceptance of the apology. B is also required to acknowledge an even greater fault (that his or her 'forgetting' is not a momentary lapse but a habitual behaviour). Therefore, even when an utterance seems to satisfy a set of objective conditions for an apology, there is no guarantee that it will be accepted as such by the recipient.

A number of scholars have attempted to formulate the 'felicity conditions' for apologies. Owen (1983), for example, offers this simple set of criteria:

❏   The act A specified in the propositional content is an offence against addressee H.
❏   H would have preferred S's not doing A to S's doing A and S believes H would have preferred S's not doing A to his doing A.
❏   A does not benefit H and S believes A does not benefit H.
❏   S regrets (is sorry for) having done A.
❏   (The utterance) counts as an expression of regret by S for having done A.

There are at least two potential problems with this set of conditions. The first is that the propositional content of apologies (what is being apologised for) is often not explicitly stated in the apology itself but rather implied based on some previous action or utterance, and when it is stated, even if it represents an offence against the addressee, it may not be exactly the offence for which the addressee is seeking an apology. B in the above example might say, 'I'm sorry for upsetting you,' which is quite different from saying 'I'm sorry I forgot.'

The second problem has to do with what needs to be done in order for the utterance to 'count' as an expression of regret. As we saw above, the utterance 'I *am* sorry,' which is clearly an expression of regret, is not always sufficient to accomplish an apology. At the same time, there are many instances in which regret is expressed which would not be considered apologies. For example, a job applicant might receive a letter with the sentence, 'we regret to inform you that your application has not been accepted.' Even though this is an explicit expression of regret, and the addressee might indeed regard the rejection as an offence, few people would regard this as a true apology.

Cohen *et al.* (1986) have pointed out that apologies often involve one or more of the following verbal strategies:

❏   an expression of apology (I *am* sorry);
❏   an explanation or account of the situation (I've had a lot on my mind lately);
❏   an acknowledgement of responsibility (I know);
❏   an offer of repair (how can I make it up to you?);
❏   a promise of forbearance (I'll never do it again).

The 'perfect' apology, in fact, contains all of these elements, even when some or most of them are implicit rather than stated outright. For something to have the 'force' of the apology, however, only one of these strategies is necessary. In some cases in which only one strategy is used, however, the speaker leaves it up to the addressee to *infer* that an apology has been made by referring to the conversational maxims. I might, for example, say, 'I feel terrible about shouting at you yesterday,' flouting the maxim of relevance (my internal state of mind may not seem directly relevant to our conversation), leading my interlocutor to take the statement as implying something more than a simple assertion.

In many cases, however, addressees require more than one of the above strategies to be used in order to be satisfied that the apology is 'complete' and 'sincere'.

✪ Activity

One of the most famous disagreements regarding the speech act of apologising began on 1 April 2001 when a US spy plane, flying without permission in Chinese airspace, collided with a Chinese fighter jet, causing it to crash and killing the pilot. The Chinese authorities detained the crew of the US plane for 11 days while they waited for the US to 'apologise' for illegally entering their airspace and causing the death of the pilot. The incident ended when the US government issued what has come to be known as 'the letter of the two sorries'. Many on both the US and Chinese sides insisted, however, that the 'two sorries' expressed in the letter were not 'true apologies'.

The 'two sorries' were:

1) Both President Bush and Secretary of State Powell have expressed their sincere regret over your missing pilot and aircraft. Please convey to the Chinese people and to the family of pilot Wang Wei that we are very sorry for their loss.
2) We are very sorry the entering of Chinese air space and the landing did not have verbal clearance, but are pleased the crew landed safely.

(United States Government 2001)

Based on Owen's felicity conditions for an apology and Cohen and his colleagues' list of strategies, decide whether or not you think these 'sorries' constitute true apologies. Give reasons for your decision. You should particularly consider:

❏ if the propositional content referred to matches with the offences perceived by the Chinese side;
❏ if enough of the strategies for apologising are expressed or implied to make the apologies convincing.

Interpreting threats

Threats suffer from a similar ambiguity as apologies because people often depend a great deal on implicature when issuing them. Consequently, as with apologies, how they are interpreted by those to whom they are issued matters a great deal.

In some ways the felicity conditions for threatening are quite similar to those for promising, warning and advising. All of these speech acts have to do with something that will or will not happen in the future, depending on whether or not certain conditions are met. In fact, very often words such as 'promise', 'advise' and 'warn' are used to issue threats, as in:

I'm warning you. If I see you around here again, I promise you, I'll kill you.

and

If you value your life, I advise you to pay what you owe.

The main differences between a threat and these other three speech acts are that: 1) unlike a promise, what is threatened is harmful rather than beneficial to the addressee; 2) unlike a warning, the action requested is for the benefit of the speaker rather than the addressee; and, 3) unlike advice, the speaker takes his or her own perspective, not the hearer's, and he or she controls the outcome rather than the hearer.

The linguist Roger Shuy summarises these differences in Table C5.1.

Table C5.1 Comparison of threatening, warning, advising and promising (adapted from Shuy 1993: 98)

	Threatening	Warning	Advising	Promising
To the speaker's benefit	✓			
To the hearer's benefit		✓	✓	✓
To the hearer's detriment	✓			
From speaker's perspective	✓	✓		✓
From hearer's perspective			✓	
Speaker controls outcome	✓			✓
Hearer controls outcome		✓	✓	

Roger Shuy is a forensic linguist, the kind of language expert who is sometimes called upon by courts and law enforcement officers to make judgements about what people meant, in order to determine if they have committed a crime. In his book *Language Crimes* (1993), he relates the case of a man named Don Tyner, who was accused of making threats to a business associate named Vernon Hyde, who resigned from his organisation after securing ownership of a number of shares in a racehorse. After Hyde's resignation, Tyner repeatedly contacted Hyde and accused him of lying and swindling his company. Hyde interpreted these accusations as threats, though Tyner repeatedly denied threatening Hyde. On one occasion, after Hyde had accused Tyner of threatening him several times, the following exchange occurred:

Tyner: How's David?

Hyde: Do what?

Tyner: How's David?

Hyde: You mean my son?

Tyner: Yep.

Hyde: Don, don't threaten my son. Do a lot of things but don't ever threaten my son.

Tyner: I didn't threaten anybody, I just said, 'How's David?'

(from Shuy 1993: 109)

Without more complete evidence, of course, it is impossible to determine whether or not Tyner was really threatening Hyde or his son. Instead, consider what you think might have led Hyde to interpret the statement 'How's David?' as a threat based on your knowledge of:

❏   the cooperative principle and conversational maxims;
❏   the felicity conditions for a threat.

Find a suggested analysis of this conversation online.

Do more activities online.

ANALYSING CONVERSATIONAL STRATEGIES   C6

In this unit you will have a chance to apply some of the ideas about conversational strategies that were introduced in A6 and B6. The kinds of interaction we explore, however, are not face-to-face conversations, but rather computer-mediated interactions, in particular, interactions using Facebook and MSN Messenger.

As noted in A6, mediated interactions are different from face-to-face spoken conversations in a number of ways. For one thing, in much computer-mediated communication, people type their 'utterances' rather than speaking them. In addition, these interactions rarely involve the same kind of synchrony that face-to-face conversation does. Whereas face-to-face interactions occur in 'real time', giving us access to other people's utterances as they are forming them, most computer-mediated interactions are asynchronous, involving a 'time lag' between production and reception, whether it be the momentary lag between the time when one party types a message and the other person reads it, which we experience in instant messaging, or the much longer time lags associated with email, blogs and social networking sites.

Perhaps the most important difference between face-to-face interaction and computer-mediated interaction is that many of the non-verbal and paralinguistic resources available in face-to-face communication are not available in text-based computer-mediated communication. This is significant because these are precisely the resources people often use as *contextualisation cues* to frame their conversational activities, and they can also play an important role in the face strategies of *involvement* and *independence*. Users of text-based communication tools, then, need to make use of different resources such as graphics, emoticons, orthography and punctuation to fulfil the functions that non-verbal and paralinguistic communication do in face-to-face encounters.

Face strategies on Facebook

Perhaps more than any other kind of computer-mediated communication, social networking sites are designed to give users tools to communicate about and manage their social relationships with others. Facebook is about 'face' precisely in the sense in which we defined it in unit A6: 'the negotiated public image mutually granted to each other by participants in a communicative event'. Users of Facebook are centrally concerned with constructing and maintaining their 'public images', with saving face and with 'giving face' to others.

It is not uncommon for people to have many Facebook 'friends' (hundreds or even thousands), and yet they do not enjoy the same kind of relationships with all of these 'friends': with some of them they are socially close and with others they are socially distant; some of them are their social equals, while others are in a hierarchical relationship with them. The problem with Facebook, however, is that it is biased towards a face system of symmetrical solidarity. Nearly all of the resources it makes available, from the initial mechanism of 'friending', to photo sharing, to the exchange of virtual tokens such as 'pokes' and 'vampire bites' are designed to express involvement. Some (see for example Kiesler 1986; Landow 1992) have even suggested that it is a fundamental characteristic of all computer-mediated communication that it flattens hierarchies and encourages self-disclosure, a phenomenon Joseph Walther (1996) calls 'hyperpersonal communication'.

For some users this is not a problem – the whole point of a social networking site for them is to help them get closer to those in their social network – and it certainly is not a problem for the company that runs Facebook, since the more people share with one another using involvement strategies, the more information about them is available to sell to advertisers. It does become a problem, however, when people who are accustomed to hierarchical or deference face systems in face-to-face communication have to negotiate their relationships in an environment that is biased towards involvement, as when students and professors or employees and employers become 'friends'.

These difficulties are especially salient in 'wall posts', since these constitute 'publically performed conversations' which people who are not involved in them typically have access to. Therefore, the relationships people enact in these interactions are not just negotiated between the interactants, but also displayed to a larger audience.

The example in Figure C6.1 illustrates how one of my students strategically mixed independence and involvement strategies when 'tagging' me in a picture in her photo album.

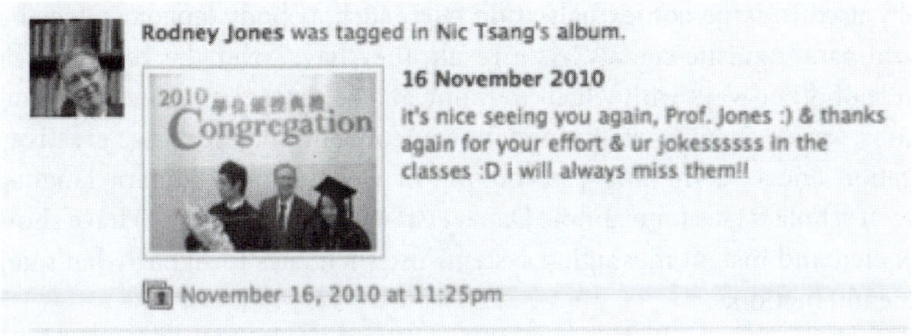

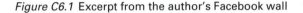

Rodney Jones was tagged in Nic Tsang's album.

16 November 2010

it's nice seeing you again, Prof. Jones :) & thanks again for your effort & ur jokessssss in the classes :D i will always miss them!!

November 16, 2010 at 11:25pm

Figure C6.1 Excerpt from the author's Facebook wall

The first thing that should be noted regarding this example is that 'tagging' someone in a photo on Facebook is a clear example of *involvement*. Not only does it assume a relationship of solidarity, but it also makes the assumption that the person tagged does not mind advertising this relationship to other users. Consequently, it is also a threat to the 'negative face' of the person who has been tagged, potentially violating their desire for autonomy and privacy. There are also other instances of involvement in this example, such as the optimistic and complimentary message, the informal language and the use of emoticons (such as :) and :D) and unconventional spelling and punctuation (like 'ur', 'jokessssss' and the repetition of the exclamation point at the end of the message).

At the same time, there are also instances of independence strategies, most notably the use of the title 'Prof. Jones' to address me. What is interesting about this is that, like many university professors, I am on a 'first-name basis' with my students. In other words, this student uses an independence strategy on Facebook which she probably would *not* use in face-to-face interaction with me. One reason for this may be to compensate for the involvement strategies that otherwise dominate the message and to mitigate the potential threat to my negative face.

✪ **Activity**

Analyse the postings on Facebook or some other social network service you use. Does this service encourage the adoption of a particular face system among users? Do the people in your network (including yourself) use different mixtures of independence and involvement strategies when interacting with people with whom they have different kinds of relationships? In particular, how do people who are socially distant or who are in hierarchal relationships manage face strategies? Can you find examples of interactions which would have been managed differently had they taken place face-to-face?

Contextualisation cues in instant messaging

As I have said above, text-based computer-mediated communication differs from face-to-face conversation in that users do not have access to many of the resources normally used to issue contextualisation cues, such as body language, facial expressions and paralinguistic signals. As a result, they have, over the years, developed a multitude of other ways with which to frame and reframe their utterances, including emoticons, screen names, status updates, unconventional spelling, creative use of punctuation and code-mixing (the mixing of words from different languages). A number of scholars (see for example Danet *et al.* 1997; Herring 2001) have shown how users of chat and instant messaging systems use such cues to signal 'what's going on' in online interaction.

Speakers of Chinese, like many of the students I teach in Hong Kong, also have at their disposal written **final particles**, sounds that often occur at the end of spoken utterances which signal the speaker's attitude towards the utterance or the hearer, which users of chat and instant messaging programs regularly insert (often in Romanised form) in their written messages (though they hardly ever appear in more formal written Chinese).

Below is an example of how such resources can be used as *contextualisation cues* in instant messaging exchanges. It is an excerpt from a conversation between two university students in Hong Kong, one a female named Tina, and the other a male named Barnett:

> Barnett: u're . . . . ~?!
> Tina: tina ar. . . . . . .
> Tina: a beautiful girl. . . . . . .
> Tina: haha . . .
> Tina: ^_^
> Barnett: ai~
> Barnett: i think i'd better leave right now. . . .^o^!

The conversation starts out with Barnett asking for clarification of Tina's identity. The tilde (~) here signifies a lengthening of the previous utterance, giving it a playful, insistent quality. Tina replies with her name, followed by a Romanised final particle ('ar'), which in Cantonese is often used to soften affirmative statements so they do not sound too abrupt, followed by a number of ellipsis marks (. . .) indicating that there is more to come. In her next message she elaborates on her identity, referring to herself as 'a beautiful girl', which might be interpreted as either a boast or an attempt at seduction. In her next two messages, however, she puts a 'joking frame' around her previous description with the words 'haha. . .' and a smiling emoticon (^_^). Barnett replies with 'ai', a Romanisation of the Cantonese word 哎, often used as an expression of pain, frustration or indignation, which he lengthens with a tilde (~) in the same way it might be if spoken in a particularly exaggerated way. He then adds, in the next message, that he thinks he had better leave the conversation, but reframes this as a playful threat with the humorous emoticon ^o^, which represents the face of a clown.

What is going on in this short exchange, of course, has very little to do with Tina giving an objective appraisal of her looks or even boasting, or with Barnett expressing concern and threatening to terminate the conversation. Instead, this is clearly an episode of playful teasing or flirting. Without the contextualisation cues supplied by such things as punctuation, emoticons and tokens such as 'haha', however, the conversation would take on a very different meaning.

★ **Activity**

a) Choose an utterance which you might send to your friend via instant messaging such as 'u finish hw?' ('have you finished the homework?) and discuss how the message could be 'framed' differently (as, for example, a warning, an offer, a boast, a complaint, a sympathetic remark, etc.) by attaching to it one of the emoticons from the range of default choices offered by MSN Messenger (Figure C6.2).

Figure C6.2 MSN Messenger emoticons

b) Save an instant messaging conversation as a 'history file' and analyse it in terms of how things such as code choice, spelling, punctuation, capitalisation and emoticons are used to strategically frame and re-frame messages.

 **Do more activities online.**

ANALYSING CONTEXTS   C7

Analysing the communicative competence that members of a particular speech community bring to a particular speech event requires more than just the analysis of texts or transcripts (though one can often tell a lot from such an analysis). It requires observing people interacting in the speech event and talking to them about what they

C7

think they need to know in order to participate in it successfully. Often one must talk with multiple participants in order to find out what it is like for people playing different roles in the event.

The anthropologist Gregory Bateson and the psychiatrist Jurgen Ruesch (Ruesch and Bateson 1968) say that there are at least four kinds of information an ethnographer should gather: 1) members' generalisations (what participants think other people need to know and do to participate in the speech event); 2) individual experiences (the specific, concrete knowledge and experiences of individual people who have participated in the speech event in the past); 3) 'objective' observation (the observation of people participating in the speech event); and 4) the analyst's comparison of what he or she has observed and heard from participants with his or her own knowledge and behaviour in similar speech events in his or her own speech community. Sometimes these different kinds of information contradict one another: participants, for example, may attribute certain behaviour to other members of their speech community but say that they themselves do things differently, or they may say they behave in a particular way but can be observed behaving in an entirely different way. The important thing for the analyst is not to privilege any of these four kinds of information, but to take them together in order to get a full picture of what is going on from the point of view of the participants. It is important to remember that the ethnographer of speaking is less interested in what is 'objectively' occurring in a speech event as in what participants *think* is occurring and what they need to *know* to participate as legitimate members of their group.

Sample analysis: 'don't bite my shit'

It would be impossible to conduct a full ethnographic analysis of a speech event in the space of this unit. What I can do, however, is discuss the meaning and significance of a particular utterance in the social and cultural context in which it occurs. The utterance, one which I heard frequently during my ethnographic study of urban skateboarders in Hong Kong (reported in Jones 2008; 2011), is: 'Hey man, don't bite my shit.' I heard this utterance or some variation of it many times during my fieldwork, sometimes uttered in a playful manner and sometimes with deadly seriousness. In order to understand the meaning of the utterance and the kinds of cultural expectations that underpin it, it is necessary to understand something about the cultural context in which it occurs.

Skateboarding in Hong Kong, as in most places, takes place within the context of a speech situation called a 'skate session'. These sessions usually occur at skate parks, but sometimes occur in other places such as on sidewalks, in parking lots and in city squares. Skaters regard the skating that goes on in parks and that which goes on in these other places to be two different *genres* of skating, one which is called 'park skating' and the other which is called 'street skating'. In Hong Kong, 'park skating' always occurs during the day when the skate parks are open and 'street skating' almost always occurs at night when fewer people are around to interfere with the activity. Skate sessions can last many hours and sometimes involve skaters moving from setting to setting. They may, for example, begin a session in the skate park in the afternoon and then move to the street after the skate park closes (*setting*).

Skaters generally participate in skate sessions in 'crews' or 'posses', groups of people who usually skate together and who often share a certain style of dressing or acting (for example 'punk' or 'hip-hop') and are usually of a similar level of skill (*participants*). People hardly ever skate alone. One reason for this is that among the main aims of a skating session is to let others witness one performing daring or difficult tricks (*ends*). This aim of making oneself a spectacle for others is reinforced by the fact that skaters often bring video cameras with them during skate sessions to film one another (*instrumentalities*).

At a skate park at any given time there are likely to be multiple 'crews' and one of the core competencies for members of this community is understanding how to manage the use of space in order to avoid conflicts among crews. In street skating sessions these conflicts can sometimes become intense if one crew claims the exclusive right to skate at a particular spot and tries to deny access to other crews. At skate parks, this does not happen since these parks are public property and the right for all skaters to use them is policed by park attendants and security guards. Therefore, different crews must cooperate and carefully negotiate the use of space (*norms*).

Skate sessions normally consist of multiple 'speech events' including conversations, horseplay, games of 'SKATE' (a highly structured game in which skaters compete in performing tricks) and 'doing lines'. 'Doing lines' involves skaters taking turns executing 'lines' upon various obstacles (such as rails, stairs and ramps). A 'line' is one or more 'tricks' (most of which have names such as 'ollie' and 'kickflip') done in succession. Skaters work to compose lines which showcase their skill and imagination. Often members of different crews will occupy different parts of the park and content themselves with different obstacles. Sometimes, however, people from different crews make use of the same obstacle, having to take turns with one another (*act sequence*). It is in the mechanism of turn-taking among members of different crews that the notion of 'biting someone's shit' becomes relevant.

'Biting someone's shit' in the context of the 'speech event' of 'doing lines' refers to the action of imitating or repeating the line executed by the previous person in the queue. The meaning of this action depends crucially on the relationship between the person who does it and the person whose line has been imitated. When it is done by a member of a different crew, it can be taken as a challenge or sign of disrespect – a transgression of the rules of etiquette associated with 'doing lines'. In this case, the utterance 'Hey man, don't bite my shit,' can be interpreted as a warning or a threat. In cases where the person who 'bites one's shit' is a member of one's own crew, it can be seen as a matter of friendly competition or even a way of showing respect for one's crew member by emulating him. In this case, the utterance 'Hey man, don't bite my shit,' might be uttered in a more playful *key* and interpreted as teasing. In the context of a different speech event, such as a game of 'SKATE', repeating the trick that the previous person has done is expected and so does not constitute 'biting someone's shit'.

The point that this example illustrates is that the meaning of an utterance such as 'don't bite my shit' cannot be interpreted with reference to only one component of the SPEAKING model, but can only be understood as a matter of the *interaction* among multiple components: place, participants, goals, the expected sequence of acts, the tone in which the utterance is said, the various media involved in the communication (including things such as participants' dress, and their skateboards, and other things such as video cameras), norms about what constitutes 'showing respect' to others, and the genre – whether it is 'park skating' or 'street skating'. More importantly, successful use of and interpretation of this speech act incorporates a complex range of cultural knowledge regarding the values, identities and norms of conduct of this particular community of young (mostly male) skateboarders in Hong Kong.

Activity ✪

Choose a speech event in which people that you know normally participate but with which you are not entirely familiar. Interview the people involved with the aim of finding out what their expectations are about who should say what to whom, when, how and why. Use the components of the SPEAKING model as a guide for your questioning. Ask people both about the kinds of communicative competences most members of their speech community have and about their own personal experiences with this particular speech event.

After that, see if you can find an occasion to observe people taking part in this speech event. Notice not just what is said, but who says it, when and how. Fill out Table C7.1 with information from both your interviews and your observation.

Table C7.1 Analysing a speech event

Date and time of observation:
Name of event:

Setting
Participants
Ends
Act sequence
Key
Instrumentalities
Norms
Genre

Refining your analysis

The greatest danger in using a model such as Hymes's SPEAKING model is that the analyst simply describes the expectations participants have regarding each of the components in a rather mechanical way, like filling out a checklist, without offering much in the way of analysis. While this can at least provide a general idea of how the speech event happens, it does not tell us very much about *why* it happens the way it does. The analyst cannot stop at just describing the various components, but also needs to ask: 1) *why* different components have particular expectations associated with them; 2) *how* the expectations associated with different components interact and affect one another; and 3) *why* certain components seem more important and other components less important to participants.

Below are some useful tips to help you avoid falling into the trap of mechanical description.

Be specific

It is important for the analyst to be as specific as possible in his or her description of the expectations people have about the different components. This sometimes involves asking probing questions or observing what people say or do carefully, paying close attention to detail.

Remember that all components are not equal

One of the most important things an analyst will want to notice is that participants may regard the expectations governing some components to be stricter than those governing others and that some behaviour might be regarded as more or less 'compulsory', while other behaviour might be regarded as 'optional'. It is also important to note how expectations regarding one component can affect the kinds of expectations participants have about other components. In other words, it is important to notice which kinds of behaviour tend to co-occur in speech events (for example, the genre of a joke may tend to co-occur with a humorous or light-hearted key).

Compare and contrast

One way to really understand whether the communicative competencies you have uncovered through your analysis are really significant is to compare and contrast different speech events or the different experiences and perspectives of different participants engaged in the same speech event. One of the reasons Ruesch and Bateson recommend that analysts compare the speech event they are studying with one that is more familiar to them is to help them to better notice those aspects of the speech event which they might be misunderstanding or taking for granted.

Explore transgressions

One good way to understand what people are expected to do in a particular situation is to find out what happens when they fail to do what they are expected to do. This is because, while appropriate behaviour usually passes unremarked upon, inappropriate behaviour is often an occasion for participants to explicitly discuss their otherwise tacit assumptions and expectations. Therefore, noticing or talking with participants about mistakes, transgressions, inappropriate behaviour or 'incompetence' can be a good way to clarify what they regard as appropriate and why.

Activity ✪

Further refine the analysis you did in the last activity by doing the following:

❏ Talk to your participants about what you have written down for each component and ask them if they think it is accurate. See if they can help you to make your descriptions of the knowledge that members need about each component more specific.

❏ Try to determine what kind of knowledge is most important for successful participation in the speech event. Is knowledge about some components more important than knowledge about others?

❏ Try to determine what the relationships among components might be and how they affect one another.

❏ Compare and contrast this speech event with a similar speech event that you are also familiar with. How can you account for the similarities and differences?

❏ Ask your participants what would happen if any of the conventions associated with this speech event were violated? How would people react? What would need to be done to repair such a violation?

🕸 **Do more activities online.**

C8   DOING MEDIATED DISCOURSE ANALYSIS

In this unit you will explore how to apply the tools of mediated discourse analysis to the analysis of social actions, social practices and *sites of engagement*. The three concepts that we will be working with are:

1 the notion of *affordances* and *constraints*: the idea that different kinds of cultural tools make certain kinds of actions and certain kinds of social identities associated with those actions either more or less possible;

2 the notion of *social practices*: the idea that certain actions combined with other actions and with certain cultural tools come to be regarded as recognisable social practices and that discourse can play an important role in maintaining and promoting these social practices;

3 the notion of *sites of engagement*: the idea that actions take place at the *nexus* of cultural tools, social relationships and the experiences, knowledge and skill of individual social actors, and the way these three elements come together can help us to understand how a particular social action will be performed.

'Fifty ways to leave your lover'

In her book *The Breakup 2.0*, Ilana Gershon discusses how different kinds of media affect the way people perform the action of 'breaking up' with a romantic partner and the way they come to regard this action as a particular kind of *social practice*. Of course there are many ways this action could be performed. One might confront the person with whom one wishes to break up face-to-face, either in public or in a private place, call him or her on the telephone, or send what is known as a 'Dear John Letter'. Technology has introduced a number of new cultural tools with which to perform this action: one could send an email, for example, negotiate the break-up using instant messaging or mobile phone-based text messaging, or one could post a message or change one's 'relationship status' on Facebook.

Gershon interviewed a large number of people about their ideas about and experiences of breaking up and found that people had very strong feelings about how the medium used can affect the action of breaking up. In particular, they felt that people who used the 'wrong' medium risked enacting the 'wrong' kind of social identity, that is, being considered 'the wrong kind of person' by others.

⭐ **Activity**

Think about the *affordances* and *constraints* of the different kinds of media one might use to accomplish the action of breaking up. For example, breaking up face-to-face makes it easier for the person doing the breaking up to gauge the other person's reaction and adapt his or her message accordingly, but it can make it more difficult to end the conversation (and the relationship) quickly and easily. This medium also makes it easier for the person being 'broken up with' to respond and ask for reasons and clarification, but it may make it more difficult for him or her to hide any feelings of disappointment or sadness that might arise. Because of these affordances and constraints, people tend to think some media are 'better' for breaking up than other media and associate different media for breaking up with different 'kinds of people'.

Fill in Table C8.1 based on your own beliefs and experiences about the things different media make harder or more difficult to do during the breaking-up process. Then *rank* the different media in terms of: 1) how much you would prefer to use it if you are breaking up with someone; and 2) how much you would prefer it to be used if you are the one being broken up with. Note if there is a difference in your ranking for these two situations. How do you account for this difference? What does this tell you about the relationship between cultural tools and social identities?

Compare your answers with those of someone else and discuss if and why you have different opinions about the kinds of people associated with different media for breaking up.

Table C8.1 Cultural tools for breaking up

Medium	Affordances and constraints	Rank	
		(1)	*(2)*
Face-to-face conversation			
Telephone conversation			
Letter or email			
Instant messaging conversation			5
Text message			4
Facebook relationship status			6

Of course, most of the time when people engage in a complex social practice such as breaking up with a lover, they use a combination of cultural
tools, including a combination of media. They might begin breaking up
with a text message, continue the negotiation of the break-up through an
instant messaging conversation and complete the process in a face-to-face
meeting.

Think about how the social practice of breaking up is constructed in
your social circle. What smaller actions are usually included in this practice
(such as 'making an appointment to meet' or 'apologising for hurting the
other person's feelings') and how are these usually combined? What sorts of
cultural tools (such as objects, media, genres, social languages, gestures or
facial expressions) are used and how do these tools affect how the practice is
accomplished?

Being 'in a relationship' on Facebook

Just as breaking-up is a complex social practice, entering into a romantic relationship
with someone can also be complicated. The people involved must negotiate the point
at which they are prepared to express to each other and to other people that they know
that they are 'in a relationship'. This is accomplished differently in different societies.
In North America when I was growing up, boys usually gave their girlfriends their
school ring, which the girl would wear around her neck to announce that she was
'going steady' with the owner of the ring.

The ways the social practice of entering into a relationship have changed as a
result of new media such as Facebook is also a topic Gershon takes up in her book.
Facebook provides a specific tool for people to accomplish the action of announcing
their 'relationship status' to others, allowing them to indicate on their profiles if they
are 'single', 'in a relationship', 'engaged', 'married', 'in a civil union', 'in a domestic
partnership', 'it's complicated', 'in an open relationship', 'widowed', 'separated' or
'divorced'.

This tool itself comes with a number of obvious affordances and constraints. While it allows users to indicate that they are in certain kinds of relationships, it makes it more difficult for them to indicate that they are in other kinds of relationships that may not be covered by the choices in the drop-down menu. It also makes ambiguity in relationships more difficult by putting social pressure on users to announce their status to others in their social network. Gershon talks about the negotiations couples go through about when to make their relationship 'Facebook official', as well as the complications that arise when they end up breaking up and having to decide how and when to change their relationship status back to 'single'.

The problem is that one cannot fully understand how this cultural tool has affected the practices of entering into and maintaining romantic relationships just by looking at these choices, because not everybody uses them in the same way. Different people and groups have different ways of using the 'relationship status' on Facebook. Some people use it not to announce romantic relationships but to avoid having to give information about their romantic entanglements by, for example, indicating that they are 'married' to their best friend. The only way to understand how social practices of relationship management have changed because of Facebook is to consider the interaction among the cultural tools the website makes available, the relationships among the people in a particular social network, and the knowledge, habits and norms associated with the 'historical bodies' of specific users.

> ✪ **Activity**
>
> Consider your social network on Facebook or some other social networking site as a *site of engagement*. Think about how you and your friends use and interpret the 'relationship status' function (or some other equivalent function on another site). Analyse how the accomplishment of the social practice of using this function depends on: 1) the affordances and constraints built into the technology itself; 2) the actual relationships among the people who belong to your social network, especially those who are associated with each other using this function; and 3) your own habits, knowledge and experiences associated with this function.

🕸 **Do more activities online.**

ANALYSING MULTIMODALITY C9

In this section you will practise applying some of the ideas introduced in units A9 and B9 to the analysis of multimodality in a text and a face-to-face interaction. You will explore how the analysis of multimodality can not just help us understand how texts and interactions are structured, but also how they promote certain ideologies and power relationships.

Multimodal discourse analysis is a complex and rapidly developing field, and it would be impossible to demonstrate all of the many tools and concepts analysts have developed for the analysis of things such as images, gestures, gaze and posture. Instead I will introduce a few basic tools and key questions that can guide you in this kind of analysis and encourage you to refer to the sources in the list of further reading for information on other tools and procedures.

'It's nice to be chased'

This first example is an advertisement that appeared in the stations of the Mass Transit Railway in Hong Kong in 2005. It portrays a woman with wings in the foreground and two men in the background holding butterfly nets. The setting of the picture seems to be a wooded area reminiscent of the setting of fairy tales, and this 'fairy tale feeling' is increased by the unconventional dress of the participants and the wings on the woman's back. Underneath the two men appears the slogan: 'It's nice to be chased. Butterfly Bra by Wacoal' (Figure C9.1).

Figure C9.1 Wacoal Bra advertisement (1)

Ideational function

This picture contains three participants – one woman and the two men – who are interacting with one another in a kind of narrative. The image shows one moment in the story, which the viewer is invited to imagine as part of a more extended (perhaps endless) 'chase'. As a narrative, however, it is interesting because the main action consists only of 'gazing'; the viewer is asked to infer the higher-level action of 'chasing' from the information in the slogan, the butterfly nets and his or her own world knowledge.

The main action vectors are formed by the gazes of the two men towards the woman, who is looking away rather than retuning the gaze (see Figure C9.2). At first this seems to be a one-sided action, as the woman does not return the gaze. However, the words help to give the impression that the woman actually *is* aware of the men's gaze but is pretending not to be. Rather than returning their gaze, she is 'playing hard to get', responding to the gaze by 'posing'.

The thing that makes this picture interesting and problematic is a second set of vectors moving downward from each of the men's shoulders with their arms moving towards one another. This gives the impression that they might be holding hands, although their hands are obscured by foliage. And so the status of the participants becomes ambiguous – the vector from their eyes moves towards the woman. The vector from their arms moves towards each other. Aside from the hint of a homo-sexual relationship, this ambiguity constructs these figures as both cooperating to catch the woman and competing with each other.

Figure C9.2 Wacoal Bra advertisement (2)

Interpersonal function

None of the participants in the picture looks at the viewer. The men look towards the woman and the woman looks up into space. This gives the viewer the feeling of looking at a private scene. In other words, the viewer takes the position of *a voyeur*. Positioning the reader like this reinforces the theme of the picture – 'watching'. The men are secretly watching the woman. The woman is secretly pretending not to know she is being watched. And the viewer is secretly watching the whole scene. Thus, although the viewer is not connected to the characters through gaze, he or she is nevertheless made to feel somehow part of the image by being placed into this voyeur-like position.

The woman is positioned in the foreground of the image, closer to the viewer, and, although she is not looking at him or her, this creates an increased feeling of intimacy and identification with this character. The intimacy is increased because we can see her face and the men cannot, and also because she is (presumably) 'speaking' to us through the printed text.

Although the forest vegetation and the men are shown in photographic accuracy, the picture does not seem to present a 'true' or realistic world, but rather a dream world. This impression is reinforced by the high colour saturation and the non-realistic elements (such as the woman's wings).

Textual function

The woman is obviously the most important character in the story as she is placed in the foreground of the picture with her whole body displayed while the men are in the background with half of their bodies obscured. The woman is also placed in the lower left quadrant of the picture, the quadrant of the 'given' and the 'real', while the men occupy the upper right quadrant of the picture, where the 'new' and the 'ideal' usually appear. There are a number of possible reasons for this. One is that the woman in the picture is intended to be portrayed as passive, earth-like and 'natural', and the men as active, thinking, rational, intellectual. Another reason might be that the woman (and her bra) are presented as a *cause* and the men chasing her are presented as a *result* of this cause. Still another possibility is that the intended viewer of the image (probably a woman) is likely be more interested in the men – and if she 'reads' the picture in the expected way, her eye moves across and upward towards the men in the upper part of the picture. The irony is that while the image portrays men looking at a woman, the composition of the image is such that the gaze of the viewer moves away from the woman and towards the men.

Ideology

This picture is rich in imagery from both science and literature. The scene reminds the viewer of fairy tales and myths containing forest nymphs. At the same time, there is the clear hint of sexual pursuit, reinforced by the relative lack of clothing of all participants. The innocence of the 'Discourse' of fairy tales, then, is juxtaposed with the 'adultness' of the sexual narrative. There is also the 'Discourse of science' present, with the woman being portrayed as a 'specimen' for the men to catch, admire, examine and catalogue. The implication is that she is just one of many specimens that may have been caught. The ad seems to be communicating to young women that to be put in the position of the woman in this ad is desirable: to be watched (secretly) by men, to be competed over, to be 'chased' are things to which she should aspire. At the same time, although the woman in the image is passive, there is still a sense that she is in some way in control of the situation; she enjoys being chased, and catching her is likely to be difficult since she has the advantage of wings, which her pursuers lack. Thus, the product, the Butterfly Bra, like the butterfly wings, is constructed as making a woman simultaneously more desirable but less likely to be 'caught'.

Activity ✪

Find an advertisement from a magazine, website, billboard or some other medium which features one or more images and analyse it in the same way I analysed the example above, considering how the visual elements (as well as the text) create *ideational, interpersonal* and *textual* meaning. Also consider how these three kinds of meaning work together to promote a particular 'version of reality' or to create or reinforce a certain set of social relationships. Use the following sets of questions to guide your analysis:

Ideational function

❏ Who/what are the main participants in the image?
❏ Is the image a narrative image, an analytical image or a classificatory image?
❏ What are the processes portrayed in the image and how are they portrayed?
❏ What are the primary vectors formed by actions, gestures, gaze and the positioning of the figures?
❏ If there are multiple vectors, how do they interact with one another?

Interpersonal function

❏ From what perspective are the figures in the image shown? How does this create a position for the viewer?
❏ Are the figures depicted close up or far away from the viewer?
❏ Are the figures looking at the viewer or away?
❏ What kind of relationship do they establish with the viewer through things such as gaze and gesture?
❏ Does the image seem realistic, and how does this affect how the viewer relates to the figures in the image?

Textual function

❏ What are the most prominent and least prominent elements in the image?
❏ What is in the centre of the image?
❏ What is the relationship between the background and the foreground?
❏ What is in the top section of the image and what is in the bottom section?
❏ What is on the left and what is on the right?
❏ How does the placement of elements in the image affect how the viewers' eyes are likely to move across it?

Ideology

❏ How do the choices about what has been included in the image and what has been excluded portray a certain version of reality?
❏ Are the figures in the image portrayed in stereotypical or unexpected ways?
❏ Are some figures active and others passive? What is the significance of this?
❏ What do you think the image is trying to get you to think or do?

C9

Fifteen seconds in a writing centre

Now we will turn to how you might go about analysing multimodality in face-to-face interaction, using as an example just 15 seconds of interaction in a university writing centre where students go to get advice about their written assignments from peer tutors. The fact that we will only be looking at a very small segment attests to the multimodal richness of most face-to-face interaction – quite a lot can occur in just 15 seconds. At the same time, this kind of microanalysis can also be risky if the analyst loses sight of the higher-level actions that the segment under analysis is part of. Thus, in a thorough multimodal analysis of interaction, the analyst always alternates his or her attention from the small details to the 'big picture', always asking how micro-elements such as gaze and posture shifts, gesture and intonation contours help participants to accomplish the higher-level actions they are engaged in.

This example also demonstrates one way of producing a multimodal transcription. The segment of interaction to be analysed is presented in 12 frames captured from a digital video of the tutoring session (see Figure C9.3). The frames were not captured at any regular time interval. Rather, a frame was captured each time a new meaningful lower-level action such as a gaze shift, a gesture or a 'tone unit' of speech was produced. As can be seen in the images, in many of the frames, multiple meaningful actions were performed across multiple modes simultaneously. In the type of transcription demonstrated here (adapted from Norris 2004), things such as head movements, the trajectory of gestures and the direction of gaze are marked with arrows, and the speech of participants is represented in text of varying sizes above their heads, the size and direction of the letters representing stress and intonation.

The analysis I will demonstrate here will focus on *intermodal relationships*, how actions taken with different modes of communication work together and affect one another. It will make use of two basic concepts: *sequentiality* – the idea that lower-level actions are arranged in meaningful sequences to form higher-level actions – and *simultaneity* – the idea that when actions are produced at the same time, they can affect how each should be interpreted. Related to these two concepts is the notion that all actions are mutually negotiated between participants in interaction. The actions that one person performs are always in some ways influenced or constrained by the actions that the other person performs.

As mentioned above, one aim of such an analysis is to identify the lower-level actions and understand how they combine together to form higher-level actions. The ultimate aim, however, is to use such an analysis to understand how people use the many resources that are available to them to perform *social practices* and enact *social identities* in ways that promote and reinforce particular 'Discourses' or social relationships.

The two participants in this segment are the tutor (the woman seated on the right) and the client (the man seated on the left). The session begins with the tutor saying, 'so ... ummm,' and making two small **beat gestures** with her pen towards the client's essay lying on the table in time with the two syllables (frame a). *Beat gestures* are perhaps the most common kinds of gestures. We use them to keep time in interactions, often tracking the rhythm of our speech, and they are important in helping participants synchronise things such as turn-taking. They can also function to signal that a new higher-level action or a new 'frame' is being taken up, much like *discourse*

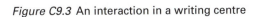

Figure C9.3 An interaction in a writing centre

markers (see B6). In this case the two beats along with the utterance signal that a new part of the tutoring session is about to start.

In frames b through f the tutor asks, 'is there anything in particular you think you want some more help with?' This utterance is accompanied by a complex combination of actions that contribute to constructing the meaning of the utterance and the relationship between the participants. As she says the words 'anything particular', the tutor points to the client's essay and inscribes a circle in the air with her pen. This is followed by a downward motion on the stressed syllable 'TIC'. Gestures like this, which involve pointing, are known as **deictic gestures**. The tutor follows this deictic gesture towards the essay with another one, pointing her pen towards the client when she says, 'YOU think.' Right after she utters the word 'think', the client leans slightly forward and raises his hand to his chin, forming the **iconic gesture** of a person deep in thought. Iconic gestures are those which symbolise some kind of abstract idea or higher-level action in a rather conventionalised way. This gesture on the part of the client is a good example of the way listeners use modes such as gesture to contribute to conversations even when they do not make use of the resource of speech.

As the tutor says 'you want some more help with', she gazes at the client, signal-ling that she is preparing to end her turn. Gaze is an important resource for the management of turn-taking in conversation, with speakers often looking away when they are speaking and then turning their gaze back to their interlocutors when they are finished. When the tutor finishes her question, she leans back slightly and brushes the hair from her face, almost as if she is clearing interactional space for the client's response as he issues a hesitant 'ummmmm'.

As she is waiting for his response, the tutor tilts her head downward and directs her gaze towards the essay, as if signalling that it is there that the client might find the answer to her questions (frame i). This is also a kind of deictic gesture, but she is using her head to point rather than her hand. The client answers this downward motion with an upward motion of his arm to touch his glasses, another iconic gesture signalling that he is 'searching' for something he would like help with. Then the client lowers his hand and asks, 'do you know the meaning of this paragraph?', inscribing exactly the same kind of circle above his essay that the tutor had made just moments before (frame k).

The modes of gaze, head movement, posture, gesture and prosody in this short segment do not just help participants to frame their utterances and organise the inter-action. These modes also work together to construct the higher-level action of 'having a tutorial' and to construct the relationship between the two participants as one of unequal power. The tutor demonstrates her power over the client in a number of small ways: through gaze (she gazes at him much more than he does at her), through her posture (she sits higher and straighter than he does), and through gestures (she frequently points at him and at his essay with her pen and her head). Furthermore, all of the client's gestures (the 'thinking' gesture, the 'searching' gesture and the imitation of the tutor's deictic circle) seem to be in response to the tutor's words or gestures, as if she is controlling him like a puppet. Another important mode the tutor uses to maintain control of the interaction, which we have not mentioned, is **object handling**. Not only does she hold a pen throughout the interaction (while the client is empty handed), but she also keeps her left hand placed on the edge of the client's essay during this entire segment as if she is prepared to take it away from him at any moment.

Activity ✪

Videotape a short interaction and divide a segment of the video into frames using an easy-to-use computer program such as iMovie (Mac) or Windows Movie Maker. Analyse how participants use the modes of gesture, gaze, posture, head movement and prosody along with the mode of spoken language to create meaning and manage the interaction. Pay attention to how lower-level actions are sequenced to form higher-level actions and how actions performed simultaneously affect one another's meaning.

 Do more activities online.

ANALYSING CORPORA   C10

In order to illustrate the procedures for corpus-assisted discourse analysis explained in unit B10, in this section I will examine a corpus of song lyrics by Lady Gaga, compare it to a more general corpus of pop music, and discuss how things such as concordances and frequency lists can be used to generate theories about texts in a corpus.

Before reading this unit I recommend that you download AntConc or some other software program for corpus analysis, and as you read, try to replicate the procedures described on a corpus of your own creation. You might, for example, create a similar corpus of lyrics from another singer and compare your findings with those generated from the Lady Gaga corpus analysed here, or you might create a corpus of post-2010 Lady Gaga songs to examine if and how this artist's music has changed.

My corpus consists of the lyrics of 59 songs released by Lady Gaga as of November 2010. Song lyrics are a good example of a type of text which might have to be 'cleaned' or otherwise altered before being suitable for inclusion in a corpus. For example, such texts often include things such as labels indicating 'chorus' or 'verse', which are not relevant to the analysis and should be removed. Sometimes repeated words or phrases are written in a kind of shorthand (e.g. I love you x 3). These need to be written out fully so that the texts reflect exactly what is sung. For my corpus, song titles and labels such as chorus and verse were deleted. Each song was saved in a separate text file and loaded into AntConc.

For my reference corpus I decided to choose a more general sampling of pop music from the same period. Thus, I compiled a corpus of the Billboard top 100 pop songs from November 2010. What this means, of course, is that my reference corpus is almost twice the size of my primary corpus. This is, in fact, normal, since a reference corpus generally contains a broader sampling of texts. These texts were prepared in the same manner as the texts for the Lady Gaga corpus. For your own reference corpus you might follow a similar procedure, or you might use one of the publicly available corpora, links to which are provided on the companion website to this book.

Table C10.1 Size of corpora and type token ratio

	No. of texts	No. of tokens	No. of types	Type token ratio
Lady Gaga songs	59	19,601	1,713	11.44
Top 100 hits (11/11)	100	33,412	3,680	9.07

Table C10.1 shows the number of texts as well as the number of tokens and types in each corpus. It also shows the type token ratio for each corpus. Note that the type token ratio for both of these corpora is rather low compared with the BNC written (45.53) and spoken (32.96) corpora. This is not surprising. Pop music generally involves quite a lot of repetition and a fairly narrow range of topics. As can be seen from the chart, the type token ratio for the Lady Gaga corpus is slightly higher than the reference corpus, suggesting that Lady Gaga's lyrics might exhibit more lexical complexity than other pop music produced around the same time.

Table C10.2 Top five function words

100 top songs				Lady Gaga songs			
Word	*Rank*	*Freq.*	*% of tokens*	*Word*	*Rank*	*Freq.*	*% of tokens*
I	1	1,709	5.11	I	1	866	4.41
you	2	1,167	3.49	you	2	718	3.66
the	3	870	2.6	the	3	463	2.36
and	4	687	2.05	oh	4	433	2.2
it	5	629	1.88	me	5	398	2.03

Table C10.2 shows the frequency of the most frequently occurring *function words* in the two corpora along with their overall ranking, their numerical frequency and the percentage of the total tokens they represent. Note that the percentage of total tokens is important when you are comparing corpora of different sizes. Some programs will calculate this for you, but with AntConc users must do this themselves.

The fact that the most frequent words in both of these corpora are 'I' and 'you' is consistent with other corpus-based studies of popular music. Murphey (1992), for example, found a similar degree of frequency for these pronouns in a corpus of English pop songs from the late 1980s. This, of course, makes sense given that pop songs usually involve a singer (or singer *persona*) singing to another person, usually a lover.

What is interesting in our findings is the relative frequency of the accusative form 'me' in the Lady Gaga corpus. In fact, the pronoun 'me' occurs almost twice as frequently in the Lady Gaga corpus (2.03% of the total tokens) than it does in the reference corpus (1.3% of the total tokens). This suggests that the singer persona in Lady Gaga's songs portrays herself more frequently in the 'object' position, the position of having things done to or for her, than singers in other songs.

Table C10.3 Top five content words

100 top songs				Lady Gaga songs			
Word	*Rank*	*Freq.*	*% of tokens*	*Word*	*Rank*	*Freq.*	*% of tokens*
like	23	234	0.70	love	17	193	0.98
baby	34	166	0.49	baby	21	158	0.80
know	36	155	0.46	want	29	109	0.56
love	39	143	0.43	know	36	91	0.46
gonna	42	127	0.38	no	37	91	0.46

Table C10.3 shows the five most frequently occurring content words in the two corpora. As you can see, content words occur much less frequently than function words. Again, the words listed are words normally associated with pop music, such as 'love' and 'baby'. One interesting finding is the greater frequency of the word 'love' in the corpus of Lady Gaga lyrics compared with the reference corpora. This might lead one to think that love is a greater preoccupation of Lady Gaga than it is of other popular singers. But the truth, of course, is more complicated than that and, as we will see below, has much to do with the way the notion of 'love' is discursively constructed in Lady Gaga's music.

Word frequency lists can often suggest suitable candidates for concordance searches and collocation analysis. In this case, I have decided to do a concordance of the word 'me', due to its relative frequency in the Lady Gaga corpus as compared with the reference corpus. Figures C10.1 and C10.2 show sections of that search, which reveal a number of different kinds of words congregating around the word 'me'. One of the most common, of course, is 'love'. Another common collocate of me is 'look' or 'looked', with the singer persona frequently talking about being looked at or *not* being looked at. Other common phrases include 'touch me', 'kiss me', 'feel me' and 'tell me'.

This initial analysis suggests some very interesting differences between the construction of 'love' in the Lady Gaga corpus and that in the reference corpus: in the Lady Gaga corpus 'love' and its associated processes of looking, touching and kissing are often portrayed as *directed towards* the singer. That is, the singer is portrayed primarily as the *object* of other people's love.

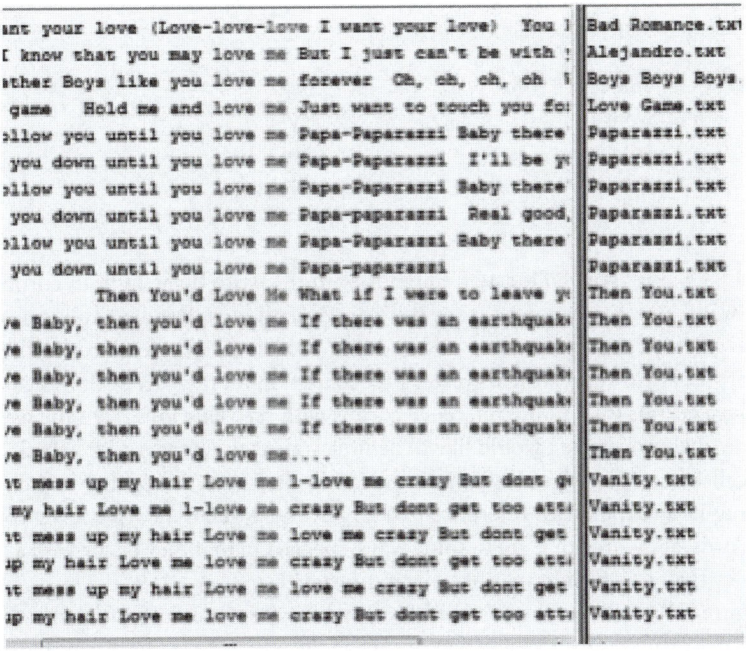

Figure C10.1 Partial concordance list for 'me' (1)

```
know you'll look for me one day  when you let love do  Let Love Down.txt
know you'll look for me one day oh yeah, it's so sad   Let Love Down.txt
before Don't look at me like that You amaze me  He at  Monster.txt
  Look at him Look at me That boy is bad And honestly   Monster.txt
. Baby don't look at me like that I don't belong to y  No Way.txt
. Baby don't look at me like that, I don't belong to   No Way.txt
could barely look at me  This time, I thought that we  Second Time Around
no one else  Look at me (watcha lookin' at) Look at m  Vanity.txt
  lookin' at) Look at me (watcha starin' at) Look at m  Vanity.txt
  starin' at) Look at me (watcha lookin' at) Look at m  Vanity.txt
  lookin' at) Look at me (watcha starin'at)  Im comin   Vanity.txt
ou'd never looked at me that way Eh eh, eh eh There's  Eh.txt
ou'd never looked at me that way Eh eh, eh eh There's  Eh.txt
ou'd never looked at me that way Eh eh, eh eh  There'  Eh.txt
ou'd never looked at me that way Eh eh, eh eh There's  Eh.txt
r when you looked at me and cried said something brok  Let Love Down.txt
ve how you looked at me With your James Dean glossy e  Speechless.txt
ve how you looked at me With your Johnnie Walker eyes  Speechless.txt
```

Figure C10.2 Partial concordance list for 'me' (2)

A collocation analysis of the word 'love' also reveals differences between the Lady Gaga corpus and the reference corpus. Table C10.4 shows the five top collocates of the word love in a span ranging from five words to the left of love and five words to the right

Table C10.4 Top five collocates of 'love' (span 5L, 5R)

Lady Gaga corpus	100 song corpus
I	I
you	you
want	my
your	the
me	me

While 'I' and 'you' collocate frequently with the word 'love' in both corpora, the words 'want' and 'your' appear as the third and fourth most frequent collocates in the Lady Gaga corpus as opposed to 'my' and 'the', which take these places in the reference corpus, again suggesting a greater preoccupation on the part of the singer in the Lady Gaga corpus than in the reference corpus with *receiving* love from the listener.

One final procedure I would like to demonstrate is the *keyword list*, which, as you will recall from B10, is generated by calculating the statistical probability of words occurring in a corpus with reference to a larger, more general corpus. Keywords, in other words, are words that are in some ways 'special', in that they occur with a greater frequency than they would in 'normal' circumstances.

Figure C10.3 shows the 22 words with the highest measure of 'keyness' in the Lady Gage corpus. Some of these words appear simply because they are unique to this collection of songs and are unlikely to occur in other songs – words such as 'Alejandro' (a man's name and the title of one of Lady Gaga's songs), and 'fu' which occurs in the lyrics: 'I want your fu-fu-fu-fu future love.'

Other words, however, while they might be common in pop songs, are words that point to topics that are particularly salient in the music of Lady Gaga, words such as 'disco', 'fame' and 'romance'. One particularly interesting finding is the high keyness of negative words such as 'dirty' and 'bad'. It is also interesting that the two words with the highest degree of 'keyness' in the corpus are the 'sound words' 'oh' and 'eh', reflecting the frequently occurring streams of nonsense syllables that characterise Lady Gaga's lyrics.

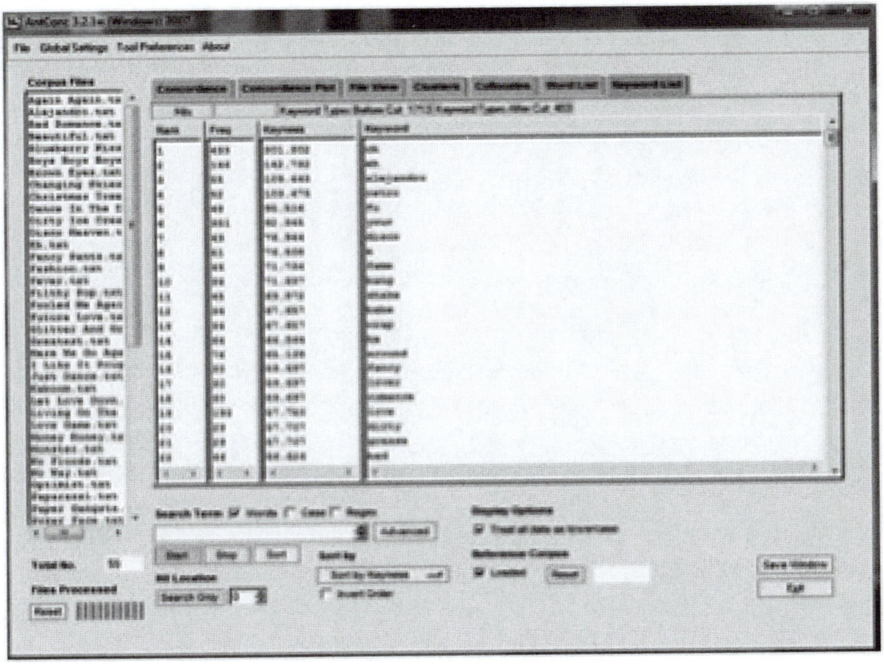

Figure C10.3 Keywords in the Lady Gaga corpus

a) Use the analysis described above as the starting point for a closer examination of Lady Gaga's song lyrics (available at http://www.ladygaga.com), using some of the principles of text analysis discussed in section B4. You might, for example, focus on things such as *transitivity, modality* and *intertextuality).* Does your close reading of the text confirm and build upon any of the findings of the corpus analysis?

b) Conduct a similar analysis using the same procedures on your own corpus of pop songs.

🕸 **Do more activities online.**

Section D
EXTENSION
READINGS IN
DISCOURSE ANALYSIS

D1

D1   **THE THREE PERSPECTIVES REVISITED**

In this section you will read three excerpts from important figures in the field of discourse analysis, each illustrating one of the three perspectives on discourse that we discussed in section B1. The first is from the famous 1952 essay by the linguist Zellig Harris in which he coined the term 'discourse analysis'. In it he outlines the limitations of traditional approaches to language and explains why we need a method to examine language beyond the level of the clause.

The second is an excerpt from the PhD dissertation of H.G. Widdowson in which he questions some of the assumptions made by Harris and argues that the analysis of discourse must go beyond just looking at how texts are put together to exploring how people use language to perform social actions. In making this argument he acknowledges his debt to the American sociolinguist William Labov, who advanced the idea that 'the object of linguistics must ultimately be the instrument of communication used by the speech community, and if we are not talking about *that* language there is something trivial in our proceedings' (1972: 187).

The last excerpt comes from the American discourse analyst and educationalist James Paul Gee. In this excerpt he defines discourse in an even broader way as the way we build social identities and social activities by combining language with 'other stuff'.

As you read these three excerpts, try to consider how these different scholars are responding to or building upon what the others have said. Think about how their respective approaches to discourse differ from one another and also ways in which they might be reconciled.

A. Discourse analysis

Zellig
Harris

Zellig Harris (reprinted from *Language 28*(1) (1952): 1–30)

The problem

One can approach discourse analysis from two types of problem, which turn out to be related. The first is the problem of continuing descriptive linguistics beyond the limits of a single sentence at a time. The other is the question of correlating 'culture' and language (i.e. non-linguistic and linguistic behavior).

The first problem arises because descriptive linguistics generally stops at sentence boundaries. This is not due to any prior decision. The techniques of linguistics were constructed to study any stretch of speech, of whatever length. But in every language it turns out that almost all the results lie within a relatively short stretch, which we may call a sentence. That is, when we can state a restriction on the occurrence of element A in respect to the occurrence of element B, it will almost always be the case that A and B are regarded as occurring within the same sentence. Of English adjectives, for instance, we can say that they occur before a noun or after certain verbs (in the same sentence): the dark clouds, the future seems bright; only rarely can we state restrictions across sentence boundaries, e.g. that if the main verb of one sentence has a given tense-suffix, the main verb of the next sentence will have a particular other tense-suffix. We cannot say that if one sentence has the form NV, the next sentence will have the form N. We can only say that most sentences are NV, some are N, and so on; and that these structures occur in various sequences.

In this way descriptive linguistics, which sets out to describe the occurrence of elements in any stretch of speech, ends up by describing it primarily in respect to other elements of the same sentence. This limitation has not seemed too serious, because it has not precluded the writing of adequate grammars: the grammar states the sentence structure; the speaker makes up a particular sentence in keeping with this structure, and supplies the particular sequence of sentences.

The other problem, that of the connection between behavior (or social situation) and language, has always been considered beyond the scope of linguistics proper. Descriptive linguistics has not dealt with the meanings of morphemes; and though one might try to get around that by speaking not of meanings, but of the social and inter-personal situation in which speech occurs, descriptive linguistics has had no equipment for taking the social situation into account: it has only been able to state the occurrence of one linguistic element in respect to the occurrence of others. Culture-and-language studies have therefore been carried on without benefit of the recent distributional investigations of linguistics. For example, they list the meanings expressed in the language by surveying the vocabulary stock; or they draw conclusions from the fact that in a particular language a particular set of meanings is expressed by the same morpheme; or they discuss the nuances of meaning and usage of one word in comparison with others (e.g. in stylistics). Culture-and-language studies have also noted such points as that phrases are to be taken in their total meaning rather than as the sum of the meanings of their component morphemes, e.g. that 'How are you?' is a greeting rather than a question about health—an example that illustrates the correlation of speech with social situation. Similarly, personality characteristics in speech have been studied by correlating an individual's recurrent speech features with recurrent features of his behavior and feeling.

Distribution within discourse

Distributional or combinatorial analysis within one discourse at a time turns out to be relevant to both of these problems. On the one hand, it carries us past the sentence limitation of descriptive linguistics. Although we cannot state the distribution of sentences (or, in general, any inter-sentence relation) when we are given an arbitrary conglomeration of sentences in a language, we can get quite definite results about certain relations across sentence boundaries when we consider just the sentences of a particular connected discourse—that is, the sentences spoken or written in succession by one or more persons in a single situation. This restriction to connected discourse does not detract from the usefulness of the analysis, since all language occurrences are internally connected. Language does not occur in stray words or sentences, but in connected discourse—from a one-word utterance to a ten-volume work, from a monolog to a Union Square argument. Arbitrary conglomerations of sentences are indeed of no interest except as a check on grammatical description; and it is not surprising that we cannot find interdependence among the sentences of such an aggregate. The successive sentences of a connected discourse, however, offer fertile soil for the methods of descriptive linguistics, since these methods study the relative distribution of elements within a connected stretch of speech.

On the other hand, distributional analysis within one discourse at a time yields information about certain correlations of language with other behavior. The reason is that each connected discourse occurs within a particular situation, whether of a person speaking, or of a conversation, or of someone sitting down occasionally over a period of months to write a particular kind of book in a particular literary or scientific tradition. To be sure, this concurrence between situation and discourse does not mean that discourses occurring in similar situations must necessarily have certain formal characteristics in common, while discourses occurring in different situations must have certain formal differences. The concurrence between situation and discourse only makes it understandable, or possible, that such formal correlations should exist. It remains to be shown as a matter of empirical fact that such formal correlations do indeed exist, that the discourses of a particular person, social group, style, or subject-matter exhibit not only particular meanings (in their selection of morphemes) but also characteristic formal features. The particular selection of morphemes cannot be considered here. But the formal features of the discourses can be studied by distributional methods within the text; and the fact of their correlation with a particular type of situation gives a meaning-status to the occurrence of these formal features.

The nature of the method

We have raised two problems: that of the distributional relations among sentences, and that of the correlation between language and social situation. We have proposed that information relevant to both of these problems can be obtained by a formal analysis of one stretch of discourse at a time. What KIND of analysis would be applicable here? To decide this, we consider what is permitted by the material.

Since the material is simply a string of linguistic forms arranged in successive sentences, any formal analysis is limited to locating linguistic elements within these sentences—that is, to stating the occurrence of elements. We cannot set up any method for investigating the nature or composition of these elements, or their correlations with non-linguistic features, unless we bring in new information from outside.

Furthermore, there are no particular elements, say but or I or communism, which have a prior importance, such as would cause us to be interested in the mere fact of their presence or absence in our text. Any analysis which aimed to find out whether certain particular words, selected by the investigator, occur in the text or not, would be an investigation of the CONTENT of the text and would be ultimately based on the MEANINGS of the words selected. If we do not depend upon meaning in our investigation, then the only morphemes or classes which we can deal with separately are those which have grammatically stated peculiarities of distribution.

Since, then, we are not in general interested in any particular element selected in advance, our interest in those elements that do occur cannot be merely in the tautologic statement THAT they occur, but in the empirical statement of HOW they occur: which ones occur next to which others, or in the same environment as which others, and so on—that is, in the relative occurrence of these elements with respect to each other. In this sense, our method is comparable to that which is used, in the case of a whole language, in compiling a grammar (which states the distributional relations among elements), rather than in compiling a dictionary (which lists all the elements that are found in the language, no matter where).

Finally, since our material is a closed string of sentences, our statement about the distribution of each element can only be valid within the limits of this succession of sentences, whether it be a paragraph or a book. We will see, we can sometimes use information about the distribution of an element outside our material; but this can be only an external aid, brought in after the distribution of the element within the discourse has been completely stated.

Issues to consider

❑ For Harris, one of the aims of discourse analysis is to *describe* texts in the same way linguists describe sentences, by explaining the occurrences of elements in relation to the occurrence of other elements. What might be the advantages of trying to discover the 'rules' that govern the ways texts are put together in the same way we can talk about the 'rules' that govern the way sentences are put together? What could such knowledge be used for? Do you think the logic that governs the way we look at sentence-level grammar can be extended to longer stretches of text or conversation?

❑ Harris suggests that by studying the formal distribution of elements in texts used in different social situations we will be able to discover correlations between certain kinds of structures and certain kinds of social behaviour. Can you think of some examples of text structures that nearly always occur in connections with certain kinds of social practices? What are some of the limitations of this approach?

B. An applied linguistic approach to discourse analysis

Henry G. Widdowson (reprinted from his unpublished doctoral dissertation 1973)

(Harris's) aim is simply to establish formal patterns without reference to meaning. But Harris nevertheless believes that his analysis has some bearing on how discourse is understood as communication. At first sight it would appear that his aim is to contribute to studies of contextualized language in both of the senses distinguished at the beginning of this chapter. In a prolegomenon to his actual analysis he makes the comment:

> One can approach discourse analysis from two types of problem, which turn out to be related. The first is the problem of continuing descriptive linguistics beyond the limits of a single sentence at a time. The other is the question of correlating "culture" and language (i.e. nonlinguistic and linguistic behavior).
>
> (Harris 1952/1964: 356)

It turns out, however, that what Harris has in mind in the second of these problems is something very like the Hallidaian notion of register. He appears to believe that the kind of distributional analysis of morpheme sequences that he proposes will provide a

Henry G.
Widdowson

basis for correlating the formal properties of different pieces of language with the social situations in which they occur.

******

Since Harris has taken a considerable number of steps in the description of discourse, the question naturally arises as to how he has managed to do this without considering speech events and social contexts at all, even though, as we have seen, he acknowledges that his description should bear upon the problem of how language is understood in social situations.

The answer to this question is, of course, that whereas Harris conceives of discourse as contextualized language data in one of the senses we have distinguished, Labov thinks of it as contextualized language data in the other sense. Harris looks for patterns of linguistic elements which link sentences together into a larger formal structure, and Labov looks at the way linguistic elements are used to perform communicative acts, and this kind of enquiry takes him outside the actual linguistic properties of the text not, as with Harris, to the linguistic properties of the code but to the extra-linguistic factors of the social situation. Labov's emphasis, therefore, is on the performance of social actions rather than on the incidence of linguistic forms

*****

It seems clear, then, that we are confronted here with two quite different kinds of enquiry both contending for the same name. A terminological distinction seems to be called for. The kind of investigation carried out by Harris into the formal structure of a piece of language might be called text analysis. Its purpose is to discover the patterning of linguistic elements beyond the limit of the sentence, and what it is that provides a text with its cohesion. Thus what Harris calls 'discourse analysis' will be referred to as 'text analysis'. One is to some degree justified in thus taking liberties with Harris's terminology by the fact that Harris himself appears to use the terms 'text' and 'discourse' interchangeably, as for example, in the following quotation:

> The formal features of the discourses can be studied by distributional methods within the text. (Harris 1952/1964: 357)

We may now use the term discourse analysis to refer to the kind of investigation proposed by Labov into the way linguistic elements are put to communicative use in the performing of social actions. Its purpose is to discover what sentences count as utterances and what it is that provides a discourse with its coherence as a piece of communication.

Issues to consider
❑ Widdowson contrasts Harris's view of discourse, which focuses on linguistic patterns and tries to correlate them to different social situations with that of Labov, who focuses on how language is used to perform particular communicative acts. What arguments could be made for and against these two contrasting views? Is there any way they could be fruitfully combined or are they mutually exclusive?

❑   Widdowson associates the perspective of Harris (discourse as language beyond the clause) more with the study of *cohesion* and the perspective of Labov (discourse as language in use) more with the study of the *coherence* of discourse 'as a piece of communication'. How can you explain this distinction based on the discussion of cohesion and coherence in section B2?

C. Discourses

James Paul Gee (reprinted from *Introduction to Discourse Analysis* (2010): 28–29)

James Paul Gee

People build identities and activities not just through language, but by using language together with other "stuff" that isn't language. If you want to get recognized as a street-gang member of a certain sort you have to speak in the "right" way, but you also have to act and dress in the "right" way, as well. You also have to engage (or, at least, behave as if you are engaging) in characteristic ways of thinking, acting, interacting, valuing, feeling, and believing. You also have to use or be able to use various sorts of symbols (e.g., graffiti), tools (e.g., a weapon), and objects (e.g., street corners) in the "right" places and at the "right" times. You can't just "talk the talk", you have to "walk the walk" as well.

The same is true of doing/being a corporate lawyer, Marine sergeant, radical feminist, or a regular at the local bar. One and the same person might talk, act, and interact in such a way as to get recognised as a "street gang member" in one context and, in another context, talk, act, and interact in quite different ways so as to get recognised as a "gifted student". And, indeed, these two identities, and their concomitant ways of talking, acting, and interacting, may well conflict with each other in some circumstances (where different people expect different identities from the person), as well as in the person's own mind.

I use the term "Discourse", with a capital "D", for ways of combining and integrating language, actions, interactions, ways of thinking, believing, valuing, and using various symbols, tools, and objects to enact a particular sort of socially recognisable identity. Thinking about the different Discourses a piece of language is part of is another tool for engaging in discourse analysis.

*****

A Discourse is a characteristic way of saying, doing, and being. When you speak or write anything, you use the resources of English to project yourself as a certain kind of person, a different kind in different circumstances. You also project yourself as engaged in a certain practice or activity. If I have no idea who you are and what you are doing, then I cannot make sense of what you have said, written, or done.

You project a different identity at a formal dinner party than you do at the family dinner table. And, though these are both dinner, they are nonetheless different practices or activities (different "games"). The fact that people have differential access to different identities and practices, connected to different sorts of status and social goods, is a root source of inequality in society. Intervening in such matters can be a contribution to social justice. Since different identities and activities are enacted in and

**James Paul
Gee**

through language, the study of language is integrally connected to matters of equity and justice.

Issues to consider

❏ 'Discourses' are larger systems for making meaning and enacting social identities in which language plays a part, along with other things such as dress, behaviour, attitude, etc. You can list the languages that you speak (such as English, Japanese and Korean). Can you list some 'Discourses' that you 'speak'?

❏ Gee says that sometimes the way we 'talk, act, and interact' in order to 'do/be' one kind of person might conflict with the way we 'talk, act, and interact' in order to 'do/be' another kind of person, and that sometimes this causes problems in regard to things such as social equity and justice. Can you think of any examples of this?

D2   **TWO PERSPECTIVES ON TEXTURE**

In this section we have included excerpts from two classic texts which address the problem of *texture*. The first is from *Cohesion in English* by M.A.K. Halliday and Ruqauya Hasan. In this excerpt the authors explain their basic idea of cohesion and the different kinds of devices that create cohesion in texts. The second is from the article 'Notes on a Schema for Stories' by David Rumelhardt in which the author argues that our ability to understand stories depends on us having in our minds the basic structure or 'schema' for stories.

A. The concept of cohesion

**Michael
Halliday and
Ruqaiya
Hasan**

Michael Halliday and Ruqaiya Hasan (reprinted from *Cohesion in English*, 1976, London: Longman, pp. 1–9)

1.1.1 Text

If a speaker of English hears or reads a passage of the language which is more than one sentence in length, he can normally decide without difficulty whether it forms a unified whole or is just a collection of unrelated sentences. This book is about what makes the difference between the two.

The word TEXT is used in linguistics to refer to any passage, spoken or written, of whatever length, that does form a unified whole. We know, as a general rule, whether any specimen of our own language constitutes a TEXT or not. This does not mean there can never be any uncertainty. The distinction between a text and a collection of unrelated sentences is in the last resort a matter of degree, and there may always be instances about which we are uncertain—a point that is probably familiar to most teachers from reading their students' compositions. But this does not invalidate the general observation that we are sensitive to the distinction between what is text and what is not.

Michael
Halliday and
Ruqaiya
Hasan

This suggests that there are objective factors involved—there must be certain features which are characteristic of texts and not found otherwise; and so there are. We shall attempt to identify these, in order to establish what are the properties of texts in English, and what it is that distinguishes a text from a disconnected sequence of sentences. As always in linguistic description, we shall be discussing things that the native speaker of the language 'knows' already—but without knowing that he knows them.

A text may be spoken or written, prose or verse, dialogue or monologue. It may be anything from a single proverb to a whole play, from a momentary cry for help to an all-day discussion on a committee. A text is a unit of language in use. It is not a grammatical unit, like a clause or a sentence; and it is not defined by its size. A text is sometimes envisaged to be some kind of super-sentence, a grammatical unit that is larger than a sentence but is related to a sentence in the same way that a sentence is related to a clause, a clause to a group and so on: by CONSTITUENCY, the composition of larger units out of smaller ones. But this is misleading. A text is not something that is like a sentence, only bigger; it is something that differs from a sentence in kind.

A text is best regarded as a SEMANTIC unit: a unit not of form but of meaning. Thus it is related to a clause or sentence not by size but by REALIZATION, the coding of one symbolic system in another. A text does not CONSIST OF sentences; it is REALIZED BY, or encoded in, sentences. If we understand it in this way, we shall not expect to find the same kind of STRUCTURAL integration among the parts of a text as we find among the parts of a sentence or clause. The unity of a text is a unity of a different kind.

1.1.2 Texture

The concept of TEXTURE is entirely appropriate to express the property of 'being a text'. A text has texture, and this is what distinguishes it from something that is not a text. It derives this texture from the fact that it functions as a unity with respect to its environment.

What we are investigating in this book are the resources that English has for creating texture. If a passage of English containing more than one sentence is perceived as a text, there will be certain linguistic features present in that passage which can be identified as contributing to its total unity and giving it texture.

Let us start with a simple and trivial example. Suppose we find the following instructions in the cookery book:

[1:1] Wash and core six cooking apples. Put them into a fireproof dish.

It is clear that them in the second sentence refers back to (is ANAPHORIC to) the six cooking apples in the first sentence. This ANAPHORIC function of them gives cohesion to the two sentences, so that we interpret them as a whole; the two sentences together constitute a text. Or rather, they form part of the same text; there may be more of it to follow.

The texture is provided by the cohesive RELATION that exists between them and six cooking apples. It is important to make this point, because we shall be constantly focusing attention on the items, such as them, which typically refer back to something that has gone before; but the cohesion is effected not by the presence of the referring

Michael
Halliday and
Ruqaiya
Hasan

item alone but by the presence of both the referring item and the item that it refers to. In other words, it is not enough that there should be a presupposition; the presupposition must also be satisfied. This accounts for the humorous effect produced by the radio comedian who began his act with the sentence

[1:2] So we pushed him under the other one.

This sentence is loaded with presuppositions, located in the words so, him, other and one, and, since it was the opening sentence, none of them could be resolved.

What is the MEANING of the cohesive relation between them and six cooking apples? The meaning is that they refer to the same thing. The two items are identical in reference, or COREFERENTIAL. The cohesive agency in this instance, that which provides the texture, is the coreferentiality of *them* and *six cooking apples*. The signal, or the expression, of this coreferentiality is the presence of the potentially anaphoric item *them* in the second sentence together with a potential target item *six cooking apples* in the first.

Identity of reference is not the only meaning relation that contributes to texture; there are others besides. Nor is the use of a pronoun the only way of expressing identity of reference. We could have had:

[1:3] Wash and core six cooking apples. Put the apples into a fireproof dish.

Here the item functioning cohesively is the apples, which works by repetition of the word apples accompanied by the as an anaphoric signal. One of the functions of the definite article is to signal identity of reference with something that has gone before. (Since this has sometimes been said to be its only function, we should perhaps point out that it has others as well, which are not cohesive at all; for example none of the instances in (a) or (b) has an anaphoric sense:

[1:4] a. None but the brave deserve the fair.
       b. The pain in my head cannot stifle the pain in my heart.

1.1.3 Ties

We need a term to refer to a single instance of cohesion, a term for one occurrence of a pair of cohesively related items. This we shall call a TIE. The relation between them and six cooking apples in example [1:1] constitutes a tie.

We can characterize any segment of a text' in terms of the number and kinds of ties which it displays. In [1:1] there is just one tie, of the particular kind which we shall be calling REFERENCE. In [1:3], there are actually two ties, of which one is of the 'reference' kind, and consists in the anaphoric relation of *the* to *six cooking apples*, while the other is of a different kind and consists in the REPETITION of the word apples, a repetition which would still have a cohesive effect even if the two were not referring to the same apples.

The concept of a tie makes it possible to analyse a text in terms of its cohesive properties, and give a systematic account of its patterns of texture. Various types of question can be investigated in this way, for example concerning the difference

Michael
Halliday and
Ruqaiya
Hasan

between speech and writing, the relationship between cohesion and the organization of written texts into sentences and paragraphs, and the possible differences among different genres and different authors in the numbers and kinds of tie they typically employ.

The different kinds of cohesive tie are: reference, substitution, ellipsis, conjunction, and lexical cohesion.

1.1.4 Cohesion

The concept of cohesion is a semantic one; it refers to relations of meaning that exist within the text, and that define it as a text.

Cohesion occurs where the INTERPRETATION of some element in the discourse is dependent on that of another. The one PRESUPPOSES the other, in the sense that it cannot be effectively decoded except by recourse to it. When this happens, a relation of cohesion is set up, and the two elements, the presupposing and the presupposed, are thereby at least potentially integrated into a text.

This is another way of approaching the notion of a tie. To return to example [1:1], the word *them* presupposes for its interpretation something other than itself. This requirement is met by the *six cooking apples* in the preceding sentence. The presupposition, and the fact that it is resolved, provide cohesion between the two sentences, and in so doing create text.

As another example, consider the old piece of schoolboy humour:

[1:5] Time flies.
      -You can't; they fly too quickly.

The first sentence gives no indication of not being a complete text; in fact it usually is, and the humour lies in the misinterpretation that is required if the presupposition from the second sentence is to be satisfied. Here, incidentally the cohesion is expressed in no less than three ties: the elliptical form *you can't*, the reference item *they* and the lexical repetition *fly*.

Cohesion is part of the system of a language. The potential for cohesion lies in the systematic resources of reference, ellipsis and so on that are built into the language itself. The actualization of cohesion in any given instance, however, depends not merely on the selection of some option from within these resources, but also on the presence of some other element which resolves the presupposition that this sets up. It is obvious that the selection of the word *apples* has no cohesive force by itself; a cohesive relation is set up only if the same word, or a word related to it such *fruit*, has occurred previously. It is less obvious, but equally true, that the word them has no cohesive force either unless there is some explicit referent for it within reach. In both instances, the cohesion lies in the relation that is set up between the two.

Like other semantic relations, cohesion is expressed through the stratal organization of language. Language can be explained as a multiple coding system comprising three levels of coding, or 'strata': the semantic (meanings), the lexicogrammatical (forms) and the phonological and orthographic (expressions). Meanings are realized (coded) as forms, and forms are realized in turn (recoded) as expressions. To put this in everyday terminology, meaning is put into wording, and wording into sound or writing:

Michael
Halliday and
Ruqaiya
Hasan

meaning	(the semantic system)
↘	
wording	(the lexicogrammatical system, grammar and vocabulary)
↘	
sounding/writing	(the phonological and orthographic systems)

The popular term 'wording' refers to lexicogrammatical form, the choice of words and grammatical structures. Within this stratum, there is no hard-and-fast division between vocabulary and grammar; the guiding principle in language is that the more general meanings are expressed through the grammar, and the more specific meanings through the vocabulary.

Cohesive relations fit into the same overall pattern. Cohesion is expressed partly through the grammar and partly through the vocabulary. We can refer therefore to GRAMMATICAL COHESION and LEXICAL COHESION. In example [1:3], one of the ties was grammatical (reference, expressed by *the*), the other lexical (repetition, expressed by *apples*). The distinction between grammatical and lexical is really only one of degree, and we need not make too much of it here. It is important to stress, however, that when we talk of cohesion as being 'grammatical or lexical', we do not imply that it is a purely formal relation, in which meaning is not involved. Cohesion is a semantic relation. But, like all components of the semantic system, it is realized through the lexicogrammatical system; and it is at this point that the distinction can be drawn. Some forms of cohesion are realized through the grammar and others through the vocabulary.

Issues to consider

❑ Halliday and Hasan emphasise a number of times in this excerpt that *cohesion* is a *semantic* concept rather than just a formal property of texts. What do they mean by this and what does it reveal about their perspective on discourse?

❑ Halliday and Hasan say that 'A text does not CONSIST OF sentences; it is REALIZED BY, or encoded in, sentences.' What exactly is meant by this distinction? How can it be related to the contrasting views of Harris and Widdowson (and Labov) that we saw in the last section?

B. Story schema

David
Rumelhart

David Rumelhart (reprinted from Notes on a schema for stories, 1975. In D. Bobrow and A. Collins (eds) *Representation and Understanding: Studies in cognitive science*. New York: Academic Press, pp. 211–216)

Just as simple sentences can be said to have an internal structure, so too can stories be said to have an internal structure. This is so in spite of the fact that no one has ever been able to specify a general structure for stories that will distinguish the strings of sentences which

David
Rumelhart

form stories from strings which do not. Nevertheless, the notion of "well-formedness" is nearly as reasonable for stories as it is for sentences. Consider the following examples:

> (1) Margie was holding tightly to the string of her beautiful new balloon. Suddenly, a gust of wind caught it. The wind carried it into a tree. The balloon hit a branch and burst. Margie cried and cried.

> (2) Margie cried and cried. The balloon hit a branch and burst. The wind carried it into a tree. Suddenly a gust of wind caught it. Margie was holding tightly to the string of her beautiful new balloon.

Here we find two strings of sentences. One, however, also seems to form a sensible whole, whereas the other seems to be analyzable into little more than a string of sentences. These examples should make clear that some higher level of organization takes place in stories that does not take place in strings of sentences. The purpose of this chapter is to illustrate that point, to develop some notions of the sorts of structures that might be involved, and to illustrate, how these structures can be used to produce cogent summaries of stories.

To begin, it is clear that simple sentences are not the highest level of structured linguistic input. Sentences themselves can serve as arguments for higher predicates and thus form more complex sentences. For example,

> (3) Margie knew that her balloon had burst.

Here we have one sentence about the bursting of Margie's balloon embedded as the argument of a higher verb. Sentences such as these, of course, occur with high frequency. Another case in which sentences occur as arguments of higher predicates is

> (4) Margie cried and cried because her balloon broke.

In this case the predicate "because" takes two sentences as arguments. Now consider the following pair of sentences:

> (5a) Margie's balloon broke.

> (5b) Margie cried and cried.

It seems clear that the sentence pair (5a) and (5b) have almost the same meaning as (4) and ought therefore to have the same underlying structure. Thus if we are to understand correctly (5a) and (5b) we must infer the causal relationship between the propositions. This, I suspect, is but a scratch on the surface of the kinds of "suprasentential" relationships that are implied and understood in ordinary discourse. In particular, I suggest that the structure of stories is ordinarily more than pairwise relationships among sentences. Rather, strings of sentences combine into psychological wholes. In the following section I explore the nature of these wholes and propose a simple story grammar which accounts for many of the salient facts about the structure of simple stories and which will serve as the basis for a theory of summarization.

David
Rumelhart

II. A simple story grammar

A. The grammar rules

In this section I will develop a grammar which I suggest accounts in a reasonable way for the structure of a wide range of simple stories. The grammar consists of a set of syntactical rules which generate the constituent structure of stories and a corresponding set of semantic interpretation rules which determine the semantic representation of the story. The symbol "+" is used to form two items in a sequence; the symbol "|" is used to separate mutually exclusive alternatives. A "*" following a structure name indicates one or more of those units; for example, A * is one or more As.

> Rule 1: Story -> Setting + Episode

The first rule of our grammar says simply that stories consist of a Setting followed by an Episode. The Setting is a statement of the time, and place of a story as well as an introduction to its main characters. The Setting corresponds to the initial section of stories such as:

> Once upon a time, in a far away land there lived a good king, his beautiful queen, and their daughter Princess Cordelia.

The setting is usually just a series of stative propositions, often terminated by phrases such as:

> One day, as Princess Cordelia was walking near the palace.

In the story illustrated in the first example—the Margie story—the setting consisted of the sentence:

> Margie was holding the string of her beautiful new balloon.

The remainder of the story is an Episode. The simple semantic rule corresponding to Rule 1 is:

> Rule 1': ALLOW (Setting, Episode)

Semantically, the setting forms a structure into which the remainder of the story can be linked. It plays no integral part in the body of the story and under certain conditions can be eliminated without adversely effecting (sic) the story: In such cases, the characters and their relevant characteristics must be introduced in the body of the story.

> Rule 2: Setting -> (State)*

Rule 2 simply expresses the assumption that settings consist of a set of stative propositions.

> Rule 2': AND (State, State, . . .)

David
Rumelhart

Semantically, the states are represented as a set of conjoined propositions entered into the data base.

The first real substantive rule in our rewrite for Episode is:

Rule 3: Episode -> Event + Reaction

Episodes are special kinds of events which involve the reactions of animate (or anthro-pomorphized) objects to events in the world. The episode consists merely of the occurrence of some event followed by the reaction of the hero of the episode to the event. Our semantic rule corresponding to Rule 3 is:

Rule 3': INITIATE (Event, Reaction)

That is, the relationship between the external event and the hero's reaction is one that I call INITIATE. I have taken the term from Schank (1973), although my use is slightly different from his. I use the term INITIATE to represent a kind of causal relationship between an external event and the willful reaction of a thinking being to that event. In the Margie story illustrated in (1), I assume that the relationship between Margie's crying and the breaking of her balloon is the INITIATE relationship. Presumably, the crying is mediated by an internal mental response such as "sadness".

Event is the most general category of our entire grammar. The following rule expresses the structure of an event:

Rule 4: Event -> {Episode | Change-of- state | Action | Event + Event}

Thus an Event can be any of the alternatives, an episode, a simple change of state, or an action that people carry out. All are special kinds of events. Furthermore, a sequence of events also can constitute an event. The first three parts of Rule 4 require no semantic interpretation rules. Our semantic rule corresponding to the fourth rewrite for event is:

Rule 4': CAUSE (Event, Event) or ALLOW (Event, Event)

The rule states that a sequence of two events can either be interpreted as one event CAUSE a second event or they can be interpreted as the first event ALLOW the second. The term CAUSE is used when the relationship between the events is one of physical causation as in the balloon hitting the branch causing the balloon to break in the Margie story. (The CAUSE predicate is similar to Schank's (1973) RESULT.) ALLOW is a relationship between two events in which the first makes the second possible, but does not cause it; thus the relationship between the wind catching the balloon and the wind carrying it into the tree I would say is ALLOW. (Here again my usage of ALLOW is clearly closely related to Schank's ENABLE, but is probably not identical.)

Rule 5: Reaction -> Internal Response + Overt Response

Thus a reaction consists of two parts, an internal and an overt response. The semantic relation between these two responses is:

**David
Rumelhart**

Rule 5': MOTIVATE (Internal Response, Overt Response)

MOTIVATE is the term used to relate thoughts to their corresponding overt actions.

Presumably there are a large variety of types of internal responses. The two most common, however, seem to be emotions and desires. Thus we have:

Rule 6: Internal Response $\rightarrow$ {Emotion | Desire}

Presumably other internal responses can be aroused, but in the stories I have analyzed these two have been sufficient. The overt response is, of course, semantically constrained to be a plausible response for our particular internal response.

Issues to consider

❏ Can you think of any stories you have read or heard that do *not* conform to Rumelhart's model? Does the fact that they do not conform make these stories in any way special or unusual? How do you react as a reader or listener when a story does not follow the structure you expect?

❏ These two excerpts approach the problem of *texture* from two very different disciplinary perspectives, one from the perspective of linguistics and the other from the perspective of cognitive science. What do you think are the advantages and limitations of these two different perspectives? Can you think of certain kinds of texts for which one perspective seems more suited than the other?

D3
GENRES, DISCOURSE COMMUNITIES AND POWER

The two excerpts below are from two important figures in the field of genre analysis. In the first, John Swales, clarifies the concept of 'discourse community' by providing six 'defining characteristics' having to do with people's relationships to one another and to the texts that they use together. In the second, Vijay Bhatia discusses the tension between creativity and conformity in genre and how this relates to issues of power and politics among members of a discourse community.

A. A conceptualisation of discourse community

John Swales

John Swales (reprinted from J. Swales, *Genre Analysis*, Cambridge: Cambridge University Press, 1990, pp. 24–27)

I would now like to propose six defining characteristics that will be necessary and sufficient for identifying a group of individuals as a discourse community.

1. A discourse community has a broadly agreed set of common public goals

John Swales

These public goals may be formally inscribed in documents (as is often the case with associations and clubs), or they may be more tacit. The goals are *public,* because spies may join speech and discourse communities for hidden purposes of subversion, while more ordinary people may join organizations with private hopes of commercial or romantic advancement. In some instances, but not in many, the goals may be high level or abstract. In a Senate or Parliament there may well exist overtly adversarial groups of members, but these adversaries may broadly share some common objective as striving for improved government. In the much more typical non-adversarial discourse communities, reduction in the broad level of agreement may fall to a point where communication breaks down and the discourse community splits. It is commonality of goal, not shared object of study that is criterial, even if the former often subsumes the latter. But not always. The fact that the shared object of study is, say, the Vatican, does not imply that students of the Vatican in history departments, the Kremlin, dioceses, birth control agencies and liberation theology seminaries form a discourse community.

2. A discourse community has mechanisms of intercommunication among its members

The participatory mechanisms will vary according to the community: meetings, tele-communications, correspondence, newsletters, conversations and so forth. This criterion is quite stringent because it produces a negative answer to the case of 'The Cafe Owner Problem' (Najjar, personal communication). In generalized form, the problem goes as follows: individuals A, B, C and so on occupy the same professional roles in life. They interact (in speech and writing) with the same clienteles; they originate, receive and respond to the same kind of messages for the same purposes; they have an approxi-mately similar range of genre skills. And yet, as cafe owners working long hours in their own establishments, and not being members of the Local Chamber of Commerce, A, Band C never interact with one another. Do they form a discourse community? We can notice first that 'The Cafe Owner Problem' is not quite like those situations where A, Band C operate as 'point'. A, Band C may be lighthouse keepers on their lonely rocks, or missionaries in their separate Jungles, or neglected consular officials in their rotting outposts. In all these cases, although A, B and C may never interact, they all have lines of communication back to base, and presumably acquired discourse community membership as a key element in their initial training. Bizzell (1987) argues that the cafe owner kind of social group will be a discourse community because 'its members may share the social-class based or ethnically-based discursive practices of people who are likely to become cafe owners in their neighborhood' (1987: 5). However, even if this sharing of discursive practice occurs, it does not resolve the logical problem of assigning membership of a community to individuals who neither admit nor recognize that such a community exists.

3. A discourse community uses its participatory mechanisms primarily to provide information and feedback

Thus, membership implies uptake of the informational opportunities. Individuals might pay an annual subscription to the *Acoustical Society of America* but if they never open any of its communications they cannot be said to belong to the discourse community, even though they are formally members of the society. The secondary purposes of the information exchange will vary according to the common goals: to improve performance in a football squad or in an orchestra, to make money in a brokerage house, to grow better roses in a gardening club, or to dent the research front in an academic department.

4. A discourse community utilizes and hence possesses one or more genres in the communicative furtherance of its aims

A discourse community has developed and continues to develop discoursal expectations. These may involve appropriacy of topics, the form, function and positioning of discoursal elements, and the roles texts play in the operation of the discourse community. In so far as 'genres are how things get done, when language is used to accomplish them' (Martin, 1985: 250), these discoursal expectations are created by the *genres* that articulate the operations of the discourse. community. One of the purposes of this criterion is to question discourse community status for new or newly-emergent groupings. Such groupings need, as it were, to settle down and work out their communicative proceedings and practices before they can be recognized as discourse communities. If a new grouping 'borrows' genres from other discourse communities, such borrowings have to be assimilated.

5. In addition to owning genres, a discourse community has acquired some specific lexis

This specialization may involve using lexical items known to the wider speech communities in special and technical ways, as in information technology discourse communities, or using highly technical terminology as in medical communities. Most commonly, however, the inbuilt dynamic towards an increasingly shared and specialized terminology is realized through the development of community-specific abbreviations and acronyms. The use of these (ESL, EAP, WAC, NCTE, TOEFL, etc.) is, of course, driven by the requirements for efficient communication exchange between "experts." It is hard to conceive, at least in the contemporary, English-speaking world, of a group of well-established members of a discourse community communicating among themselves on topics relevant to the goals of the community and not using lexical items puzzling to outsiders. It is hard to imagine attending perchance the convention of some group of which one is an outsider and understanding every word, if it were to happen—as might occur in the inaugural meeting of some quite new grouping—then that grouping would not yet constitute a discourse community.

6. A discourse community has a threshold level of members with a suitable degree of relevant content and discoursal expertise

Discourse communities have changing memberships; individuals enter as apprentices and leave by death or in other less involuntary ways. However, survival of the community depends on a reasonable ratio between novices and experts.

An example of a discourse community

As we have seen, those interested in discourse communities have typically sited their discussions within academic contexts, thus possibly creating a false impression that such communities are only to be associated with intellectual paradigms or scholarly cliques. Therefore, for my principal example of a discourse community, I have deliberately chosen one that is not academic, but which nevertheless is probably typical enough of many others. The discourse community is a hobby group and has an 'umbrella organisation' called the Hong Kong Study Circle, of which I happen to be a member. The aims of the HKSC (note the abbreviation) are to foster interest in and knowledge of the stamps of Hong Kong (the various printings, etc.) and of their uses (postal rates, cancellations, etc.). Currently there are about 320 members scattered across the world, but with major concentrations in Great Britain, the USA and HK (China) itself and minor ones in Holland and Japan. Based on the membership list, my guess is that about a third of the members are non-native speakers of English and about a fifth women. The membership varies in other ways: a few are rich and have acquired world-class collections of classic rarities, but many are not and pursue their hobby interest with material that costs very little to acquire. Some are full-time specialist dealers, auctioneers and catalogue publishers, but most are collectors. From what little I know, the collectors vary greatly in occupation. One standard reference work was co-authored by a stamp dealer and a dean at Yale; another was written by a retired lieutenant-colonel. The greatest authority on the nineteenth-century carriage of Hong Kong mail, with three books to his credit, has recently retired from a lifetime of service as a signalman with British Rail. I mention these brief facts to show that the members of the discourse community have, superficially at least, nothing in common except their shared hobby interest, although Bizzell (1992) is probably correct in pointing out that there may be psychological predispositions that attract particular people to collecting and make them 'kindred spirits'.

Issues to consider

❏ The second criterion for a discourse community discussed by Swales is that members must have a means of intercommunication among members. He then, however, gives an example of people in the same profession (cafe owners) who do not necessarily have a means of communicating with one another. Do you think this group constitutes a discourse community? Why or why not? Can you think of other groups that have a similar ambiguous status based on this criterion or other criteria listed by Swales?

❏ What groups do you belong to that you think can be considered discourse communities? What genres are associated with these communities and how do you learn to use them? Swales says the newly formed groups take time to 'settle down' and establish themselves as discourse communities. Can you think of any groups that are in the process of becoming discourse communities but have not yet attained full status?

B. The power and politics of genre

Vijay K. Bhatia (reprinted from *World Englishes 16*(3): 359–371)

Complexity of generic forms

Although generic forms are products of conventional knowledge embedded in disciplinary cultures, they are dynamic constructs. Typical realizations of these institutionalized forms are often characterized by their generic integrity, on the one hand, and their propensity for innovation, on the other (see Bhatia, 1993, 1995). These two aspects of genre may appear to be somewhat contradictory at first, but as we shall soon discover, these two characteristics are complementary to each other. In fact, it will not be inaccurate to suggest that one is, in a way, an essential prerequisite to the other. Generic integrity is the product of the conventional features of a specific generic construct. Although these conventions are embedded in the rhetorical context, they often constrain the use of linguistic resources (lexico-grammatical as well as discoursal), and are frequently invoked to arrive at a reasonable interpretation of the genre or even determine the choice of the genre to suit a particular context. Within generic boundaries, experienced users of genre often manage to exercise considerable freedom to manipulate generic conventions to respond to novel situations, to mix what Bhatia (1993) calls 'private intentions' with socially recognized communicative purposes, and even to produce new forms of discourse.

Therefore the tension between conformity and creativity, so often made an issue of in applied discourse studies, is not necessarily real. As Dubrow (1982: 39) points out, 'a concern for generic traditions, far from precluding originality, often helps to produce it.' Similarly, Fowler (1982: 31) points out:

> Far from inhibiting the author, genres are a positive support. They offer room, as one might say, for him to write in—a habitation of mediated definiteness, a proportioned mental space; a literary matrix by to order his experience during composition . . . The writer is invited to match experience and form in a specific yet undetermined way. Accepting the invitation does not solve his problems of expression . . . But it gives him access to formal ideas as to how a variety of constituents might suitably be combined. Genre also offers a challenge by provoking a free spirit to transcend the limitations of previous examples.

In fact, a subtle exploitation of a certain aspect of generic construct is always seen as tactically superior and effective. It is almost like the advertiser's exploitation of the cliché *the shape of things to come* in the following opening headline of an advertisement for a car.

The shape of things to come: Mitsubishi Cordia

Or, the use of the famous statement about the British colonial empire in the Lufthansa advertisement *The sun never sets on Lufthansa territory,* or in the following slogan for energy conservation, which says, *Don't be fuelish,* where the whole idea of waste of energy is lost unless it is associated with 'Don't be foolish.'

Vijay K.
Bhatia

The whole point about such associations is that they communicate best in the context of what is already familiar. In such contexts, words on their own carry no meanings; it is the experience which gives them the desired effect. Therefore, if one is not familiar with the original, the value of the novel expression is undermined. Just as the advertiser makes use of the well-known and the familiar in existing knowledge, a clever genre writer makes use of what is conventionally available to a discourse community to further his or her own subtle ends. The innovation, the creativity or the exploitation becomes effective only in the context of the already available and familiar. The main focus of this paper is on these two interrelated aspects of genre theory, i.e., the constraints on generic construction, a pre-knowledge of which gives power to insiders in specific discourse communities, and the exploitation of this power by experienced and expert members of such disciplinary cultures to achieve their 'private intentions' within 'socially recognized communicative purposes.'

Organizational preferences and generic controls

The other interesting area of generic variation, although within a restricted range, one finds in organizational preferences. In the case of academic publications, we often come across what we commonly refer to as housestyles. Although every single journal claims to have its own style sheet, most of them can be characterized more by their overlap rather than variation.

Similarly, in the case of newspaper genres, especially the news reports and the editorials, we find an unmistakable 'generic identity' (Bhatia, 1993) in almost all of the exploits of these genres from various newspapers, although all of them have their own preferences in terms of style, stance and substance. Some may be more objective, while others more interpretative; some more socially responsible, while others more sensational. In spite of all these differences, most of them display common characteristics in terms of their use of generic resources, in terms of their structure, interpretation and communication of intentions. These somewhat different orientations to the events of the day do not make their stories very different in terms of their generic form.

Even in the case of business communities, we often find different organizations displaying their unique identities through their organizational preferences in the matters of their choice of generic forms, but the broad range of genres they tend to exploit to further their organizational objectives show remarkable similarities rather than differences.

All these areas of generic use indicate that although their preferred generic forms show a subtle degree of variation for what could be seen as 'tactical advantage,' they never disregard some of the basic features of individual generic constructs, which give these genres their essential identities.

The power of genre

There is no better illustration of the saying 'knowledge is power' than the one in the case of generic power. Power to use, interpret, exploit and innovate novel generic forms is the function of generic knowledge which is accessible only to the members of disciplinary communities.

Vijay K.
Bhatia

Maintaining generic integrity: editorial intervention

In some forms of academic discourse, especially the research articles, one can see generally two kinds of mechanism in place to ensure generic integrity: the peer review process, and editorial intervention. Both these mechanisms, though operating at different levels, are actively invoked to ensure that all accounts of new knowledge conform to the standards of institutionalized behaviour that is expected by a community of established peers in a specific discipline. Although individual judgements can vary within the membership of specific disciplinary communities, a high degree of consensus is often ensured by selecting like-minded scholars from within well-defined disciplinary boundaries.

After peer review, the second most important intervention comes from the editors, who enjoy all the power one can imagine to maintain the identity and integrity of the research article genre. Berkenkotter and Huckin (1995) document an in-depth and fascinating study of this kind of editorial control to maintain generic integrity. They point out that for the construction and dissemination of knowledge 'textual activity' is as important as the 'scientific activity.'

Generic conventions as authority: the case of citations and references

To us academics, the power of genre is nowhere better illustrated than in the publication of research articles. Swales in his research report *Aspects of Research Article Introductions* (1981) was the first one to point out the importance of the description of previous research on the rhetorical activity of knowledge dissemination as distinct from knowledge creation. In order to become acceptable to the specialist community of fellow researchers, one must relate his or her knowledge claims to the accumulated knowledge of the discipline, without which his or her claims in the field are unlikely to find recognition through publication.

Power to innovate (mixing and embedding)

Although this pressure for the 'democratisation' (Fairclough, 1992) of discourse is becoming increasingly intense in some countries, especially in the USA, it is unlikely to make a significant dent in the so-called integrity of professional genres, at least not in the foreseeable future. However, one can see an increasing 'fragmentation of discursive norms and conventions' (Fairclough, 1992: 221), often leading to genre-mixing and embedding in institutionalized orders of discourse (see Bhatia, 1994, for a detailed discussion of this), on the one hand, and creation of new genres, on the other. To a large extent, these changes in discursive practices are making professional genres increasingly dynamic and complex.

The dynamic complexity of academic and professional communication is further increased by the role of multimedia, the explosion of information technology, the multidisciplinary contexts of the world of work, the increasingly competitive professional environment, and above all, the overwhelmingly compulsive nature of promotional and advertising activities, so much so that our present-day world of work is being increasingly identified as a 'consumer culture' (Featherstone, 1991). The inevitable result of this is that many of the institutionalized genres, whether they are social, professional or academic, are seen as incorporating elements of promotion. Fairclough (1992: 207) rightly associates some of these changes with what he calls 'commodification' of

Vijay K.
Bhatia

institutional orders of discourse. Referring to such changes in discourse practices, he (1993: 141) points out, . . . there is an extensive restructuring of boundaries between orders of discourse and between discursive practices, for example, the genre of consumer advertising has been colonising professional and public service orders of discourse on a massive scale, generating many new hybrid partly promotional genres . . . As an instance of such a hybrid genre, Fairclough (1993) discusses the case of contemporary university prospectuses, where he highlights an increasing tendency towards marketization of the discursive practices of British universities. Bhatia (1995), in his discussion of genre-mixing in professional discourse, gives examples from several settings, where genre-mixing and embedding is becoming increasingly common. He also mentions several instances where one may find an increasing use of promotional strategies in genres which are traditionally considered non-promotional in intent, especially academic introductions, including book introductions, forewords, prefaces of various kinds, which are becoming increasingly difficult to distinguish from publishers' blurbs.

Shared knowledge – privileged access/insider information

If generic conventions, on the one hand, give suitable expression to the communicative intentions of genre writers (who are members of a particular discourse community), on the other hand, they also match their intentions against their intended reader's expectations. This is possible only when all the participants share, not only the code, but also the knowledge of the genre, which includes the knowledge of its construction, interpretation and use. A necessary implication of this shared genre knowledge is that it is not routinely available to the outsiders, which creates a kind of social distance between the legitimate members of a discourse community and those who are considered outsiders. Although this creates conditions of homogeneity between the insiders, at the same time it also increases social distance between them and the outsiders, sometimes resulting in disastrous consequences for the one who does not have access to such shared knowledge. This shared knowledge could be in the form of linguistic resources used to construct a generic form, or it could be in the awareness of the rules of language use, some of which are socially learnt, as the ones associated with classroom discourse and academic genres, while others can be legally enforced, such as the ones associated with courtroom procedures.

Maintaining solidarity within a professional community

One of the most noticeable characteristics of any professional or academic discourse community is the availability and typical use of a range of appropriate genres, which their members think serve the goals of their community. The recurrent use of such discoursal forms creates solidarity within its membership giving them their most powerful weapon to keep the outsiders at a safe distance. Hudson (1979: 1) rightly claims,

> If one wished to kill a profession, to remove its cohesion and its strength, the most effective way would be to forbid the use of its characteristic language.

In this context, it is hardly surprising that most of the attempts by the powerful reformist lobbies in many Western democracies to introduce plain English in

Vijay K. Bhatia

legislative contexts are seen as imposition from outside and have been firmly rejected by the professional legal community.

Issues to consider

❏ According to Bhatia, genres are defined by the tension between their 'generic integrity' and their potential for innovation. In fact, he argues that these two aspects of genre work together: that generic conventions provide the basis for innovation. What happens when genres lose their generic integrity? What happens when they lose their propensity for innovation?

❏ 'There is no better illustration of the saying "knowledge is power",' says Bhatia, 'than the one in the case of generic power.' This is particularly true, he says, when it comes to professional genres. Can you think of examples of how the power to use, interpret and innovate particular genres allows certain people to exert power or control over other people?

D4   **IDEOLOGIES IN DISCOURSE**

The excerpts presented in this section discuss some of the basic conceptual and analytical tools you can use to do critical discourse analysis. The first is from Norman Fairclough's *Discourse and Social Change*, one of the classic works in discourse analysis devoted to the study of discourse and ideology. In this excerpt Fairclough explains the concept of intertextuality and its relationship with ideology. The second excerpt is from James Paul Gee's book *Social Linguistics and Literacies*. In this excerpt Gee also takes up the topic of intertextuality, or, as he calls it, *heteroglossia*, in his analysis of a label on an aspirin bottle. He also discusses 'cultural models' (see section A4) and their relationship to power and ideology.

A. Intertextuality

Norman Fairclough

Norman Fairclough (reprinted from *Discourse and Social Change*, Cambridge: Polity Press, 1992, pp. 101–102)

The term 'intertextuality' was coined by Kristeva in the late 1960s in the context of her influential accounts for western audiences of the work of Bakhtin (see Kristeva 1986a, actually written in 1966). Although the term is not Bakhtin's, the development of an intertextual (or in his own terms 'translinguistic') approach to analysis of texts was a major theme of his work throughout his academic career, and was closely linked to other important issues including his theory of genre (see Bakhtin 1986, a paper he wrote in the early 1950s).

Bakhtin points to the relative neglect of the communicative functions of language within mainstream linguistics, and more specifically to the neglect of ways in which texts and utterances are shaped by prior texts that they are 'responding' to,

Norman
Fairclough

and by subsequent texts that they 'anticipate'. For Bakhtin, all utterances, both spoken and written, from the briefest of turns in a conversation to a scientific paper or a novel, are demarcated by a change of speaker (or writer), and are oriented retrospectively to the utterances of previous speakers (be they turns, scientific articles, or novels) and prospectively to the anticipated utterances of the next speakers. Thus 'each utterance is a link in the chain of speech communication.' All utterances are populated, and indeed constituted, by snatches of others' utterances, more or less explicit or complete: 'our speech . . . is filled with others' words, varying degrees of otherness and varying degrees of "our-own-ness", varying degrees of aware-ness and detachment. These words of others carry with them their own expression, their own evaluative tone, which we assimilate, rework, and reaccentuate' (Bakhtin 1986: 89). That is utterances—'texts' in my terms—are inherently intertextual, constituted by elements of other texts. Foucault adds the refinement of distinguishing within the intertextual aura of a text different 'fields' of 'presence', 'concomitance', and memory.

The salience of the concept of intertextuality in the framework I am developing accords with my focus upon discourse and social change. Kristeva observes that inter-textuality implies 'the insertion of history (society) into a text and of this text into history' (1986: 39). By 'the insertion of history into a text', she means that the text absorbs and is built out of texts from the past (texts being the major artefacts that constitute history). By 'the insertion of the text into history', she means that the text responds to, reaccentuates, and reworks past texts, and in so doing helps to make history and contributes to wider processes of change, as well as anticipating and trying to shape subsequent texts. This inherent historicity of texts enables them to take on the major roles they have in contemporary society at the leading edge of social and cultural change. The rapid transformation and restructuring of textual traditions and orders of discourse is a strong contemporary phenomenon, which suggests that intertextuality ought to be a major focus in discourse analysis.

Issues to consider

❑   In this excerpt, Fairclough quotes Kristiva as saying that intertextuality involves 'the insertion of history (society) into a text and of this text into history'. How do you interpret this statement? What role can texts play in affecting the way we interpret past events and past texts? What role can they play in affecting future events, that is, creating social change?

B. Ideology, social languages and cultural models

James Paul Gee (reprinted from *Social Linguistics and Literacies*, London: Taylor and Francis, 1996, pp. 69–79)

James Paul
Gee

Heteroglossia

It is important to extend our discussion of social languages by pointing out that they are very often 'impure'. That is, when we speak or write, we very often mix together different social languages. This is a practice that the Russian literary theorist Mikhail

James Paul
Gee

Bakhtin (1981, 1986) called heteroglossia (multiple voices) . . . To see a clear example of such heteroglossia, and its ties to sociopolitical realities, consider the following warning(s) taken from a bottle of aspirin.

> Warnings: **Children and teenagers should not use this medication for chicken pox or flu symptoms before a doctor is consulted about Reye Syndrome, a rare but serious illness reported to be associated with aspirin.** Keep this and all drugs out of the reach of children. In case of accidental overdose, seek professional assistance or contact a poison control center immediately. As with any drug, if you are pregnant or nursing a baby, seek the advice of a health professional before using this product. IT IS ESPECIALLY IMPORTANT NOT TO USE ASPIRIN DURING THE LAST 3 MONTHS OF PREGNANCY UNLESS SPECIFICALLY DIRECTED TO DO SO BY A DOCTOR BECAUSE IT MAY CAUSE PROBLEMS IN THE UNBORN CHILD OR COMPLICATIONS DURING DELIVERY. See carton for arthritis use and Important Notice.

This text starts with a sentence of very careful and very specific information indeed: the initial sentence talks (in bold) about 'children *and* teenagers'; it specially says '*this* medication'; gives us an exclusive list of two relevant diseases, 'chicken pox *or* flu'; mentions a specific syndrome, Reye Syndrome, and explicitly tells us that it is 'rare *but* serious'. Then, all of a sudden, with the second sentence we enter a quite different sort of language, marked both by the phrasing and by the disappearance of the bold print. Now, the text talks not about aspirin specifically, as in the first sentence, but about 'this and *all* drugs' (second sentence) and '*any* drug' (fourth sentence). We are told to keep 'this and all drugs' out of the reach of 'children', but what now has happened to the teenagers? We get three different references to the medical profession, none of them as direct and specific as 'doctor' (which was used in the first sentence): 'professional assistance', 'poison control center', and 'health professional'. We are told to seek help in case of 'accidental overdose', making us wonder what should happen if the overdose was not accidental. The language of this middle part of the text speaks out of a (seemingly not all that dangerous) world where institutional systems (companies, professionals, centers) take care of people who only through ignorance (which these systems can cure) get themselves into trouble. Then, all of a sudden, again, we make a transition back to the social language of the opening of the text, but this time it is shouted at us in bold capitals. We are confronted with the phrase 'especially important'. We return to quite specific language: we again get 'aspirin', rather than 'all drugs' or 'any drug', time is handled quite specifically ('last 3 months'), we no longer 'seek assistance or advice' from 'professionals', rather we once again consult with our 'doctor' and do not take the aspirin 'unless specifically directed'. This is, once again, a dangerous world in which we had better do what (and only what) the doctor says. This dire warning about pregnancy, however, does make us wonder why a rather general and gentle warning about pregnancy and nursing is embedded in the more moderate language of the middle of the text. The text ends with small print, which appears to tell us to look on the carton for an 'Important Notice' (weren't these 'warnings' the important notice?).

So, in this text we have at least two rather different social languages (voices) inter-mingled, juxtaposed rather uncomfortably side by side. Why? At one time, the aspirin bottle had only the middle text (sentences 2, 3, and 4) on it as a 'warning' (singular). Various medical, social, cultural, and political changes, including conflicts between and among governmental institutions, medical workers, consumers, and drug compa-nies, have led to the intrusion of the more direct and sharper voice that begins and ends the 'warnings'. Thus, we see, the different social languages in this text are sedimented there by social, political, and cultural happenings unfolding in history. In fact, even what looks like a uniform social language—for example, the moderate middle of this text—is very often a compendium of different social languages with different histor-ical, social, cultural, and political sources, and looks to us now to be uniform only because the workings of multiple social languages have been forgotten and effaced.

Similarity in the 'eye of the beholder'

One of the key ways humans think about the world is through seeking out similarities (Hofstadter and the fluid Analogies Research Group 1995; Holyoak and Thagard 1995). We try to understand something new in terms of how it resembles something old. We attempt to see the new thing as a type, thus, like other things of the same or similar type. And very often a great deal hangs on these judgments: for example, is spanking a child a type of discipline or a type of child abuse? When we answer this question we claim either that spanking a child is more similar to paradigmatic instances of discipline or to paradigmatic instances of child abuse.

Judgments like whether spanking is discipline or child abuse are still 'open' and widely discussed in the culture thanks to on-going social changes. However, any language is full of such similarity judgments that have been made long ago in the history of the language—in another time and another place—and which are now taken for granted and rarely reflected upon by current speakers of the language.

Let me take another example that is relevant to those of us interested in language and learning. Consider a sentence like 'The teacher taught the students French' (see also Birch 1989: pp. 25–29; Halliday 1976). This sentence has the same grammar as (the language treats it the same as) sentences like 'John handed Mary the gun', 'John gave Mary the gun', 'John sent Mary the gun', and many more. This type of sentence seems to mean (if we consider prototypical cases like 'give', 'hand', and 'send') that an agent transfers something to someone.

And so we are led to think of teaching French as transferring something (French) from one person (the teacher) to someone else (the student), though this transfer is a mental one, rather than a physical one. This suggestion (about the meaning of teaching languages), which we pick up from our grammar, happens to fit with one of the most pervasive ways of thinking, (what I will later call a master myth) embedded in our language and in culture. We tend to think of meaning as something speakers or writers take out of their heads (its original container), package, like a gift, into a package or container (i.e., words and sentences) and convey (transfer) to hearers, who unpackage it and place its contents (i.e., 'meaning') into their heads (its final container).

This container/conveyor metaphor (Lakoff and Johnson 1980; Reddy 1979) is, as we will see below, a fallacious view of meaning. It gives rise to idioms like 'I catch your meaning', 'I can't grasp what you are saying', 'I've got it', 'Let me put the matter in

James Paul Gee

James Paul Gee

plain terms', 'I can't put this into words', and a great many more. So, it is easy for us to accept the suggestion of our grammar and see teaching languages as a form of mental transference of neatly wrapped little packages (drills, grammar lessons, vocabulary lists) along a conveyor belt from teacher to student.

At a more subtle level, the fact that 'The teacher teaches the students French' has the same grammar as 'The teacher teaches the students history (physics, linguistics, algebra)' suggests that teaching a language (like French) is a comparable activity to teaching a disciplinary content like physics (Halliday 1976). Our schools, with their classrooms, curricula, discrete class hours (five times a week for an hour we learn French), encourage us further to think that, since all these teachers are standing in the same sort of space, playing the same sort of role in the system, they could be or even must be doing the same (sort of) thing.

We note, as well, that the driving teacher spends too much time in a car and the coach spends too much time on the field to be respected as *teachers*. Note, too, that we don't say things like 'The coach teaches football'—football cannot be taught, one can only help someone master it in a group with other apprentices. Our mental model of teaching makes us compare 'teaching French' to 'teaching history' and not to 'coaching football' or 'training someone to drive', despite the fact that it may well be that learning a language is a lot more like learning to drive a car or play football than it is like learning history or physics.

What we see here, then, is that language encapsulates a great many frozen theories (generalizations about what is similar to what)—we have just witnessed frozen theories of communication and language acquisition. We do not have to accept the theories our various social languages offer us. Though we can hardly reflect on them all, we can reflect on some of them and come to see things in new ways.

Meaning

Having established the context of social languages, we can turn directly to meaning. Meaning is one of the most debated terms in linguistics, philosophy, literary theory, and the social sciences. To start our discussion of meaning, let us pick a word and ask what it means. Say we ask: 'What does the word *sofa* mean?'

Imagine that my friend Susan and I go into my living room, where I have a small white, rather broken down seat big enough for more than one person, and a larger and nicer one. I point to the larger, nicer one and say, 'That sofa has a stain on it.' Susan sees nothing exceptional about what I have said, assumes we both mean the same thing by the word 'sofa', and points to the smaller object, saying, 'Well, that sofa has a lot more stains on it.' I say, 'That's not a sofa, it's a settee.' Now Susan realizes that she and I do not, in fact, mean the same thing by the word 'sofa'.

Why? The reason is that I am making a distinction between two words, 'sofa' and 'settee', where something is either the one or the other, and not both, while Susan does not make such a distinction, either because she does not have the word 'settee' or because she uses it in the same way as she uses 'sofa'. When I use the word 'sofa', I mean it to exclude the word 'settee' as applicable; when I use the word 'settee', I mean it to exclude the word 'sofa'. Susan, of course, does not exactly know the *basis* on which I make the distinction between 'sofa' and 'settee' (how and why I distinguish 'sofa' and 'settee'), a matter to which we will turn in the next section.

James Paul Gee

Now someone else, Kris, comes in, having overheard our conversation, and says, 'That's not a settee, nor a sofa, it's a divan.' I and Susan now realize that when Kris uses the word 'divan', she distinguishes among the words 'sofa', 'settee', and 'divan'.

Now, assume that I say 'Well they are both couches,' and we all agree on this. This shows that my use of the word 'couch' does not exclude 'sofa' or 'settee' as (also possibly) applicable, nor do these words exclude 'couch', though they exclude each other. And for Susan and Kris the use of the word 'couch' does not exclude their other words (which are different than mine), nor do their other words exclude 'couch' (though their other words exclude each other). Thus, by default almost, we mean (pretty much) the same thing by 'couch'.

What is emerging here is that what we mean by a word depends on which other words we have available to us and which other words our use of the word (e.g., 'sofa') is meant to exclude or not exclude as possibly also applying (e.g., 'sofa' excludes 'settee', but not 'couch'). It also depends on which words are 'available' to me in a given situation. For example, I may sometimes use the word 'love seat', which I consider a type of settee, but in the above situation with Susan and Kris I may have not viewed this as a possible choice, perhaps because I am reluctant to use the term in front of close friends who might think it too 'fancy'. This is to say that I am currently using a social language in which 'love seat' is not available.

The sorts of factors we have seen thus far in our discussion of 'sofa' reflect one central principle involved in meaning, a principle I will call the *exclusion principle*. Susan, Kris, and I all have the word 'sofa', but it means different things to each of us because each of has a different set of related words. The exclusion principle says that the meaning of a word is (in part—there are other principles) a matter of what other words my use of a given word in a given situation is intended to exclude or not exclude as also possibly applicable (though not actually used in this case). Meaning is always (in part) a matter of intended exclusions and exclusions (contrasts and lack of contrasts) within the assumed semantic field.

*****

Cultural models as the basis of meaning choices and guesses

So far I have left out one crucial principle of meaning. This is the principle that determines what I have called the basis of the distinctions we make (e.g., 'sofa' versus 'settee', with 'couch' applicable to both). Why do we mean the way we do?

To get at what constitutes the basis of our choices and assumptions in the use of words, let us consider what the word 'bachelor' means (Fillmore 1975; Quinn and Holland 1987). All of us think we know what the word means. Dictionaries say it means 'an unmarried man' *(Webster Handy College Dictionary, 1972)*, because it seems clear that in most contexts in which the word is used it excludes as applicable words like 'woman', 'girl', 'boy', and 'married': Let me ask you, then, is the Pope a bachelor? Is a thrice-divorced man a bachelor? Is a young man who has been in an irreversible coma since childhood a bachelor? What about a eunuch? A committed gay man? An elderly senile gentleman who has never been married? The answer to all these questions is either 'no' or 'I'm not sure' (as I have discovered by asking a variety of people). Why? After all, all these people are unmarried men.

James Paul Gee

The reason why the answer to these questions is 'no', despite the fact that they all involve cases of clearly unmarried males, is that in using the word 'bachelor' we are making exclusions we are unaware of and are assuming that the contexts in which we use the word are clear and transparent when they are not. Context has the nasty habit of almost always seeming clear, transparent, and unproblematic, when it hardly ever actually is.

Our meaningful distinctions (our choices and guesses) are made on the basis of certain beliefs and values. This basis is a type of theory . . ., in the case of many words a social theory. The theories that form the basis of such choices and assumptions have a particular character. They involve (usually unconscious) assumptions about models of simplified worlds. Such models are sometimes called cultural models, folk theories, scenes, schemas, or frames. I will call them *cultural models*.

I think of cultural models as something like movies or videotapes in the mind. We all have a vast store of these tapes, each of which depicts prototypical (what we take to be 'normal') events in a simplified world. We all have a vast store of these tapes, each of which depicts prototypical (what we take to be 'normal') events in a simplified world. We conventionally take these simplified worlds to be the 'real' world, or act as if they were. We make our choices and guesses about meaning in relation to these worlds.

These cultural models are emblematic visions of an idealized, 'normal', 'typical' reality, in much the way that, say, a Bogart movie is emblematic of the world of the 'tough guy' or an early Woody Allan movie of the 'sensitive, but klutzy male'. They are also variable, differing across different cultural groups, including different cultural groups in a society speaking the same language. They change with time and other changes in the society, but we are usually quite unaware we are using them and of their full implications.

These cultural models are, then, pictures of simplified worlds in which prototypical events unfold. The most commonly used cultural model for the word 'bachelor' is (or used to be) something like the following (Fillmore 1975): Men marry women at a certain age; marriages last for life; and in such a world, a bachelor is a man who stays unmarried beyond the usual age, thereby becoming eminently marriageable. We know that this simplified world is not always true, but it is the one against which we use the word 'bachelor', that is, make choices about what other words are excluded as applicable or not, and make assumptions about what the relevant context is in a given case of using a word. Thus, the Pope is not a bachelor because he just isn't in this simplified world, being someone who has vowed not to marry at any age. Nor are gay men, since they have chosen not to marry women.

Such cultural models involve us in exclusions that are not at first obvious and which we are often quite unaware of making. In the case of 'bachelor' we are actually excluding words like 'gay' and 'priest' as applying to ('normal') unmarried men, and in doing so, we are assuming that men come in two ('normal') types: ones who get married early and ones who get married late. This assumption *marginalizes* people who do not want to get married or do not want to marry members of the opposite sex. It is part of the function of such cultural models to set up what count as central, typical cases, and what count as marginal, non-typical cases.

There is even a more subtle exclusion being made via this cultural model. If men become 'eminently marriageable' when they stay unmarried beyond the usual age, then this can only be because we have assumed that after that age there is a shortage of 'desirable' men and a surplus of women who want them, women who, thus, are not 'eminently marriageable', or, at least, not as 'eminently marriageable' as the men. Hence, we get the most common cultural model associated with 'spinster'. So we see that our usual use of 'bachelor' involves also an exclusion of the phrase 'eminently marriageable' as applicable to 'older' women, and the assumption that the reverse of 'bachelor', namely 'spinster', *is* applicable.

Such hidden exclusions are . . . ideological. They involve social theories (remember, cultural models are a type of theory), quite tacit ones involving beliefs about the distribution of goods—prestige, power, desirability, centrality in society. Furthermore, the fact that we are usually unaware of using these cultural models and of their full implications means that the assumptions they embody are the distribution of social goods appear to us natural, obvious, just the ways things are, inevitable, even appropriate. And this is so despite the fact that cultural models vary across both different cultures and different social groups.

Issues to consider

❏ The mixing of 'social languages' that Gee observes on the bottle of aspirin is also a kind of intertextuality, sometimes called *interdiscursivity*. This kind of intertextuality occurs when larger aspects of discourse such as speech styles, social languages, genres and even ideologies are borrowed from others. What do you think the reason for and effect of mixing social languages were in this text? Can you think of other texts that mix broader aspects of discourse (such as social languages or genres) in order to strategically advance a particular ideology or to present the authors or the readers as certain kinds of people?

❏ Gee says that our choices of and assumptions about the meanings of words are often determined by 'cultural models', which are idealised versions of 'normal, typical reality'. Cultural models often involve ideas about certain 'types' of people, such as 'bachelors' and how they are supposed to act. Consider the cultural models surrounding some kind of important event or activity in your society (such as studying in university or getting married). What sorts of cultural models does your society associate with these events or activities? What kinds of people do the cultural models include, and what kinds of people do they marginalise or exclude?

TWO PERSPECTIVES ON CONVERSATION

The two readings in this section represent two different perspectives on conversation. The first, by John Austin, is a basic outline of the principles of speech act theory. In particular, Austin makes an argument about why a perspective which focuses only on the propositional content of utterances cannot adequately explain how people actually use language. The second excerpt is from a classic article by conversation analyst

D5

Emanuel Schegloff. The focus of the article is conversational closings, but Schegloff uses this topic to illustrate one of the basic principles of adjacency pairs, the principle of *conditional relevance*.

A. How to do things with words

John L. Austin

John L. Austin (reprinted from *How to do Things with Words*, Oxford: Oxford University Press, 1990, pp. 359–371)

What I shall have to say here is neither difficult nor contentious; the only merit I should like to claim for it is that of being true, at least in parts. The phenomenon to be discussed is very widespread and obvious, and it cannot fail to have been already noticed, at least here and there, by others. Yet I have not found attention paid to it specifically.

It was for too long the assumption of philosophers that the business of a 'statement' can only be to 'describe' some state of affairs, or to 'state some fact', which it must do either truly or falsely. Grammarians, indeed, have regularly pointed out that not all 'sentences' are (used in making) statements: there are, traditionally, besides (grammarians') statements, also questions and exclamations, and sentences expressing commands or wishes or concessions. And doubtless philosophers have not intended to deny this, despite some loose use of 'sentence' for 'statement'. Doubtless, too, both grammarians and philosophers have been aware that it is by no means easy to distinguish even questions, commands, and so on from statements by means of the few and jejune grammatical marks available, such as word order, mood, and the like: though perhaps it has not been usual to dwell on the difficulties which this fact obviously raises. For how do we decide which is which? What are the limits and definitions of each?

But now in recent years, many things which would once have been accepted without question as 'statements' by both philosophers and grammarians have been scrutinized with new care. . . . It has come to be commonly held that many utterances which look like statements are either not intended at all, or only intended in part, to record or impart straightforward information about the facts: for example, 'ethical propositions' are perhaps intended, solely or partly, to evince emotion or to prescribe conduct or to influence it in special ways. . . . We very often also use utterances in ways beyond the scope at least of traditional grammar. It has come to be seen that many specially perplexing words embedded in apparently descriptive statements do not serve to indicate some specially odd additional feature in the reality reported, but to indicate (not to report) the circumstances in which the statement is made or reservations to which it is subject or the way in which it is to be taken and the like. To overlook these possibilities in the way once common is called the 'descriptive' fallacy; but perhaps this is not a good name, as 'descriptive' itself is special. Not all true or false statements are descriptions, and for this reason I prefer to use the word 'Constative'. . . . Utterances can be found . . . such that:

> A. they do not 'describe' or 'report' or constate anything at all, are not 'true or false'; and

B. the uttering of the sentence is, or is a part of, the doing of an action, which again would not normally be described as, or as 'just', saying something.

John L. Austin

Examples:

(a) 'I do (sc. take this woman to be my lawful wedded wife)' – as uttered in the course of the marriage ceremony.
(b) 'I name this ship the Queen Elizabeth' – as uttered when smashing the bottle against the stern.
(c) 'I give and bequeath my watch to my brother' – as occurring in a will.
(d) 'I bet you sixpence it will rain tomorrow.'

In these examples it seems clear that to utter the sentence (in, of course, the appropriate circumstances) is not to describe my doing of what I should be said in so uttering to be doing or to state that I am doing it: it is to do it. None of the utterances cited is either true or false: I assert this as obvious and do not argue it.

It needs argument no more than that 'damn' is not true or false: it may be that the utterance 'serves to inform you' – but that is quite different. To name the ship is to say (in the appropriate circumstances) the words 'I name, etc.'. When I say, before the registrar or altar, 'I do', I am not reporting on a marriage: I am indulging in it.

What are we to call a sentence or an utterance of this type? I propose to call it a performatire sentence or a performative utterance, or, for short, 'a performative'. The term 'performative' will be used in a variety of cognate ways and constructions, much as the term 'imperative' is. The name is derived, of course, from 'perform', the usual verb with the noun 'action': it indicates that the issuing of the utterance is the performing of an action – it is not normally thought of as just saying something. Are we then to say things like this:

'To marry is to say a few words', or
'Betting is simply saying something'?

Such a doctrine sounds odd or even flippant at first, but with sufficient safeguards it may become not odd at all.

*****

The uttering of the words is, indeed, usually a, or even the, leading incident in the performance of the act (of betting or what not), the performance of which is also the object of the utterance, but it is far from being usually, even if it is ever, the sole thing necessary if the act is to be deemed to have been performed. Speaking generally, it is always necessary that the circumstances in which the words are uttered should be in some way, or ways, appropriate, and it is very commonly necessary that either the speaker himself or other persons should also perform certain other actions, whether 'physical' or 'mental' actions or even acts of uttering further words. Thus, for naming the ship, it is essential that I should be the person appointed to name her; for (Christian) marrying, it is essential that I should not be already married with a wife living, sane and undivorced, and so on; for a bet to have been made, it is generally necessary for the

John L.
Austin

offer of the bet to have been accepted by a taker (who must have done something, such as to say 'Done'); and it is hardly a gift if I say, 'I give it you' but never hand it over. . . .

But we may, in objecting, have something totally different, and this time quite mistaken, in mind, especially when we think of some of the more awe-inspiring performatives such as 'I promise to . . .'. Surely the words must be spoken 'seriously' and so as to be taken 'seriously'? This is, though vague, true enough in general – it is an important commonplace in discussing the purport of any utterance whatsoever. I must not be joking, for example, nor writing a poem. . . .

Well we shall next consider what we actually do say about the utterance concerned when one or another of its normal concomitants is absent. In no case do we say that the utterance was false but rather that the utterance – or rather the act, e.g., the promise – was void, or given in bad faith, or not implemented, or the like. In the particular case of promising, as with many other performatives, it is appropriate that the person uttering the promise should have a certain intention, viz. here to keep his word: and perhaps of all concomitants this looks the most suitable to be that which 'I promise' does describe or record. Do we not actually, when such intention is absent, speak of a 'false' promise? Yet so to speak is not to say that the utterance 'I promise that . . .' is false, in the sense that though he states that he does he doesn't, or that though lie describes he misdescribes – misreports. For he does promise: the promise here is not even void, though it is given in bad faith. His utterance is perhaps misleading, probably deceitful and doubtless wrong, but it is not a lie or a misstatement. At most we might make out a case for saying that it implies or insinuates a falsehood or a misstatement (to the effect that he does intend to do something): but that is a very different matter. Moreover, we do not speak of a false bet or a false christening; and that we do speak of a false promise need commit us no more than the fact that we speak of a false move. 'False' is not necessarily used of statements only.

*****

Besides the uttering of the words of so-called performative, a good many other things have as a general rule to be right and to go right if we are to be said to have happily brought off our action. What these are we may hope to discover by looking at and classifying types of case in which something goes wrong and the act – marrying, betting, bequeathing, christening, or what not – is therefore at least to some extent a failure: the utterance is then, we may say, not indeed false but in general unhappy. And for this reason we call the doctrine of the things that can be and go wrong on the occasion of such utterances, the doctrine of the infelicities.

Suppose we try first to state schematically – and I do not wish to claim any sort of finality for this scheme – some at least of the things which are necessary for the smooth or 'happy' functioning of a performative (or at least of a highly developed explicit performative, such as we have hitherto been alone concerned with), and then give examples of infelicities and their effects . . .

A.1   There must exist an accepted conventional procedure having a certain conventional effect, that procedure to include the uttering of certain words by certain persons in certain circumstances, and further,

A.2 the particular persons and circumstances in a given case must be appropriate for the invocation of the particular procedure invoked.

B.1 The procedure must be executed by all participants both correctly and

B.2 completely.

C.1 Where, as often, the procedure is designed for use by persons having certain thoughts or feelings, or for the inauguration of certain consequential conduct on the part of any participant, then a person participating in and so invoking the procedure must in fact have those thoughts or feelings, and the participants must intend so to conduct themselves, and further

C.2 must actually so conduct themselves subsequently.

Now if we sin against any one (or more) of these six rules, our performative utterance will be (in one way or another) unhappy.

Issues to consider

❑ Some of the felicity conditions for speech acts are external, that is, they can be determined through observation. Things such as the time, place and people involved are examples. But some are internal, having to do with the intentions, thoughts, feelings and even 'sanity' of the person issuing the speech act or the person to whom it is being issued. What complications does this introduce for the successful interpretation of speech acts?

❑ The feminist critic Judith Butler (1990/2006) says that when a doctor announces the gender of a newborn baby (e.g. 'It's a girl!'), he or she is issuing a performative. It is by naming the child's gender that gender is assigned. Do you agree with this interpretation? What conditions do you think must be met for such a speech act to be felicitous?

B. Opening up closings

Emanuel A. Schegloff and Harvey Sacks (reprinted from *Semiotica 7*, 1973: 289–327)

It seems useful to begin by formulating the problem of closing technically in terms of the more fundamental order of organization, that of turns. Two basic features of conversation are proposed to be: (1) at least, and no more than, one party speaks at a time in a single conversation; and (2) speaker change recurs.

The achievement of these features singly, and especially the achievement of their cooccurrence, is accomplished by co-conversationalists through the use of a 'machinery' for ordering speaker turns sequentially in conversation. The turn-taking machinery includes as one component a set of procedures for organizing the selection of 'next speakers', and, as another, a set of procedures for locating the occasions on which transition to a next speaker may or should occur. The turn-taking machinery operates utterance by utterance. That is to say, it is within any current utterance that possible next speaker selection is accomplished, and upon possible completion of any current utterance that such selection takes effect and transition to a next speaker becomes relevant. We shall speak of

**Emanuel A.
Schegloff
and Harvey
Sacks**

this as the 'transition relevance' of possible utterance completion . . . Whereas these basic features . . . deal with a conversation's ongoing orderliness, they make no provision for the closing of conversation. A machinery that includes the transition relevance of possible utterance completion recurrently for any utterance in the conversation generates an indefinitely extendable string of turns to talk. Then, an initial problem concerning closings may be formulated: HOW TO ORGANIZE THE SIMULTANEOUS ARRIVAL OF THE CO-CONVERSATIONALISTS AT A POINT WHERE ONE SPEAKER'S COMPLETION WILL NOT OCCASION ANOTHER SPEAKER'S TALK, AND THAT WILL NOT BE HEARD AS SOME SPEAKER'S SILENCE. The last qualification is necessary to differentiate closings from other places in conversation where one speaker's completion is not followed by a possible next speaker 's talk, but where, given the continuing relevance of the basic features and the turn-taking machinery, what is heard is not termination but attributable silence, a pause in the last speaker's utterance, etc. It should suggest why simply to stop talking is not a solution to the closing problem: any first prospective speaker to do so would be hearable as 'being silent' in terms of the turn-taking machinery, rather than as having suspended its relevance . . .

How is the transition relevance of possible utterance completion lifted? A proximate solution involves the use of a 'terminal exchange' composed of conventional parts, e.g., an exchange of 'good -byes' . . . We note first that the terminal exchange is a case of a class of utterance sequences which we have been studying for some years, namely, the utterance pair, or, as we shall refer to it, the adjacency pair . . . Briefly, adjacency pairs consist of sequences which properly have the following features: (1) two utterance length, (2) adjacent positioning of component utterances, (3) different speakers producing each utterance. The component utterances of such sequences have an achieved relatedness beyond that which may otherwise obtain between adjacent utterances. That relatedness is partially the product of the operation of a typology in the speakers' production of the sequences. The typology operates in two ways: it partitions utterance types into 'first pair parts' (i.e., first parts of pairs) and second pair parts; and it affiliates a first pair part and a second pair part to form a 'pair type'. 'Question-answer', 'greeting-greeting', 'offer-acceptance/refusal' are instances of pair types. Adjacency pair sequences, then, exhibit the further features (4) relative ordering of parts (i.e. first pair parts precede second pair parts) and (5) discriminative relations (i.e., the pair type of which a first pair part is a member is relevant to the selection among second pair parts) . . .

In the case of that type of organization which we are calling 'overall structural organization', it may be noted that at least initial sequences (e.g., greeting exchanges), and ending sequences (i.e., terminal exchanges) employ adjacency pair formats. It is the recurrent, institutionalized use of adjacency pairs for such types of organization problems that suggests that these problems have, in part, a common character, and that adjacency pair organization . . . is specially fitted to the solution of problems of that character.

But it may be wondered why are two utterances required for either opening or closing? . . . What two utterances produced by different speakers can do that one utterance cannot do it: by an adjacently positioned second, a speaker can show that he understood what a prior aimed at, and that he is willing to go along with that. Also, by virtue of the occurrence of an adjacently produced second, the doer of a first can see that what he intended was indeed understood, and that it was or was not accepted.

Emanuel A.
Schegloff
and Harvey
Sacks

We are then proposing: If WHERE transition relevance is to be lifted is a systematic problem, an adjacency pair solution can work because: by providing that transition relevance is to be lifted after the second pair part's occurrence, the occurrence of the second pair part can then reveal an appreciation of, and agreement to, the intention of closing NOW which a first part of a terminal exchange reveals its speaker to propose. Given the institutionalization of that solution, a range of ways of assuring that it be employed have been developed, which make drastic difference between one party saying "good-bye" and not leaving a slot for the other to reply, and one party saying "good-bye" and leaving a slot for the other to reply.

The former becomes a distinct sort of activity, expressing anger, brusqueness, and the like, and available to such a use by contrast with the latter. It is this consequentiality of alternatives that is the hallmark of an institutionalized solution . . .

In referring to the components of terminal exchanges, we have so far employed "good-bye" as an exclusive instance. But, it plainly is not exclusively used. Such other components as "ok", "see you", "thank you", "you're welcome", and the like are also used. Since the latter items are used in other ways as well, the mere fact of their use does not mark them as unequivocal parts of terminal exchanges. The adjacency pair is one kind of 'local', i.e., utterance, organization. It does NOT appear that FIRST parts of terminal exchanges are placed by reference to that order of organization. While they, of course, occur after some utterance, they are not placed by reference to a location that might be formulated as 'next' after some 'last' utterance or class of utterances. Rather, their placement seems to be organized by reference to a properly initiated closing SECTION.

The [relevant] aspect of overall conversational organization concerns the organization of topic talk. . . . If we may refer to what gets talked about in a conversation as 'mentionables', then we can note that there are considerations relevant for conversationalists in ordering and distributing their talk about mentionables in a single conversation. There is, for example, a position in a single conversation for 'first topic'. We intend to mark by this term not the simple serial fact that some topic gets talked about temporally prior to others, for some temporally prior topics such as, for example, ones prefaced by "First, I just want to say . . .", or topics that are minor developments by the receiver of the conversational opening of "how are you" inquiries, are not heard or treated as 'first topic' is to accord it to a certain special status in the conversation. Thus, for example, to make a topic 'first topic' may provide for its analyzability (by coparticipants) as 'the reason for' the conversation, that being, furthermore, a preservable and reportable feature of the conversation. In addition, making a topic 'first topic' may accord it a special importance on the part of its initiator. These features of 'first topics' may pose a problem for conversationalists who may not wish to have special importance accorded some 'mentionable', and who may not want it preserved as 'the reason for the conversation'. It is by reference to such problems affiliated with the use of first topic position that we may appreciate such exchanges at the beginnings of conversations in which news IS later reported, as:

A: What's up.
B: Not much. What's up with you?
A: Nothing.

**Emanuel A.
Schegloff
and Harvey
Sacks**

Conversationalists, then, can have mentionables they do not want to put in first topic position, and there are ways of talking past first topic position without putting them in.

A further feature of the organization of topic talk seems to involve 'fitting' as a preferred procedure. That is, it appears that a preferred way of getting mentionables mentioned is to employ the resources of the local organization of utterances in the course of the conversation. That involves holding off the mention of a mentionable until it can 'occur naturally', that is, until it can be fitted to another conversationalist's prior utterance . . .

There is, however, no guarantee that the course of the conversation will provide the occasion for any particular mentionable to 'come up naturally'.

This being the case, it would appear that an important virtue for a closing structure designed for this kind of topical structure would involve the provision for placement of hitherto unmentioned mentionables. The terminal exchange by itself makes no such provision. By exploiting the close organization resource of adjacency pairs, it provides for an immediate (i.e., next turn) closing of the conversation. That this close-ordering technique for terminating not exclude the possibility of inserting unmentioned mentionables can be achieved by placement restrictions on the first part of terminal exchanges, for example, by requiring 'advance note' or some form of foreshadowing.

Issues to consider

❏ Sacks and Schegloff say that adjacency pairs always play a part in the beginning and ending of conversations. Why is this necessary? Can you think of any situations in which this is not the case? What kind of effect is produced? Do people perform openings and closing differently in situations other than face-to-face communication (for example, text messaging or telephone conversations)?

❏ According to Sacks and Schegloff, closing sequences are designed the way they are in order to help participants manage topics in conversations (that is, to make sure neither of the parties wishes to introduce a new topic). What role do adjacency sequences that occur at the beginnings of conversations have in helping people to manage topics? Which person – the initiator of the conversation or the responder – is usually the person who introduces the topic in face-to-face communication? Is this the same in other kinds of interaction such as instant messaging?

FRAMES IN INTERACTION

In the following classic article by Deborah Tannen and her collaborator Cynthia Wallat, the authors give a clear and accessible definition of *interactive frames* and the theoretical basis for this concept. They then go on to illustrate how interactive frames operate in a medical examination between a paediatrician and a child. As you read, pay attention to the strategies the doctor uses to shift frames from 'playing' with the child to explaining the child's condition to the mother, and how the doctor and the child's mother negotiate conflicting frames.

Interactive frames and knowledge schemas in interaction: examples from a medical examination/interview

Deborah Tannen and Cynthia Wallat (reprinted from *Social Psychology Quarterly* *50*(2), 1987: 205–216)

Deborah
Tannen and
Cynthia
Wallat

Interactive frames

The interactive notion of frame refers to a definition of what is going on in interaction, without which no utterance (or movement or gesture) could be interpreted. To use Bateson's classic example, a monkey needs to know whether a bite from another monkey is intended within the frame of play or the frame of fighting. People are continually confronted with the same interpretative task. In order to comprehend any utterance, a listener (and a speaker) must know within which frame it is intended: for example, is this joking? Is it fighting? Something intended as a joke but interpreted as an insult (it could of course be both) can trigger a fight.

Goffman (1974) sketched the theoretical foundations of frame analysis in the work of William James, Alfred Schutz and Harold Garfinkel to investigate the socially constructed nature of reality. Building on their work, as well as that of linguistic philosophers John Austin and Ludwig Wittgenstein, Goffman developed a complex system of terms and concepts to illustrate how people use multiple frameworks to make sense of events even as they construct those events. Exploring in more detail the linguistic basis of such frameworks, Goffman (1981) introduced the term "footing" to describe how, at the same time that participants frame events, they negotiate the interpersonal relationships, or "alignments," that constitute those events.

The interactive notion of frame, then, refers to a sense of what activity is being engaged in, how speakers mean what they say. As Ortega y Gas'set (1959: 3), a student of Heidegger, puts it, "Before understanding any concrete statement, it is necessary to perceive clearly 'what it is all about' in this statement and 'what game is being played.'" Since this sense is gleaned from the way participants behave in interaction, frames emerge in and are constituted by verbal and nonverbal interaction.

*****

One author (Tannen) was talking to a friend on the telephone, when he suddenly yelled, "YOU STOP THAT!" She knew from the way he uttered this command that it was addressed to a dog and not her. She remarked on the fact that when he addressed the dog, he spoke in something approximating a southern accent. The friend explained that this was because the dog had learned to respond to commands in that accent, and, to give another example, he illustrated the way he plays with the dog: "I say, 'GO GIT THAT BALL!'" Hearing this, the dog began running about the room looking for something to fetch. The dog recognized the frame "play" in the tone of the command; he could not, however, understand the words that identified an outer frame, "*referring* to playing with the dog," and mistook the reference for a literal invitation to play.

This example illustrates, as well, that people (and dogs) identify frames in interaction by association with linguistic and paralinguistic cues – the way words are uttered – in addition to what they say. That is, the way the speaker uttered "You stop

Deborah
Tannen and
Cynthia
Wallat

that!" was associated with the frame "disciplining a pet" rather than "chatting with a friend." Tannen drew on her familiarity with the use of linguistic cues to signal frames when she identified her friend's interjection "You stop that!" as addressed to a dog, not her. But she also drew on the knowledge that her friend was taking care of someone's dog. This was part of her knowledge schema about her friend. Had her schema included the information that he had a small child and was allergic to dogs, she might have interpreted the same linguistic cues as signaling the related frame, "disciplining a misbehaving child." Furthermore, her expectations about how any speaker might express orders or emotions, i.e. frame such expressions, were brought to bear in this instance in conjunction with her expectations about how this particular friend is likely to speak to her, to a dog and to a child; that is, a schema for this friend's personal style. Thus frames and schemas interacted in her comprehension of the specific utterance.

Interactive frames in the pediatric examination

Linguistic registers

A key element in framing is the use of identifiable linguistic registers. Register, as Ferguson (1985) defines it, is simply "variation conditioned by use," conventionalized lexical, syntactic and prosodic choices deemed appropriate for the setting and audience. . . . In addressing the child, the pediatrician uses "motherese": a teasing register characterized by exaggerated shifts in pitch, marked prosody (long pauses followed by bursts of vocalization), and drawn out vowel sounds, accompanied by smiling.

For example, while examining Jody's ears with an ophthalmoscope (ear light), the pediatrician pretends to be looking for various creatures, and Jody responds with delighted laughter:

Doctor: Let me look in your ear. Do you have a monkey in your ear?
Child: [laughing] No::::.
Doctor: No:::? . . . Let's see . . . . I . . see . . . . . a birdie!
Child: ⌈[laughing] No:::.
Doctor: ⌊[smiling] No.

In stark contrast to this intonationally exaggerated register, the pediatrician uses a markedly flat intonation to give a running account of the findings of her examination, addressed to no present party, but designed for the benefit of pediatric residents who might later view the video-tape in the teaching facility. We call this "reporting register." For example, looking in Jody's throat, the doctor says, with only slight stumbling:

Doctor: Her canals are are fine, they're open, urn her tympanic membrane was thin, and light.

Finally, in addressing the mother, the pediatrician uses conventional conversational register, as for example:

Doctor: As you know, the important thing is that she does have difficulty with the use of her muscles.

Register shifting

Throughout the examination the doctor moves among these registers. Sometimes she shifts from one to another in very short spaces of time, as in the following example in which she moves smoothly from teasing the child while examining her throat, to reporting her findings, to explaining to the mother what she is looking for and how this relates to the mother's expressed concern with the child's breathing at night.

[Teasing register]

Doctor: Let's see. Can you open up like this, Jody. Look.
          [Doctor opens her own mouth]
Child: Aaaaaaaaaaaaaah.
Doctor: Good. That's good.
Child: Aaaaaaaaaaaah

[Reporting register]

Doctor: /Seeing/ for the palate, she has a high arched palate →
Child: Aaaaaaaaaaaaaaaaaaaaaaaaaah
Doctor: but there's no cleft,
          [maneuvers to grasp child's jaw]

[Conversational register]

    . . . what we'd want to look for is to see how she . . . moves her
    palate. . . . Which may be some of the difficulty with breathing that
    we're talking about.

The pediatrician's shifts from one register to another are sometimes abrupt (for example, when she turns to the child and begins teasing) and sometimes gradual (for example, her reporting register in "high arched palate" begins to fade into conversational register with "but there's no cleft," and come to rest firmly in conversational register with "what we'd want to look for . . ."). In the following example, she shifts from entertaining Jody to reporting findings and back to managing Jody in a teasing tone:

[Teasing register]

Doctor: That's my light.
Child: /This goes up there./
Doctor: It goes up there. That's right.

[Reporting register]

    Now while we're examining her head we're feeling for lymph nodes in
    her neck . . . or for any masses . . . okay . . . also you palpate the
    midline for thyroid, for goiter . . . if there's any.

[Teasing register]

    Now let us look in your mouth. Okay? With my light. Can you open up
    real big? . . . Oh, bigger. . . . Oh bigger. . . . Bigger.

Deborah
Tannen and
Cynthia
Wallat

Frame shifting

Although register shifting is one way of accomplishing frame shifts, it is not the only way. Frames are more complex than register. Whereas each audience is associated with an identifiable register, the pediatrician shifts footings with each audience. In other words, she not only talks differently to the mother, the child and the future video audience, but she also deals with each of these audiences in different ways, depending upon the frame in which she is operating.

The three most important frames in this interaction are the social encounter, examination of the child and a related outer frame of its videotaping, and consultation with the mother. Each of the three frames entails addressing each of the three audiences in different ways. For example, the social encounter requires that the doctor entertain the child, establish rapport with the mother and ignore the video camera and crew. The examination frame requires that she ignore the mother, make sure the video crew is ready and then ignore them, examine the child, and explain what she is doing for the future video audience of pediatric residents.

The consultation frame requires that she talk to the mother and ignore the crew and the child—or, rather, keep the child "on hold," to use Goffman's term, while she answers the mother's questions. These frames are balanced nonverbally as well as verbally. Thus the pediatrician keeps one arm outstretched to rest her hand on the child while she turns away to talk to the mother, palpably keeping the child "on hold."

Juggling frames

Often these frames must be served simultaneously, such as when the pediatrician entertains the child and examines her at the same time, as seen in the example where she looks in her ear and teases Jody that she is looking for a monkey. The pediatrician's reporting register reveals what she was actually looking at (Jody's ear canals and tympanic membrane). But balancing frames is an extra cognitive burden, as seen when the doctor accidentally mixes the vocabulary of her diagnostic report into her teasing while examining Jody's stomach:

[Teasing register]

Doctor: Okay. All right. Now let me /?/ let me see what I can find in there. Is
          there peanut butter and jelly?
          Wait a minute.⌐
Child: └No⌐
Doctor: └No peanut butter and jelly in there?
Child: No.

[Conversational register]

Doctor: Bend your legs up a little bit. . . . That's right.

[Teasing register]

          Okay? Okay. Any peanut butter and jelly in here?⌐
Child: └No⌐
Doctor: └No.
          No. There's nothing in there. Is your spleen palpable over there?⌐
Child: └No.

Deborah
Tannen and
Cynthia
Wallat

The pediatrician says the last line, "Is your spleen palpable over there?" in the same teasing register she was using for peanut butter and jelly, and Jody responds with the same delighted giggling "No" with which she responded to the teasing questions about peanut butter and jelly. The power of the paralinguistic cues with which the doctor signals the frame "teasing" is greater than that of the words spoken, which in this case leak out of the examination frame into the teasing register.

In other words, for the pediatrician, each interactive frame, that is, each identifiable activity that she is engaged in within the interaction, entails her establishing a distinct footing with respect to the other participants.

The interactive production of frames

Our analysis focuses on the pediatrician's speech because our goal is to show that the mismatch of schemas triggers the frame switches which make this interaction burdensome for her. Similar analyses could be performed for any participant in any interaction. Furthermore, all participants in any interaction collaborate in the negotiation of all frames operative within that interaction. Thus, the mother and child collaborate in the negotiation of frames which are seen in the pediatrician's speech and behavior.

For example, consider the examination frame as evidence in the pediatrician's running report of her procedures and findings for the benefit of the video audience.

Although the mother interrupts with questions at many points in the examination, she does not do so when the pediatrician is reporting her findings in what we have called reporting register. Her silence contributes to the maintenance of this frame. Furthermore, on the three of seventeen occasions of reporting register when the mother does offer a contribution, she does so in keeping with the physician's style: Her utterances have a comparable clipped style.

The homonymy of behaviors

Activities which appear the same on the surface can have very different meanings and consequences for the participants if they are understood as associated with different frames. For example, the pediatrician examines various parts of the child's body in accordance with what she describes at the start as a "standard pediatric evaluation." At times she asks the mother for information relevant to the child's condition, still adhering to the sequence of foci of attention prescribed by the pediatric evaluation. At one point, the mother asks about a skin condition behind the child's right ear, causing the doctor to examine that part of Jody's body. What on the surface appears to be the same activity—examining the child—is really very different. In the first case the doctor is adhering to a preset sequence of procedures in the examination, and in the second she is interrupting that sequence to focus on something else, following which she will have to recover her place in the standard sequence.

Conflicting frames

Each frame entails ways of behaving that potentially conflict with the demands of other frames. For example, consulting with the mother entails not only interrupting the examination sequence but also taking extra time to answer her questions, and this means that the child will get more restless and more difficult to manage as the examination proceeds. Reporting findings to the video audience may upset the mother,

Deborah
Tannen and
Cynthia
Wallat

necessitating more explanation in the consultation frame. Perhaps that is the reason the pediatrician frequently explains to the mother what she is doing and finding and why.

Another example will illustrate that the demands associated with the consultation frame can conflict with those of the examination frame, and that these frames and associated demands are seen in linguistic evidence, in this case by contrasting the pediatrician's discourse to the mother in the examination setting with her report to the staff of the Child Development Center about the same problem. Having recently learned that Jody has an arteriovenous malformation in her brain, the mother asks the doctor during the examination how dangerous this condition is. The doctor responds in a way that balances the demands of several frames:

> Mother: I often worry about the danger involved too. →
> Doctor: ⌊Yes.
>   Cause she's well I mean like right now, . . . uh . . . in her present
>   condition. →
> Doctor: ⌊mhm
> Mother: I've often wondered about how dangerous they they are to her right
>   now.
> Doctor: We:ll . . . um . . . the only danger would be from bleeding. . . . From
>   them. If there was any rupture, or anything like that. Which CAN
>   happen . . . um . . .| that would be the danger.
> Mother: ⌊mhm
> Doctor: . . . For that. But they're . . . . . . mm . . . not going to be something
>   that will get worse as time goes on.
> Mother: Oh I see.
> Doctor: But they're just there. Okay?

The mother's question invoked the consultation frame, requiring the doctor to give the mother the information based on her medical knowledge, plus take into account the effect on the mother of the information that the child's life IS in danger. However, the considerable time that would normally be required for such a task is limited because of the conflicting demands of the examination frame: the child is "on hold" for the exam to proceed. (Notice that it is the admirable sensitivity of this doctor that makes her aware of the needs of both frames. According to this mother, many doctors have informed her in matter-of-fact tones of potentially devastating information about her child's condition, without showing any sign of awareness that such information will have emotional impact on the parent. In our terms, such doctors acknowledge only one frame—examination— in order to avoid the demands of conflicting frames—consultation and social encounter. Observing the burden on this pediatrician, who successfully balances the demands of multiple frames, makes it easy to understand why others might avoid this.)

The pediatrician blunts the effect of the information she imparts by using circumlocutions and repetitions; pausing and hesitating; and minimizing the significant danger of the arteriovenous malformation by using the word "only" ("only danger"), by using the conditional tense ("that would be the danger"), and by stressing what sounds positive, that they're not going to get worse. She further creates a reassuring effect by smiling, nodding and using a soothing tone of voice.

Deborah
Tannen and
Cynthia
Wallat

In reviewing the video-tape with us several years after the taping, the pediatrician was surprised to see that she had expressed the prognosis in this way—and furthermore that the mother seemed to be reassured by what was in fact distressing information. The reason she did so, we suggest, is that she was responding to the immediate and conflicting demands of the two frames she was operating in: consulting with the mother in the context of the examination.

Evidence that this doctor indeed felt great concern for the seriousness of the child's condition is seen in her report to the staff regarding the same issue:

> Doctor: . . . uh: I'm not sure how much counseling has been done, . . . with these parents, . . . around . . . the issue . . . of the a-v malformation. Mother asked me questions, . . . about the operability, inoperability of it, . . . u:m . . . which I was not able to answer. She was told it was inoperable, and I had to say well yes some of them are and some of them aren't. . . . And I think that this is a . . . a . . . an important point. Because I don't know whether . . . the possibility of sudden death, intracranial hemorrhage, if any of this has ever been discussed with these parents.

Here the pediatrician speaks faster, with fluency and without hesitation or circumlocution. Her tone of voice conveys a sense of urgency and grave concern. Whereas the construction used with the mother, "only danger," seemed to minimize the danger, the listing construction used with the staff ("sudden death, intracranial hemorrhage"), which actually refers to a single possible event, gives the impression that even more dangers are present than those listed.

Thus the demands on the pediatrician associated with consultation with the mother; those associated with examining the child and reporting her findings to the video audience; and those associated with managing the interaction as a social encounter are potentially in conflict and result in competing demands on the doctor's cognitive and social capacities.

Issues to consider

❏ The different frames the doctor uses with the young patient and with her mother also involve different face strategies of independence and involvement. What do you think the relationship between framing strategies and face strategies is? How do they work together in interactions? How does this relate to Goffman's concept of 'footing'?

❏ The way we interpret frames depends crucially on our 'knowledge schema' for different situations. How do the knowledge schema the participants in the interaction described have about medical consultations affect how they produce and interpret contextualisation cues? Can you think of a situation in which you or someone you know approached a situation with an incomplete or faulty knowledge schema? What were the consequences?

❏ At one point in this interaction the doctor mixes a formal medical register ('Is your spleen palpable over there?') with a 'teasing frame', and the child reacts as if this is part of the game. The authors use this as an example of how non-verbal contextualisation cues can sometimes be so powerful as to override the actual content of an utterance. Why do you think this is? Can you think of any examples of this from your own experience?

❑ Sometimes we have to manage the demands of two or more frames at one time. In this interaction, for example, the doctor has to manage communicating medical information to both the mother and the students watching the video and, at the same time, manage her young patient. In what way are the demands of these three different frames incompatible? What kinds of miscommunication can potentially arise from such situations?

THE ETHNOGRAPHY OF COMMUNICATION

The two readings that follow come from two classic volumes on the ethnography of communication: *Directions in Sociolinguistics*, edited by John Gumperz and Dell Hymes, and *The Ethnography of Communication* by Muriel Saville-Troike. In the first excerpt, Hymes lays out the distinction among speech situations, speech events and speech acts. In the second excerpt, Muriel Saville-Troike discusses the concept of communicative competence. One important point she makes is that since we are all members of multiple speech communities, we all must obtain multiple competences and sometimes negotiate among them, something that is particularly true for second language learners.

A. Speech situations, speech events and speech acts

Dell Hymes **Dell Hymes** (reprinted from *Directions in Sociolinguistics,* John J. Gumperz and Dell Hymes (eds), Oxford: Basil Blackwell, 1986, pp. 52–65)

Speech situation
Within a community one readily detects many situations associated with (or marked by the absence of) speech. Such contexts of situation will often be naturally described as ceremonies, fights, hunts, meals, lovemaking, and the like. It would not be profitable to convert such situations en masse into parts of a sociolinguistic description by the simple expedient of relabeling them in terms of speech. (Notice that the distinctions made with regard to speech community are not identical with the concepts of a general communicative approach, which must note the differential range of communication by speech, film, art object, music.) Such situations may enter as contexts into the statement of rules of speaking as aspects of setting (or of genre). In contrast to speech events, they are not in themselves governed by such rules, or one set of such rules throughout. A hunt, e.g., may comprise both verbal and nonverbal events, and the verbal events may be of more than one type.

In a sociolinguistic description, then, it is necessary to deal with activities which are in some recognizable way bounded or integral. From the standpoint of general social description they may be registered as ceremonies, fishing trips, and the like; from particular standpoints they may be regarded as political, esthetic, etc., situations, which serve as contexts for the manifestation of political, esthetic, etc., activity. From the sociolinguistic standpoint they may be regarded as speech situations.

Dell Hymes

Speech event

The term speech event will be restricted to activities, or aspects of activities, that are directly governed by rules or norms for the use of speech. An event may consist of a single speech act, but will often comprise several. Just as an occurrence of a noun may at the same time be the whole of a noun phrase and the whole of a sentence (e.g., "Fire!"), so a speech act may be the whole of a speech event, and of a speech situation (say, a rite consisting of a single prayer, itself a single invocation). More often, however, one will find a difference in magnitude: a party (speech situation), a conversation during the party (speech event), a joke within the conversation (speech act). It is of speech events and speech acts that one writes formal rules for their occurrence and characteristics.

Notice that the same type of speech act may recur in different types of speech event, and the same type of speech event in different contexts of situation. Thus, a joke (speech act) may be embedded in a private conversation, a lecture, a formal introduction. A private conversation may occur in the context of a party, a memorial service, a pause in changing sides in a tennis match.

Speech act

The speech act is the minimal term of the set just discussed, as the remarks on speech events have indicated. It represents a level distinct from the sentence, and not identifiable with any single portion of other levels of grammar, nor with segments of any particular size defined in terms of other levels of grammar. That an utterance has the status of a command may depend upon a conventional formula ("I hereby order you to leave this building"), intonation ("Go!" vs. "Go?"), position in a conversational exchange ["Hello" as initiating greeting or as response (perhaps used when answering the telephone)], or the social relationship obtaining between the two parties (as when an utterance that is in the form of a polite question is in effect a command when made by a superior to a subordinate). The level of speech acts mediates immediately between the usual levels of grammar and the rest of a speech event or situation in that it implicates both linguistic form and social norms.

To some extent speech acts may be analyzable by extensions of syntactic and semantic structure. It seems certain, however, that much, if not most, of the knowledge that speakers share as to the status of utterances as acts is immediate and abstract, depending upon an autonomous system of signals from both the various levels of grammar and social settings. To attempt to depict speech acts entirely by postulating an additional segment of underlying grammatical structure (e.g., "I hereby X you to . . .") is cumbersome and counterintuitive. (Consider the case in which "Do you think I might have that last bit of tea?" is to be taken as a command.)

An autonomous level of speech acts is in fact implicated by that logic of linguistic levels according to which the ambiguity of "the shooting of the blacks was terrible" and the commonality of "topping Erv is almost impossible" and "it's almost impossible to top Erv" together requires a further level of structure at which the former has two different structures, the latter one. The relation between sentence forms and their status as speech acts is of the same kind. A sentence interrogative in form may be now a request, now a command, now a statement; a request may be manifested by a sentence that is now interrogative, now declarative, now imperative in form.

Discourse may be viewed in terms of acts both syntagmatically and paradigmatically; i.e., both as a sequence of speech acts and in terms of classes of speech acts among which choice has been made at given points.

Issues to consider

❏ The distinction between speech events and speech situations is potentially ambiguous. Hymes says that what distinguishes speech events from speech situations is that speech situations are not governed by one set of rules throughout. What distinguishes a speech event from a speech situation, then, is very much dependent on the distinctions that members of a speech community themselves make regarding things such as setting and genre. What are some ways an analyst can go about determining the boundaries of a speech event?

❏ Hymes's understanding of *speech acts* differs somewhat from the formulation we are familiar with from Austin (see section B5). Rather than understanding speech acts in relation to 'felicity conditions', Hymes suggests that we interpret speech acts in terms of the speech events in which they are embedded, just as we interpret speech events in terms of the broader speech situations in which they are embedded. What differences does this reveal between the way the ethnography of communication and other approaches to spoken discourse such as pragmatics and conversation analysis understand communication?

B. Communicative competence

Muriel Saville-Troike (reprinted from *The Ethnography of Communication*, Oxford: Blackwell, 2003, pp. 18–22)

Hymes (1966) observed that speakers who could produce any and all of the grammatical sentences of a language (per Chomsky's 1965 definition of *linguistic competence*) would be institutionalized if they indiscriminately went about trying to do so without consideration of the appropriate contexts of use. *Communicative competence* involves knowing not only the language code but also what to say to whom, and how to say it appropriately in any given situation. Further, it involves the social and cultural knowledge speakers are presumed to have which enables them to use and interpret linguistic forms. Hymes (1974, 1987) augmented Chomsky's notion of linguistic competence (knowledge of systematic potential, or whether or not an utterance is a possible grammatical structure in a language) with knowledge of appropriateness (whether and to what extent something is suitable), occurrence (whether and to what extent

Muriel
Saville-
Troike

something is done), and feasibility (whether and to what extent something is possible under particular circumstances). The concept of communicative competence (and its encompassing congener, social competence) is one of the most powerful organizing tools to emerge in the social sciences in recent years.

Communicative competence extends to both knowledge and expectation of who may or may not speak in certain settings, when to speak and when to remain silent, to whom one may speak, how one may talk to persons of different statuses and roles, what nonverbal behaviors are appropriate in various contexts, what the routines for turn-taking are in conversation, how to ask for and give information, how to request, how to offer or decline assistance or cooperation, how to give commands, how to enforce discipline, and the like—in short, everything involving the use of language and other communicative modalities in particular social settings.

Clear cross-cultural differences can and do produce conflicts or inhibit communication. For example, certain American Indian groups are accustomed to waiting several minutes in silence before responding to a question or taking a turn in conversation, while the native English speakers they may be talking to have very short time frames for responses or conversational turn-taking, and find long silences embarrassing. . .

The concept of communicative competence must be embedded in the notion of cultural competence, or the total set of knowledge and skills which speakers bring into a situation. This view is consonant with a semiotic approach which defines culture as meaning, and views all ethnographers (not just ethnographers of communication) as dealing with symbols (e.g. Douglas 1970; Geertz 1973). The systems of culture are patterns of symbols, and language is only one of the symbolic systems in this network. Interpreting the meaning of linguistic behavior requires knowing the meaning in which it is embedded.

Ultimately all aspects of culture are relevant to communication, but those that have the most direct bearing on communicative forms and processes are the social and institutional structure, the values and attitudes held about language and ways of speaking, the network of conceptual categories which results from experiences, and the ways knowledge and skills (including language) are transmitted from one generation to the next and to new members of the group. Shared cultural knowledge is essential to explain the shared presuppositions and judgments of truth value which are the essential undergirdings of language structures, as well as of contextually appropriate usage and interpretation.

While referential meaning may be ascribed to many of the elements in the linguistic code in a static manner, situated meaning must be accounted for as an emergent and dynamic process. Interaction requires the perception, selection, and interpretation of salient features of the code used in actual communicative situations, integrating these with other cultural knowledge and skills, and implementing appropriate strategies for achieving communicative goals.

The phonology, grammar, and lexicon which are the target of traditional linguistic description constitute only a part of the elements in the code used for communication. Also included are the paralinguistic and nonverbal phenomena which have conventional meaning in each speech community, and knowledge of the full range of variants in all elements which are available for transmitting social, as well as

Muriel
Saville-
Troike

referential, information. Ability to discriminate between those variants which serve as markers of social categories or carry other meaning and those which are insignificant, and knowledge of what the meaning of a variant is in a particular situation, are all components of communicative competence.

The verbal code may be transmitted on oral, written, or manual (signed) channels. The relative load carried on each channel depends on its functional distribution in a particular speech community, and thus they are of differential importance in the linguistic repertoire of any individual or society. Full participation in a deaf speech community requires ability to interpret language on the manual channel but not the oral, for instance; a speech community with a primarily oral tradition may not require interpretation of writing; and a speech community which relegates much information flow to the written channel will require literacy skills for full participation. Thus, the traditional linguistic description which focuses only on the oral channel will be too narrow to account for communicative competence in most societies.

Although it may cause some terminological confusion, references to *ways of speaking* and *ethnography of speaking* should be understood as usually including a much broader range of communicative behavior than merely speech. The typical descriptive focus on oral production has tended to treat language as a unidirectional phenomenon. In considering the nature and scope of communicative competence, it is useful to distinguish between *receptive* and *productive* dimensions (Troike 1970); only shared receptive competence is necessary for successful communication. Knowledge of rules for appropriate communicative behavior entails understanding a wide range of language forms, for instance, but not necessarily the ability to produce them. Members of the same community may understand varieties of a language which differ according to the social class, region, sex, age, and occupation of the speaker, but only a few talented mimics will be able to speak them all. In multilingual speech communities, members often share receptive competence in more than one language but vary greatly in their relative ability to speak one or the other.

The following outline summarizes the broad range of shared knowledge that is involved in appropriate communication. From the ethnographer's perspective, this inventory also indicates the range of linguistic, interactional, and cultural phenomena which must ultimately be accounted for in an adequate description and explanation of communicative competence (see also Gumperz 1984; Hymes 1987; Duranti 1988).

1 Linguistic knowledge

(a) Verbal elements
(b) Nonverbal elements
(c) Patterns of elements in particular speech events
(d) Range of possible variants (in all elements and their organization)
(e) Meaning of variants in particular situations

2 Interaction skills

(a) Perception of salient features in communicative situations
(b) Selection and interpretation of forms appropriate to specific situations, roles, and relationships (rules for the use of speech)

(c) Discourse organization and processes
(d) Norms of interaction and interpretation
(e) Strategies for achieving goals

Muriel
Saville-
Troike

3 Cultural knowledge

(a) Social structure (status, power, speaking rights)
(b) Values and attitudes
(c) Cognitive maps/schemata
(d) Enculturation processes (transmission of knowledge and skills)

Communicative competence within the ethnography of communication usually refers to the communicative knowledge and skills shared by a speech community, but these (like all aspects of culture) reside variably in its individual members. The shared yet individual nature of competence reflects the nature of language itself, as expressed by von Humboldt (1836):

> While languages are in the ambiguous sense of the word . . . creations of nations, they still remain personal and individual creations of individuals. This follows because they can be produced in each individual, yet only in such a manner that each individual assumes a priori the comprehension of all people and that all people, furthermore, satisfy such expectation.

Considering communicative competence at an individual level, we must additionally recognize that any one speaker is not infrequently a member of more than one speech community—often to different degrees. For individuals who are members of multiple speech communities, which one or ones they orient themselves to at any given moment—which set of social and communicative rules they use—is reflected not only in which segment of their linguistic knowledge they select, but which interaction skills they utilize, and which aspects of their cultural knowledge they activate. The competence of non-native speakers of a language usually differs significantly from the competence of native speakers; the specific content of what an individual needs to know and the skills he or she needs to have depend on the social context in which he or she is or will be using the language and the purposes he or she will have for doing so.

This further emphasizes why the notion of an "ideal speaker-listener, in a completely homogeneous speech-community" (Chomsky 1965: 3) is inadequate for ethnographic purposes. Also, multilingual speakers' communicative competence includes knowledge of rules for the appropriate choice of language and for switching between languages, given a particular social context and communicative intent, as well as for the intralingual shifting among styles and registers which is common to the competence of all speakers. An extension has been made to "intercultural communicative competence," which requires an additional level of metacompetence involving explicit awareness of differential usages and ability to adapt communicative strategies to a variety of cultural situations (Kim 1991). Liu (2001) further extends the construct to "adaptive cultural competence" as a goal for second language learners, which also encompasses social identity negotiation skills and culture-sensitivity knowledge. He argues that such a

Muriel Saville-Troike

higher level competence is needed for appropriate and effective social participation of non-native speakers who are in roles of international students or immigrées.

Accounting for the nature of communicative competence ultimately "requires going beyond a concern with Language (capital L) or a language. It requires a focus on the ways in which people do use language . . ." (Hymes 1993: 13). Problems arise when individual competence is judged in relation to a presumed "ideal" monolingual speech community, or assessed with tests given in a limited subset of situations which do not represent the true range of an individual's verbal ability (Hymes 1979). The problems are particularly serious ones when such invalid judgments result in some form of social or economic discrimination against the individuals, such as unequal or inappropriate educational treatment or job placement. Awareness of the complex nature of communicative competence and the potential negative consequences of misjudgments is leading to major changes in procedures and instruments for language assessment, but no simple solutions are forthcoming (see Philips 1983; Milroy 1987; Byram 1997).

Issues to consider

❏ Saville-Troike offers a model for thinking about communicative competence which is slightly different from Hymes's SPEAKING model, one in which competence is divided into: 1) linguistic knowledge; 2) interaction skills; and 3) cultural knowledge, with each category containing a number of components. Which of these components correspond to the components in the SPEAKING model and which do not? To what extent do you think these additional components enhance the model?

❏ Saville-Troike makes the distinction between *receptive competence* and *productive competence*. How do these different kinds of competence determine the degree of participation one can have in a speech event? Are there speech events in which only receptive competence is sufficient for most participants? Are there speech events in which both kinds of competence are required for participation?

❏ At the end of this excerpt Saville-Troike discusses the implications of the idea of communicative competence for language learning and language assessment. How do you think using the idea of communicative competence as opposed to the narrower notion of linguistic competence would affect the way you might go about testing the language proficiency of an individual?

D8 **DISCOURSE AND ACTION**

In this section you will read an excerpt from *Mediated Discourse: The nexus of practice*, the book in which Ron Scollon first articulated his theory of mediated discourse analysis. As you read, notice how he distinguishes his method from other approaches to discourse analysis. At the same time, take note of the similarities this method has with other methods discussed in this book and how Scollon incorporates principles and tools from those methods into his model.

Discourse and action: a cup of coffee

Ron Scollon (reprinted from *Mediated Discourse: The nexus of practice*. London: Routledge 2001, pp. 1–8)

Ron Scollon

One morning recently in San Diego, California I had a cup of coffee at the international chain coffee shop, Starbucks®. After a short time in the queue I ordered a tall latte and another drink for my friend. I paid for the drinks and then waited a few minutes while the drinks were made and then delivered to me. We took the drinks and sat down to drink them and have a conversation. As linguists and perhaps only linguists do, in and among the other topics of conversation we talked about what was printed on the cup.

Mediated discourse analysis is a framework for looking at such actions with two questions in mind: What is the action going on here? and How does Discourse figure into these actions? In a sense there is nothing very new or different about mediated discourse analysis in that it is a remedial position that seeks to develop a theoretical remedy for discourse analysis that operates without reference to social actions on the one hand and social analysis that operates without reference to discourse on the other. Virtually all of the theoretical elements have been proposed and developed in the work of others. In this, mediated discourse analysis takes the position that social action and Discourse are inextricably linked on the one hand (Chouliaraki and Fairclough 1999) but that on the other hand these links are sometimes not at all direct or obvious, and therefore in need of more careful theorization.

In having this cup of coffee I could say there is just a single action—having a cup of coffee as is implied in the common invitation, 'Let's go have a cup of coffee.' Or I could say there is a very complex and nested set of actions—queuing, ordering, purchasing, receiving the order, selecting a table, drinking coffee, conversing, busing our trash and the rest. Likewise, I could say there is just one discourse here—a conversation among friends. Or I could say there are many complex Discourses with rampant intertextualities and interdiscursivities—international neo-capitalist marketing of coffee, service encounter talk, linguistic conference talk, family talk and the rest. Mediated discourse analysis is a position which seeks to keep all of this complexity alive in our analyses without presupposing which actions and which Discourses are the relevant ones in any particular case under study.

As a way to at least temporarily narrow the scope of my analysis here, I want to focus on the coffee cup. It can be called the primary mediational means by which the coffee has been produced as something transferable, delivered to me, and ultimately consumed. Without the cup there is no <having a cup of coffee> in the literal sense. Throughout all the other actions which take place, the cup figures as the material line that holds this all together. From the point of view of an analysis of mediated action (Wertsch 1998), then, we would want to consider the cup—a paper one in this case— absolutely central to both the narrowly viewed actions of delivery or drinking and to the more broadly viewed actions of consumer purchasing/marketing or of <having a cup of coffee> as a conversational genre.

If we come to this social interaction from the point of view of discourse analysis, and if we set aside for the moment all of the complexities of service encounter talk and of casual conversation between friends, we still find that the cup itself (with its protective

D8

Ron Scollon

sleeve) is an impressive semiotic complex of at least seven different Discourses (Gee 2010).

> Commercial branding: There is a world-wide recognizable logo which appears twice on the cup and once on the cardboard protective sleeve.

> Legal: The logo is marked as a registered property (®) and the text on the sleeve is marked as copyrighted (©). A patent number is also given. In addition, there is a warning that the contents are 'extremely hot' which derives from a famous lawsuit against another international chain where a customer had held a paper cup of their coffee between his legs while driving and been uncomfortably scorched.

> E-commerce: A website is given where the consumer can learn more, though it does not indicate what we might learn about.

> Consumer correctness: An extended text tells us that the company cares for those who grow its coffee and gives a telephone number where the consumer can call to make a donation to CARE on behalf of plantation workers in Indonesia.

> Environmental correctness: We are told that the sleeve is made of 60% recycled fiber and that it uses less material than would a second paper cup. The color scheme is in natural cardboard brown with green lettering which are widely associated with environmental friendliness.

> Service information: There is a roster of possibilities ('Decaf', 'Shots', 'Syrup', 'Milk', 'Custom', and 'Drink') printed and superimposed is the handwritten 'L' (for 'latte').

> Manufacturing information: Under the cup around the inside rim is the information about the cup itself, its size, and product labeling and number.

On the one hand we have a fairly clear and mundane social action—having a cup of coffee in a coffee shop—and a semiotic complex of Discourses which are also, at least now at the beginning of this century, rather mundane. We have an array of analytical positions from which we can analyze this action from seeing it as participating in a bit of micro-social interaction to seeing it as participating in the world-wide consumer practices of neo-capitalism. At the same time we have an array of analytical positions from which we can analyze the Discourses represented in these texts printed on this coffee cup. The problem that mediated discourse analysis is trying to engage is how we are to work out a way to understand the relationships among the actions—drinking the cup of coffee—and the Discourses. Ethnographic observation leads us to believe that, on the whole except for the odd linguist, the coffee is drunk without much attention being focused on this impressive discursive array on the cup. Correspondingly, the literature has many analyses of such Discourses in public places from the products of the news industry through to the broader popular culture industry which make scant reference at all to the actual social situations in which these Discourses are engaged in social action. Mediated discourse analysis is an attempt to theorize a way in which we can link the Discourse of commercial branding, for example, with the practice of drinking a cup of coffee in conversation without giving either undue weight to the action without reference to the Discourse or to the Discourse without reference to the actions within which it is appropriated.

Ron Scollon

A few central concepts

A mediated discourse analysis gives central importance to five concepts:

- Mediated action
- Site of engagement
- Mediational means
- Practice
- Nexus of practice

Mediated action: The unit of analysis of a mediated discourse analysis is the mediated action (not the Discourse or text or genre). That is, the focus is on social actors as they are acting because these are the moments in social life when the Discourses in which we are interested are instantiated in the social world as social action, not simply as material objects. We use the phrase 'mediated action' to highlight the unresolvable dialectic between action and the material means which mediate all social action (Wertsch 1998). That is, we take the position that action is materially grounded in persons and objects and that it is unproductive to work with purely abstracted conceptual systems of representation. Participation in the world-wide consumer society requires at some point the transfer of coins and cups, speaking and drinking. Conversely stated, this transfer of coins and cups and speaking and drinking inevitably entail participating in the consumer society. There is no action without participating in such Discourses; no such Discourses without concrete, material actions.

A site of engagement: A mediated action occurs in a social space which I have elsewhere called a 'site of engagement' (Scollon 1998, 1999). This is the real-time window that is opened through an intersection of social practices and mediational means (cultural tools) that make that action the focal point of attention of the relevant participants. The idea of the site of engagement takes from practice/activity theory (as well as from interactional sociolinguistics) the insistence on the real-time, irreversible, and unfinalizable nature of social action. A mediated action is not a class of actions but a unique moment in history. Its interpretation is located within the social practices which are linked in that unique moment. The cup of coffee/coffee conversation in San Diego is theoretically taken as unique and unfolding in that moment and bears only a loose, indirect, and highly problematical relationship with another cup of coffee at a Starbucks® in San Luis Obispo among the same participants a week later if for no other reason that the first is part of the history of the second.

Mediational means: A mediated action is carried out through material objects in the world (including the materiality of the social actors—their bodies, dress, movements) in dialectical interaction with structures of the habitus. We take these mediational means to always be multiple in any single action, to carry with them historical affordances and constraints, and to be inherently polyvocal, intertextual, and interdiscursive. Further, these multiple mediational means are organized in a variety of ways, either in hierarchical structures of activities or in relatively expectable relations of salience or importance.

Ron Scollon

While I have focused on the cup in this sketch, this cup of coffee has also equally entailed the physical spaces of the coffee shop, the coins and bills exchanged, the servers, the counters, the coffee machines, the tables and chairs, the other customers of the shop, the San Diego sunshine—a significant materiality of that particular action—and our own habitus, latte for me, chai latte for my friend. The polyvocality, intertextuality, and interdiscursivity of the cup has been noted above. To this we add the Southern California décor which sets this particular shop in its place on earth and departs so radically from the 'same' company's shops in Washington, DC, Beijing, and London.

Practice and social structure: For this mediated action to take place in this way there is a necessary intersection of social practices and mediational means which in themselves reproduce social groups, histories, and identities. A mediated discourse analysis takes it that a mediated action is only interpretable within practices. From this point of view 'having a cup of coffee' is viewed as a different action in a Starbucks®, in a cafeteria, and at home. The difference lies both in the practices (how the order is made, for example) and in the mediational means (including the range from the espresso machines to the décor of the spaces in which the action is taken). That is to say, a mediated discourse analysis does not neutralize these practices and social structures as 'context', but seeks to keep them alive in our interpretations of mediated actions.

Nexus of practice: Mediated discourse analysis takes a tight or narrow view of social practice as social practices—ordering, purchasing, handing and receiving—and so then sees these as practices (as count nouns, not as a mass noun). These practices are linked to other practices discursive and non-discursive over time to form nexus of practice. So we might loosely at least want to talk about an early 21st Century American 'designer coffee shop' nexus of practice which would provisionally include such things as pricing practices (high), ordering practices (the distinctions between caffe latte, café au lait, regular coffee with milk, cappuccino), drinking practices (alone with newspapers, in conversation with friends), discursive practices (being able to answer to 'whole or skim?', knowing that 'tall' means the smallest cup on sale or that 'for here' means in a porcelain cup rather than a paper one), physical spacing practices (that the queuing place and delivery place are different) and the rest.

The concept of the nexus of practice works more usefully than the concept of the community of practice which was the earlier framing (Scollon 1998) in that it is rather loosely structured and structured over time. That is, a nexus of practice, like practices themselves is formed one mediated action at a time and is always unfinalized (and unfinalizable). The concept of the nexus of practice is unbounded (unlike the more problematical community of practice) and takes into account that at least most practices (ordering, purchasing, handing and receiving) can be linked variably to different practices in different sites of engagement and among different participants. From this point of view, the practice of handing an object to another person may be linked to practices which constitute the action of purchasing in a coffee shop, it may be linked to practices which constitute the action of giving a gift to a friend on arriving at a birthday party, or even to handing a bit of change to a panhandler on the street. Mediated discourse analysis takes the position that it is the constellation of linked practices which make for the uniqueness of the site of engagement and the identities thus produced, not necessarily the specific practices and actions themselves.

Ron Scollon

This mediated action of having a cup of coffee and the concurrent and dialogically chained prior and subsequent mediated actions could be analyzed with a great deal more care than I have been able to do here. My purpose has been simply to make these five points:

- The mediated action (within a dialogical chain of such social actions) is the focus of mediated discourse analysis.
- The focus is on real-time, irreversible, one-time-only actions rather than objectivized, categorical analyses of types of action or discourses and texts.
- An action is understood as taking place within a site of engagement which is the real-time window opened through an intersection of social practices and mediational means.
- The mediational means are multiple in any case and inevitably carry histories and social structures with them.
- A mediated action produces and reproduces social identities and social structures within a nexus of practice.

Theoretical principles

It is only with some trepidation that I suggest that mediated discourse analysis is a theory as that word tends to evoke emotional responses only surpassed perhaps by 'patriotism' or 'plagiarism'. Nevertheless, I believe it is important to seek to make one's claims clear and then proceed with the business of discovering what is wrong with them. Here I will articulate three principles which organize mediated discourse theory. The three main principles are the principles of social action, communication, and history. I would argue that the second two are simply tautological or definitional extensions of the first principle as are the corollaries. I make no claim that these principles are unique to mediated discourse; indeed, it is my hope that the only originality, if there is originality at all in these ideas, is in the degree of explicitness of the underlying principles I am trying to achieve.

PRINCIPLE ONE: The principle of social action: Discourse is best conceived as a matter of social actions, not systems of representation or thought or values.

> COROLLARY ONE: The ecological unit of analysis
>
> The proper unit of analysis for a theory of social action is, tautologically, the social action, or as I prefer to phrase it, the mediated action; that is, the person or persons in the moment of taking an action along with the mediational means which are used by them form the 'ecological' unit of analysis, the unit of analysis in which the phenomenon exists, changes, and develops through time (Bateson 1972).
>
> COROLLARY TWO: Practice: All social action is based in tacit, normally nonconscious actions.
>
> COROLLARY THREE: Habitus: The basis of social action is the habitus (Bourdieu 1977, 1990) or the historical-body (Nishida 1958): An individual's accumulated experience of social actions.

COROLLARY FOUR: Positioning (identity claims): All social actions occur within a nexus of practice which makes implicit or explicit claims to the social groups and positions of all participants—speakers, hearers, and those talked about or in front of.

COROLLARY FIVE: Socialization: Because all social actions position the participants, all communications have the effect of socialization to nexus of practice.

COROLLARY SIX: Othering: Because of the principle of socialization, all communications have the simultaneous effect of producing 'others' who are identified by not being members of the relevant community of practice.

PRINCIPLE TWO: The principle of communication: The meaning of the term 'social' in the phrase 'social action' implies a common or shared system of meaning. To be social an action must be communicated.

COROLLARY ONE: Mediational means: The production of shared meanings is mediated by a very wide range of mediational means or cultural tools such as language, gesture, material objects, and institutions which are carriers of their sociocultural histories.

COROLLARY TWO: Organization of mediational means: The multiple mediational means involved in a mediated action are related to each other in complex ways.

PRINCIPLE THREE: The principle of history: 'Social' means 'historical' in the sense that shared meaning derives from common history or common past.

COROLLARY ONE: Interdiscursivity: Because of the principle of history, all communication is positioned within multiple, overlapping, and even conflicting discourses.

COROLLARY TWO: Intertextuality: Because of the principle of history, all communications (particular utterances) borrow from other discourses and texts and are, in turn, used in later discourses.

COROLLARY THREE: Dialogicality (or conversational or practical inference): Because of the principle of history, all communications respond to prior communications and anticipate following communications.

Issues to consider

❏ Scollon says that the main task of mediated discourse analysis is finding out a way to understand the relationship between the actions that we take and larger 'capital D Discourses' 'without giving either undue weight to the action without reference to the Discourse or to the Discourse without reference to the actions within which it is appropriated.' What are some of the challenges involved in this task? How is the way mediated discourse analysis goes about this task different from the way critical discourse analysis (see sections A4, B4, C4 and D4) does?

❏ According to Scollon, a 'nexus' of practice occurs when a number of practices are linked to other practices in predictable ways. The example he gives is 'early 21st Century American "designer coffee shop" nexus of practice'. How does this definition of nexus of practice compare to Gee's definitions of 'cultural models' and 'capital D Discourses' and with Swales's definition of 'discourse communities'?

❏ Scollon notes that when we take social actions we inevitably make claims about 'who we are', the communities to which we belong. He also notes that these same actions have the effect of producing 'others' who are constructed as not members of the relevant nexus of practice. How is the way mediated discourse analysis approaches issues of social identity similar to and different from the way interactional sociolinguistics and critical discourse analysis do?

❏ In section D4, Fairclough quoted Kristiva as saying that intertextuality involves 'the insertion of history (society) into a text and of this text into history'. How is the relationship between discourse and history explained in mediated discourse analysis?

Ron Scollon

TWO PERSPECTIVES ON MULTIMODALITY

D9

The excerpts reprinted in this section represent the two broad approaches to multimodality which were introduced in section A9. The first is from Gunther Kress and Theo van Leeuwan's classic, *Reading Images: The grammar of visual design*. In this excerpt the authors make an argument that visual design, like language, constitutes an organised system of meaningful choices which can be analysed with reference to linguistic theories. At the same time, they warn against adopting the same concepts used to analyse language to analyse other modes, which necessarily involve different kinds of resources from making meaning. They then go on to explain the 'grammar' of visual design in terms of Halliday's tripartite model of meaning: ideational meaning, interpersonal meaning and textual meaning.

In the second excerpt, Sigrid Norris makes an argument for moving beyond a view of interaction that focuses primarily on spoken language, insisting that other modes such as gesture, gaze, posture and the layout of furniture are just as important, and sometimes more important, than speech. She then goes on to explain how principles from mediated discourse analysis (see section D8) can help to organise the multimodal analysis of interactions.

As you read through these excerpts, consider not just how the two approaches differ from each other, but also how they appropriate and build upon concepts from other approaches to discourse that have been discussed in this book.

A. Reading images

Gunther Kress and Theo van Leeuwen (reprinted from *Reading Images: The grammar of visual design* 2nd edition. London: Routledge 2006, pp. 17–20, 41–43)

Gunther Kress and Theo van Leeuwen

D9

Gunther Kress and Theo van Leeuwen

In this book we take a fresh look at the question of the visual. We want to treat forms of communication employing images as seriously as linguistic forms have been. We have come to this position because of the now overwhelming evidence of the importance of visual communication, and the now problematic absence of the means for talking and thinking about what is actually communicated by images and by visual design. In doing so, we have to move away from the position which Roland Barthes took in his 1964 essay 'Rhetoric of the image' (1977: 32–51). In this essay (and elsewhere, as in the introduction to *Elements of semiology;* Barthes, 1967a), he argued that the meaning of images (and of other semiotic codes, like dress, food, etc.) is always related to and, in a sense, dependent on, verbal text. By themselves, images are, he thought, too 'polysemous', too open to a variety of possible meanings. To arrive at a definite meaning, language must come to the rescue. Visual meaning is too indefinite; it is a 'floating chain of signifieds'. Hence, Barthes said, 'in every society various techniques are developed intended to fix the floating chain of signifieds in such a way as to counter the terror of uncertain signs; the linguistic message is one of these techniques' (1977: 39). He distinguished between an image–text relation in which the verbal text extends the meaning of the image, or vice versa, as is the case, for example, with the speech balloons in comic strips, and an image–text relation in which the verbal text elaborates the image, or vice versa. In the former case, which he called relay, new and different meanings are added to complete the message. In the latter case, the same meanings are restated in a different (e.g. more definite and precise) way, as is the case, for example, when a caption identifies and/or interprets what is shown in a photograph. Of the two, elaboration is dominant. Relay, said Barthes, is 'more rare'. He distinguished two types of elaboration, one in which the verbal text comes first, so that the image forms an illustration of it, and one in which the image comes first, so that the text forms a more definite and precise restatement or 'fixing' of it (a relation he calls anchorage).

Before approximately 1600 (the transition is, of course, very gradual), Barthes argued, 'illustration' was dominant. Images elaborated texts, more specifically the founding texts of the culture—mythology, the Bible, the 'holy writ' of the culture—texts, therefore, with which viewers could be assumed to be familiar. This relation, in which verbal texts formed a source of authority in society, and in which images disseminated the dominant texts in a particular mode to particular groups within society, gradually changed to one in which nature, rather than discourse, became the source of authority. In the era of science, images, ever more naturalistic, began to function as 'the book of nature', as 'windows on the world', as 'observation', and verbal text served to identify and interpret, to 'load the image, burdening it with a culture, a moral, an imagination'.

This position does explain elements of communication. Any one of the image–text relations Barthes describes may at times be dominant, although we feel that today there is a move away from 'anchorage'. Compare, for example, the 'classic' documentary film in which the viewer is first confronted with 'images of nature', then with the authoritative voice of a narrator who identifies and interprets the images, with the modern 'current affairs' item, in which the viewer is first confronted with the anchorperson's verbal discourse and, either simultaneously or following on from the verbal introduction, with the 'images of nature' that illustrate, exemplify and authenticate the discourse. But Barthes' account misses an important point: the visual component of a text is an independently organized and structured message, connected with the verbal text, but in no way dependent on it—and similarly the other way around.

Gunther
Kress and
Theo van
Leeuwen

One important difference between the account we develop in this book and that of earlier semioticians is our use of work in linguistic theories and descriptions. This is a difficult argument to make, but worth making clearly. We think that this book would not have been possible without the achievements of linguistics, yet we do not, in the way some critics of our approach have suggested, see our approach as a linguistic one. So what have we used from linguistics, and how have we used it? And, equally, what have we not used from linguistics? To start with the latter question, we have not imported the theories and methodologies of linguistics directly into the domain of the visual, as has been done by others working in this field. For instance, we do not make a separation of syntax, semantics and pragmatics in the domain of the visual; we do not look for (the analogues of) sentences, clauses, nouns, verbs, and so on, in images. We take the view that language and visual communication can both be used to realize the 'same' fundamental systems of meaning that constitute our cultures, but that each does so by means of its own specific forms, does so differently, and independently.

To give an example, the distinction between 'subjective' and 'objective' meanings has played an important role in Western culture ever since the physical sciences began to develop in the sixteenth century. This distinction can be realized (that is, given concrete, material expression, hence made perceivable and communicable) with linguistic as well as visual means. The terms 'subjective' and 'objective' can therefore be applied to both: they belong to the meaning potential of a culture and its society. But the way the distinction is realized in language is quite different from the way it is realized in images. For example, in language an idea can be realized subjectively by using a 'mental process verb' like believe in the first person (e.g. We believe that there is a grammar of images); or objectively through the absence of such a form (e.g. There is a grammar of images). Visual representation, too, can realize both subjectivity, through the presence of a perspectival angle, and objectivity, through its absence. Mental process clauses and nominalization are unique to language. Perspective is unique to images. But the kinds of meaning expressed are from the same broad domain in each case; and the forms, different as they are, were developed in the same period, in response to the same cultural changes. Both language and visual communication express meanings belonging to and structured by cultures in the one society; the semiotic processes, though not the semiotic means, are broadly similar; and this results in a considerable degree of congruence between the two.

At the same time, however, each medium has its own possibilities and limitations of meaning. Not everything that can be realized in language can also be realized by means of images, or vice versa. As well as a broad cultural congruence, there is significant difference between the two (and other semiotic modes, of course). In a language such as English one needs to use a verb in order to make a full utterance (believe, is); and language has to use names to refer to whatever is to be represented (a grammar of images, believe, we). But language does not have or need angles of vision to achieve perspective, nor does it have or need spatial dispositions of elements to achieve the meanings of syntactic relations: images have and need both. The meaning potentials of the two modes are neither fully conflated nor entirely opposed. We differ from those

Gunther Kress and Theo van Leeuwen

who see the meaning of language as inherent in the forms and the meaning of images as derived from the context, or the meanings of language as 'conscious' and the meanings of images as 'unconscious'.

To return to the first of our two questions—What have we used from linguistics, and how have we used it?—perhaps the most significant borrowing is our overall approach, an 'attitude' which assumes that, as a resource for representation, images, like language, will display regularities, which can be made the subject of relatively formal description. We call this a 'grammar' to draw attention to culturally produced regularity. More specifically, we have borrowed 'semiotic orientations', features which we taken to be general to all human meaning-making, irrespective of mode. For instance, we think that the distinction between 'objectivity' and 'subjectivity' is a general cultural/semiotic issue which can be realized linguistically as well as visually, though differently so, as we have said. Or, as another instance, we have taken Michael Halliday's social semiotic approach to language as a model, as a source for thinking about general social and semiotic processes, rather than as a mine for categories to apply in the description of images. His model with its three functions is a starting point for our account of images, not because the model works well for language (which it does, to an extent), but because it works well as a source for thinking about all modes of representation.

*****

A social semiotic theory of communication

In order to function as a full system of communication, the visual, like all semiotic modes, has to serve several representational and communicational requirements. We have adopted the theoretical notion of 'metafunction' from the work of Michael Halliday for this purpose. The three metafunctions which he posits are the ideational, the interpersonal and the textual. In the form in which we gloss them here they apply to all semiotic modes, and are not specific to speech or writing.

The ideational metafunction

Any semiotic mode has to be able to represent aspects of the world as it is experienced by humans. In other words, it has to be able to represent objects and their relations in a world outside the representational system. That world may of course be, and most frequently is, already semiotically represented. In doing so, semiotic modes offer an array of choices, of different ways in which objects, and their relations to other objects and to processes, can be represented. Two objects may be represented as involved in a process of interaction which could be visually realized by vectors:

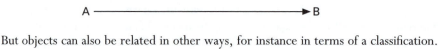

But objects can also be related in other ways, for instance in terms of a classification. They would be connected, not by a vector but, for instance, by a 'tree' structure:

The interpersonal metafunction

Gunther
Kress and
Theo van
Leeuwen

Any semiotic mode has to be able to project the relations between the producer of a (complex) sign, and the receiver/reproducer of that sign. That is, any mode has to be able to represent a particular social relation between the producer, the viewer and the object represented.

As in the case of the ideational metafunction, modes offer an array of choices for representing different 'interpersonal' relations, some of which will be favoured in one form of visual representation (say, in the naturalistic image), others in another (say, in the diagram). A depicted person may be shown as addressing viewers directly, by looking at the camera. This conveys a sense of interaction between the depicted person and the viewer. But a depicted person may also be shown as turned away from the viewer, and this conveys the absence of a sense of interaction. It allows the viewer to scrutinize the represented characters as though they were specimens in a display case.

The textual metafunction

Any semiotic mode has to have the capacity to form texts, complexes of signs which cohere both internally with each other and externally with the context in and for which they were produced. Here, too, visual grammar makes a range of resources available: different compositional arrangements to allow the realization of different textual meanings. In Figure D9.1, for example, the text is on the left and the picture on the right. Changing the layout (Figure D9.1) would completely alter the relation between written text and image and the meaning of the whole. The image, rather than the written text, would now serve as point of departure, as 'anchor' for the message.

Issues to consider

❏ In the beginning of this excerpt Kress and van Leeuwen give a historical account of the relationship between text and image beginning with the fifteenth century. How do you think the importance of images in communication has changed over time, especially in relation to media such as the Internet and mobile phones? Do you think images function differently in communication than they did before?

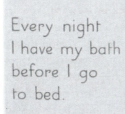

Figure D9.1

**Gunther
Kress and
Theo van
Leeuwen**

Bath

Every night
I have my bath
before I go
to bed.

Figure D9.2

❑ Kress and van Leeuwen say 'both language and visual communication express
meanings belonging to and structured by cultures in the one society.' Does this
mean that the visual grammar of different cultures is likely to be as different as
their languages? To what degree does visual communication transcend different
cultures in ways that language cannot?

❑ Look at Figures D9.1 and D9.2. Which arrangement of text and image seems
more 'natural' to you? Can you 'translate' the differences between these two
arrangements into language?

B.

Sigrid Norris

Sigrid Norris (reprinted from *Analyzing Multimodal Interaction: A methodological framework.*
London: Routledge, 2004, pp. 1–3, 9–13)

Multimodal interaction analysis

All interactions are multimodal. Imagine, for example, a simple two-person interaction, a conversation with a friend. During this interaction, you are aware of your
friend's spoken language, so that you hear the verbal choices, the content, the prosody,
and the pitch. You are also aware of the way that your friend is standing or sitting, the
way that your friend is nodding or leaning back or forward; you are aware of your
friend's facial expression, and clothing, just as you are aware of the environment in
which this interaction takes place. If there is music playing in the background, even
though you are not focusing on the music, you are aware of it. All of these elements
play a part in this conversation. You may react to the words that your friend is speaking
as much as you may react to your friend's facial expression or the posture that your
friend is taking up towards you. You may speak quickly or slowly, depending on
the music playing in the background or the given environment that the interaction
takes place in.

Sigrid Norris

Intuitively we know that we draw on all of these communicative channels or modes when interacting with others. We also know that we are aware of many things that surround us while we interact with others. Let us keep thinking about a conversation. No matter where it may take place, you are certainly aware whether other people are present in close proximity. Thus, if your conversation takes place at a table in a cafeteria, you are aware of others talking, eating, or passing by your table. You may not take much notice of these other people, because you are focused on your conversation, but you are aware of them nevertheless.

Interactional meaning

Generally it is assumed that we can communicate best through our use of language. Language seems to have the most informative content, which can easily be employed without a need for other channels. We may speak on the phone, write emails, or go to chat-rooms. In each case, we use language, either spoken or written, to communicate.

But when thinking about TV or the Internet, it is clear that we also communicate through images. Often, viewing an image may carry more. We may even feel that the image has more "reality" to it than a written description of the same image would have. This realization questions the notion that the process of communicating is dependent upon language. Just as moving images or still photos can communicate meaning to the viewer, nonverbal channels such as gesture, posture, or the distance between people can—and do—carry meaning in any face-to-face interaction.

All movements, all noises, and all material objects carry interactional meaning as soon as they are perceived by a person. Previously, language has been viewed as constituting the central channel in interaction, and nonverbal channels have been viewed as being subordinated to it. While much valuable work on the interplay between the verbal and nonverbal has been established, I believe that the view which unquestionably positions language at the center limits our understanding of the complexity of interaction.

Therefore, I will step away from the notion that language always plays the central role in interaction, without denying that it often does. Language, as Kress et al. (2001) have noted, is only one mode among many, which may or may not take a central role at any given moment in an interaction. In this view, gesture, gaze, or head movement may be subordinated to the verbal exchanges going on as has been shown in much research.

However, gesture, gaze, and head movement also may take the superior position in a given interaction, while language may be subordinated or absent altogether. Alternatively, sometimes many communicative channels play an integral part in a given interaction, without one channel being more important than another.

While we all intuitively know that people in interaction draw on a multiplicity of communicative modes, and that people in interaction are aware of much more than just what they are focused upon, an analysis of such multimodal interaction brings with it many challenges.

Structure and materiality

One challenge for the analysis of multimodal interaction is that the different communicative modes of language, gesture, gaze, and material objects are structured in significantly different ways. While spoken language is sequentially structured, gesture is

Sigrid Norris

globally synthetically structured, which means that we can not simply add one gesture on to another gesture to make a more complex one. In language, we can add a prefix to a word, making the word more complex; or we can add subordinate clauses to a main clause, making the sentence more complex. With gestures, this is not possible, since gestures that are linked to language inform about global content or intensity. Gaze, however, may be sequentially structured, and during conversation it often is. But, during other interactions, gaze can be quite random. For example, when you walk through the woods with a friend, your gaze may wander randomly, focusing on a tree, a rock, or nothing at all. Then there are other communicative modes, which are structured even more differently.

As we will see, furniture is a mode, and when thinking about it, we find a functional structure. Chairs are usually located around a table, or a reading lamp is located next to an easy chair. Thus, different modes of communication are structured in very different ways.

Another challenge for the analysis of multimodal interaction is the fact that different communicative modes possess different materiality. For example, spoken language is neither visible nor enduring, but it does have audible materiality. Gesture, however, has visible materiality but is also quite fleeting. The mode of print has more visible materiality and is also enduring; and the mode of layout, thinking about furniture, for example, has highly visible materiality and is extensively enduring.

*****

Heuristic units

The first step to a multimodal analysis of interaction is a basic understanding of an array of communicative modes. modes such as proxemics, posture, head movement, gesture, gaze, spoken language, layout, print, music, to name several, are essentially systems of representation. A system of representation or mode of communication is a semiotic system with rules and regularities attached to it (Kress and Van Leeuwen, 2001). I like to call these systems of representation *communicative modes* when I emphasize their interactional communicative function.

A communicative mode is never a bounded or static unit, but always and only a *heuristic* unit. The term "heuristic" highlights the plainly explanatory function, and also accentuates the constant tension and contradiction between the system of representation and the real-time interaction among social actors. A system of representation—a writing system, for example—is usually thought of as a given system that exists in and by itself once it is developed.

While such a system changes over time, we can describe the system in the form of dictionaries and grammars, showing the rules and regularities that exist. Taking this thought further, we could describe systems of representation like gesture, gaze, layout, etc. in a similar way to a written language, by developing certain in dictionaries and grammars of these communicative modes.

Communicative modes in interaction

When observing an interaction and trying to discern all of the communicative modes that the individuals are utilizing, we soon notice that this is a rather overwhelming task.

Sigrid Norris

People move their bodies, hands, arms, and heads, and while the observer may try to understand the content of what is being spoken, they have already missed many important messages which each speaker is sending—intentionally or not—and the other speaker is reacting to through other modes. Yet, a multimodal interactional analysis is not as impossible as one may think. First, the analyst needs to become skilled at distinguishing one communicative mode from others. Then the analyst is ready to investigate how modes play together in interaction.

When working with real-time interaction, we discover that there is constant tension and contradiction between the system of representation and the event. Individuals in interaction draw on systems of representation while at the same time constructing, adopting, and changing those systems through their actions. In turn, all actions that individuals perform are mediated by the systems of representation that they draw on.

Unit of analysis

As I mentioned in the introduction, the differing structures and materiality of modes were challenges that needed to be overcome, as an integrative multimodal approach required a single unit of analysis that allowed for the communicative modes to be structurally and materially different. In multimodal interactional analysis, the mediated action is the unit of analysis, and since every action is mediated, I will simply speak of the action as the unit of analysis. The action as unit of analysis, however, is still a complicated issue, because there are smaller (lower-level) and larger (higher-level) actions. Take, for example, a person uttering the words "good morning." This is an intonation unit, the unit that discourse analysts rely on. But this intonation unit can also be defined as an action, and more specifically, as a lower-level action. Now, take a meeting among three friends, which can be called a conversation, a moment in time, or a social encounter. This meeting can also be called an action, however, and more specifically, a higher-level action. This use of action as a unit of analysis may seem confusing at first sight. However, let us think about the specific example of a meeting among three friends—to illustrate the usefulness of this unit of analysis. The meeting is taken to be the higher-level action. This higher-level action is bracketed by an opening and a closing of the meeting and is made up of a multiplicity of chained lower-level actions. All intonation units that an individual strings together become a chain of lower-level actions. All gesture units that an individual performs become a chain of lower-level actions. All postural shifts that an individual completes become a chain of lower-level actions. All gaze shifts that an individual performs become a chain of lower-level actions, and so on. Consequently, all higher-level actions are made up of multiple chains of lower-level actions.

The chains of lower-level actions are easily understood when talking about embodied communicative modes like gaze, gesture, or spoken language. But disembodied modes can play just as important a role in interaction as do the embodied modes.

Modes like print—a magazine that participants are reading or that is just lying on a table for anyone to see; or layout—the furniture in a room, pictures hung on a wall, or a busy street with signs, buildings, and walkways, are disembodied modes. These modes can also be analyzed by using the unit of analysis, the (mediated) action. However, here the unit of analysis is the frozen action. Frozen actions

Sigrid Norris

are usually higher-level actions which were performed by an individual or a group of people at an earlier time than the real-time moment of the interaction that is being analyzed.

These actions are frozen in the material objects themselves and are therefore evident. When we see a magazine lying on a table, we know that somebody has purchased the magazine and placed it on the table. Thus, the chains of lower-level actions that somebody had to perform in order for the magazine to be present on the table are perceptible by the mere presence of the magazine itself. The same is true for furniture, pictures on walls, houses in cities, or a CD playing. Material objects or disembodied modes, which we are concerned with here because individuals draw upon them in interaction, necessarily entail higher-level actions (which are made up of chained lower-level actions).

We can think of lower-level actions as the actions that are fluidly performed by an individual in interaction. Each lower-level action is mediated by a system of representation (which includes body parts such as the lips, etc. for spoken language; or hands, arms, and fingers for manual gestures). Higher-level actions develop from a sum of fluidly performed chains of lower-level actions, so that the higher-level actions are also fluid and develop in real-time. Every higher-level action is bracketed by social openings and closings that are at least in part ritualized. When the three friends get together for their meeting, the higher-level action of that meeting is opened up by the physical coming together or the friends and by ritualized greetings. Similarly, this overarching higher-level action will be ended by ritualized greetings and a parting of the individuals. Embedded within such a higher-level action, we find other higher-level actions such as a conversation between two or three members, or another conversation among all three of them. Besides conversations, we may also find higher-level actions which develop from a sum of other lower-level actions in which there is little or no talk involved, like the higher-level action of consuming food and/or drink.

While lower-level and higher-level actions are fluidly constructed in interaction, frozen actions are higher-level actions, which are entailed in an object or a disembodied mode. To understand this concept, we can think about ice. Similarly to the freezing of water, actions are frozen in the material objects present in interaction.

Issues to consider

❑ Norris talks about how the materiality of a mode affects the way it structures meaning and action. What implications does this have when people wish to 'translate' meanings from one mode to another? Can you give some examples?

❑ 'A communicative mode,' says Norris, 'is never a bounded or static unit, but always and only a *heuristic* unit.' What does she mean by this? What are the advantages of keeping the concept of 'communicative mode' flexible and contingent?

FINDING 'DISCOURSES' WITH CORPUS-ASSISTED ANALYSIS

The following excerpt is from a study by Paul Baker and Tony McEnery on the portrayal of refugees in British newspapers and texts from the Office of the United Nations High Commission on Refugees. The excerpt included here deals only with the newspaper texts, which the authors demonstrate portray refugees as packages, invaders and pests. Baker and McEnery make the argument in this article that lexical choice plays an important role in the construction of 'Discourses' and the expression of ideology.

A corpus-based approach to discourses of refugees and asylum seekers in UN and newspaper texts

Paul Baker and Tony McEnery (reprinted from *Journal of Language and Politics* 4(2), 2005, pp. 197–226)

Paul Baker
and Tony
McEnery

Discourses

A discourse can be conceptualised as a "system of statements which constructs an object" (Parker 1992: 5). Discourse is further categorised by Burr (1995: 48) as:

> a set of meanings, metaphors, representations, images, stories, statements and so on that in some way together produce a particular version of events . . . Surrounding any one object, event, person etc., there may be a variety of different discourses, each with a different story to tell about the world, a different way of representing it to the world.

Discourses are not valid descriptions of people's 'beliefs' or 'opinions', and they cannot be taken as representing an inner, essential aspect of identity such as personality or attitude. Instead, they are connected to practices and structures that are lived out in society from day to day.

One way that researchers can be confident in their claims about the existence of discourses is to highlight "patterns of association—how lexical items tend to co-occur—are built up over large amounts of text and are often unavailable to intuition or conscious awareness. They can convey messages implicitly and even be at odds with an overt statement." (Hunston 2002: 109). In order to explore how refugees are constructed in news discourse we chose to build and use corpora of news texts.

Data and method

The British newspaper texts (referred to hereafter as the News Corpus) were collected from an internet archive called Newsbank, the criteria for selecting news articles being that the article had to contain the words *refugee(s)* or the phrases *asylum seeker(s)* and had to have been published in 2003.

D10

Paul Baker
and Tony
McEnery

Results

Concordances (tables showing all of the examples of a search term in the context that it appears in) of the words *refugee* (53 occurrences) and *refugees* (87) were carried out on the 76,205 word News Corpus. In addition, concordance searches of the words *they* and *them* uncovered anaphoric references to refugees which were also included in the analysis. In order to uncover linguistic patterns surrounding the search words, the concordances were sorted alphabetically using the words directly to the left and right of the search terms, and the descriptive clauses and phrases which were used to refer to the target words were then grouped into categories of similarity.

Table D10.1 Size of corpora and frequency of target words

	News texts
Size of corpus (words)	76,205 refugee(s)
	62,299 asylum seeker(s)
refugee	53
refugees	87
asylum seeker	10
asylum seekers	131

Quantification

An initial analysis reveals that refugees are commonly described in terms of where they are from (e.g. Sierra Leone, Bangladesh, Afghanistan, Iran, Kosovo, Algeria etc.), where they currently are (France, Sangatte, the Belgian border etc.) or where they are going. A smaller set of terms describe refugees in terms of the circumstances which created them, although these words are vague (*economic, political, war, wartime*).

One of the other most common ways of describing refugees in the News Corpus is by providing a pre-modifying quantification (Table D10.2). This is often given as a rough estimate by reporters—e.g. *tens of thousands* or *up to 100 refugees*. Sometimes numbers are described as growing: *more and more refugees*.

In some cases, these types of quantification suggest that the volume of refugees is troublesome. In the example below, the reference to the large number (*a mob, up to 100*) of refugees in the article serves to enhance their danger.

> "BRITISH journalist Robert Fisk was attacked and beaten up by a mob of Afghan refugees in Pakistan yesterday . . . He suffered head, face and hand injuries after being pelted with stones by up to 100 refugees."

Many of the attempts to quantify refugees suggest an underlying discourse concerning alarm over their growing numbers.

D10

Table D10.2 Quantification of refugees in News Corpus

Paul Baker and Tony McEnery

Pakistan hosts 3m	refugees	and Iran 2.5m, while a further 1.5m a
She was concerned for the thousands of Afghan	refugees	and she wanted to spotlight their terr
Tens of thousands of Afghan	refugees	are streaming home in the vanguard o
– 50,000 dead and more than 300,000 internal	refugees	because of Pakistan-sponsored te
Now a fascinating documentary has traced five	refugees	children who were rescued from p
in Afghanistan, which is swelling the number of	refugees	daily, and tightened security by ferry
ill be more grieving widows and children, more	refugees	fleeing in terror and dying in agony.
Our coverage of the deaths of eight	refugees	found in a container near Wexford
Four million	refugees	have fled in a quarter of a century of
terror network rages, two Afghan	refugees	in northern Iran seek solace in the scr
was attacked and beaten up by a mob of Afghan	refugees	in Pakistan yesterday.
EIGHT	refugees	, including two children, were found
"And the tragedy of 22 million	refugees	is another deep wound in our world –
juries after being pelted with stones by up to 100	refugees	. Last night Fisk was recovering in ho
TV and video equipment to help Sighthill's 1,200	refugees	learn English.
shawar, home to 300,000 Afghan	refugees	. On the ground floor two gynaeco
months before the bulk of the Shomali's 200,000	refugees	return: "The major obstacle is the pre
Eight	Refugee	Stowaways Die in Lorry
in March after 19 Kurdish	refugees	were found in the back of his lorry.
end to the problem is in sight as more and more	refugees	are delivered to northern France by t

"Mr Endres said Kabul risked straining under the weight of refugees in transit."

"The camp . . . is currently filled far beyond capacity. Because of the upheaval in Afghanistan, which is swelling the number of refugees daily . . ."

In the first example, refugees are likened to a dangerous mass or heavy load (note the use of the words *straining* and *weight*) while in the second, refugees are constructed as liquid (*filled beyond capacity, swelling*). Such a feature may not be peculiar to British newspaper texts; Reisigl and Wodak (2001: 59) note that the description of immigrants and the effects of immigration in terms of negative metaphors is a common feature of German and Austrian discourses. They list nineteen different types of metaphors, including plants, fire, blood, disease and food. We look at some of the metaphors in the News and UNHCR Corpora in the following sections.

Movement

A set of words which describe refugees are concerned with their movement (Table D10.3), often using verb phrases which suggest a range of evaluative responses which construct refugees as victims or a collective group undergoing suffering: e.g. *fleeing refugees, refugees trudge aimlessly, hunched against a biting wind, roads heave with refugees*. As with the *filled far beyond capacity* example noted earlier, a number of movement metaphors liken refugees to water in some way: *swelling the numbers of refugees, the flood of refugees, refugees are streaming home, refugees are streaming back to their homes, overflowing refugee camps*.

Streaming collocates (or significantly often co-occurs) in the BNC with the words *tears, blood, sweat, water* and *rain* and often occurs in a negative context, e.g. "tears streaming down his face". *Overflowing* collocates strongly in the BNC with *leaking* and *water*. *Swelling* (462 occurrences in the BNC) collocates most strongly with words

**Paul Baker
and Tony
McEnery**

Table D10.3 Movement of refugees in the News Corpus

and the Holy Family fleeing as	refugees	to Egypt. Jesus relives exodus and ex
I troubles of 1950, Shaw was engaged in carrying	refugees	from East Pakistan to Calcutta and t
They can also help to attract	refugees	back to their homes and thousands of
rgest oilfield, and provide a haven for	refugees	and defecting soldiers.
xt night the Taliban bombed Talin Chee, forcing	refugees	into another village and finally the ha
heated and broke down close to a village housing	refugees	who had fled across the border fro
which is swelling the number of	refugees	daily, and tightened security by ferry
and tinsel, desultory groups of	refugees	trudge aimlessly, hunched against a
alert to deal with the flood of	refugees	. Border residents also left their hom
h huge brightly painted trucks bearing returning	refugees	sitting on tottering piles of their pos
of Turkish gangsters who have been transporting	refugees	from Ankara and Istanbul via Zeebru
mbed a bridge and a tractor convoy packed with	refugees	. This time it is thought the Americ
nother day. The roads heave with	refugees	, the taxis are full and the drivers still
, the Holy Family was forced to take Him as a	refugee	to Egypt.
ed mullah had fled across the Pakistan border as a	refugee	in the company of his sen
N Pushtuns who were stranded in nearby	refugee	camps when the Taliban fled may be
starvation or disease in the overflowing	refugee	camps, then clearly the number of d
e problem is in sight as more and more	refugees	are delivered to northern France by
Tens of thousands of Afghan	refugees	are streaming back to their homes a
Tens of thousands of Afghan	refugees	are streaming home in the vanguard
hospital hit, or children crippled by landmines, or	refugees	driven from their homes by military
will be more grieving widows and children, more	refugees	fleeing in terror and dying in agony.
Four million	refugees	have fled in a quarter of a century of
n at Guantanamo Bay, where Cuban and Haitian	refugees	have previously been held, and is
	Refugees	. . . have returned to rubble
es said Kabul risked straining under the weight of	refugees	in transit.
ing a mercy mission to bring the young European	Refugees	into homes all over the country.
	Refugees	Return. Tens of thousands of Afgh
months before the bulk of the Shomali's 200,000	refugees	return: "The major obstacle is the
, and those shots of	refugees	smuggling themselves on to Eurost
s mother's necklace and trafficked in our wartime	refugees	. Yet women fell for him. On reflecti

which suggest medical contexts: e.g. *redness, bruising, pain, chest*. However, *swell* which occurs more often (566 times in the BNC) collocates with words connected to water: *waves, Atlantic, ocean, sea, water*. The phrase *flood of* collocates most strongly with *refugees* in the BNC, with *tears* and *immigrants* occurring second and third respectively. Again, *flood* is connected to water and to tragedy.

In a sense then, refugees are constructed as a 'natural disaster' like a flood, which is difficult to control as it has no sense of its own agency. Again, this is not peculiar to British newspaper texts; similar water metaphors were also found by Refaie (2001) in an analysis of Austrian newspaper articles about Kurdish asylum seekers in Italy.

Phrases such as "trudge aimlessly" help to construct refugees as having no real understanding of their situation or what motivates them. Consider the phrase "desultory groups of refugees" (Table D10.3, line 8). *Desultory* is a fairly rare word in general British English, occurring only 103 times in the BNC, and only collocating with two lexical words, *fashion* and *conversation*. Again, the word implies lack of motivation or pattern: e.g. "Because the session is informal it is liable to fragment into a desultory conversation with no clear direction."

The movement of refugees is constructed as an elemental force which is difficult to predict and has no sense of control. If refugees are likened to the movement of water, then they are dehumanised and become something that requires control in order to prevent disaster to others (e.g. non-refugees).

Paul Baker and Tony McEnery

As well as describing the movement of refugees as being almost random, a number of phrases focus on movement in terms of large quantities: e.g. *roads heave with refugees, packed with refugees*. The word *packed* collocates with words suggesting quantity or places containing large numbers of people in the BNC—*tightly, densely, closely, tight, crowd, courtroom, cinemas*, while the verb lemma *heave* collocates with words which suggest weight—*bulk, broad, deep, great* as well as the expression of emotional burdens, e.g. "Uncle Walter heaved a sigh and slumped back in the chair, his hand covering his eyes" (example taken from the BNC).

Closely related to the notion of packed refugees are another set of movement descriptors connected to refugees, associated with the transportation of objects and goods. Refugees are *delivered, transported, carried, trafficked* and *smuggled*.

> "For the locals, no end to the problem is in sight as more and more refugees are delivered to northern France by traffickers."

The highest collocate of deliver in the BNC is *goods*. *Goods* also occurs as a strong collocate of *transport*, along with *cattle, supplies* and *materials*. *Carry* occurs much more frequently and has a wider range of collocates, many of which are object-based nouns: *placards, firearms, suitcases, torches*. Finally, *smuggle* collocates most strongly with the following lexical words: *cocaine, heroin, drugs, drug* and *arms* while *traffic* collocates with *narcotics, drugs* and *arms*.

Therefore, as well as being described as an elemental force that cannot be reasoned with (water), refugees are also constructed in terms of metaphors and connotational verbs which construct them as transported goods, particularly illegal substances—again, as a token of their dehumanisation.

Tragedy

Another discourse of refugees is to construct them as 'tragic' (see Table D10.4). This involves using phrases such as the *plight of, despair of* and *tragedy of. Plight* collocates in the BNC with groups such as *homeless, refugees, blacks, women, unemployed* and *children*—all identities that could be constructed as powerless in different ways. However, three of the four strongest collocates of *plight* in the BNC are *highlighting, highlight* and *highlighted*, in sentences such as "It is 10 days since our shock issue highlighting the plight of the starving in Somalia." *Plight* is therefore often connected to attempts to heighten awareness about a group which is oppressed or unfortunate in some way.

Other words which suggest tragedy in connection with the refugee data are *scrounge, beg, tedious, tottering, solace* and *stricken*. Refugees are reported as starving, dying while locked in containers, seeking solace in religion, queuing for food and being attacked by soldiers.

Official attempts to help

Related to the presentation of refugees as tragic victims is another set of collocates which are more concerned with external efforts to help them (Table D10.5). These

**Paul Baker
and Tony
McEnery**

Table D10.4 Tragic circumstances of refugees in the News Corpus

After seeing the plight of these	refugee	children, I could not do any
king undercover to report on the plight of Afghan	refugees	. But her f
"And the tragedy of 22 million	refugees	is another deep wound in our world–
s with; cultural vandalism and the despair of its	refugees	, reports Peter Foster in Bamiyan
wounded early today as Israeli tanks moved on a	refugee	camp in the Gaza Strip.
Israel fires on	refugee	camp
Israelis attacked the Rafah	refugee	camp – thought to be a stronghold of
For in the poverty-stricken Palestinian	refugee	camps of Lebanon, giving your life t
ghans, the ones who haven't made it to the	refugee	camps and have no relatives in
Cambodian refugees	refugees	continue to starve.
widows and children, more	refugees	fleeing in terror and dying in agony.
Our coverage of the deaths of eight	refugees	found in a container near Wexford
None of the	refugees	has enough calcium.
two Afghan	refugees	in northern Iran seek solace in the sc
EIGHT	refugees	. . . were found dead
huge brightly painted trucks bearing returning	refugees	on tottering piles of their possession
THE net is closing on the gang that sent eight	refugees	to their deaths in a lorry container, it
Unusually, the	refugees	were not advised to carry mobile tele
Eight	Refugee	Stowaways Die in Lorry
It's here you find	refugee	camps that have turned into shabby c
	"They	have so little medical assistance tha
e body, not spirit, that must take precedence as	they	scrounge for scrap metal and beg for
Instead	they	live a tedious routine, queuing up to
Not only were	they	hungry, they were freezing.
inquests into the deaths of the eight recorded that	they	died at sea between Belgium and Ir

Table D10.5 Official attempts to help in the News Corpus

helped the UNHCR return	refugees	in East Timor;
Margaret Curran welcomes new funding to help	refugees	integrate into society.
Last week we looked at	Refugee	Action. Here, Belinda Beresford in
id expansion was straining resources, said the UN	refugee	agency.
Now a fascinating documentary has traced five	refugee	children who were rescued from
, who is chief executive of the Northern England	Refugee	Service, said: "If she went into Afg
Bob Dylan and Eric Clapton performed in aid of	refugees	of Bangladesh in 1971.
"She was concerned for the thousands of Afghan	refugees	and she wanted
ing a mercy mission to bring the young European	refugees	into homes all over the coun
On the first floor is the school for	refugees	and orphans.
tywest will be turned into a reception centre for	refugees	and the homeless.
hildren in India and humanitarian assistance for	refugees	in Afghanistan.
hief of mission of the UN high commissioner for	Refugees	. Agencies are racing to provide bla
agreements with the UN High Commissioner for	Refugees	on the role of the peacekeeping forc
He was filming for Comic Relief in a	refugee	camp.
the French close the Red Cross	refugee	camp at Sangatte. However, they op
into the love which feeds the hungry, shelters the	refugee	, and confronts violence and power

involve phrases such as *refugee action, refugee service, refugee agency*, describe official bodies involved in running organisations, and discuss attempts to enable refugees to 'integrate into society', particularly by learning the language of their host country or by going to school. The grammatical pattern *X for refugees* is a relatively common example of this 'helping' discourse trace. In addition, terms such as *shelter, help, concern, mercy* and *rescue* contribute to the construction of this discourse.

Crime and nuisance

Paul Baker and Tony McEnery

However, a less common discourse constructs refugees as being connected to crime and as a nuisance (Table D10.6). In this case, their presence 'pushes down' house prices or causes a steep rise in petty crime. Such fears invoke a more general discourse of capitalism, whereby refugees are seen as a threat to the capitalist way of life by reducing the value of property. As one woman is reported as saying: "they are a pest". Refugee camps are also reported as hiding grounds for extremists or militants, and refugees are also involved in plans to enter countries illegally—e.g. "to storm the channel tunnel". The use of *storm* as a verb suggests attempts to conquer—common collocates of the verb lemma *storm* in the BNC include *troops, castle, victory* and *army*. In this sense, refugees are invaders.

A final, rare use of *refugee* in the News Corpus is more metaphorical, where it is used to describe people who look like someone or something else:

> "Coming on like some refugee from the Ricky Lake Show, burly Fred spent much of the programme successfully convincing Sandra that he thought the first marriage had been annulled, and moaning to the camera that he 'shouldn't be put in jail for falling in love'."

> "Owen may look like a refugee from a Hovis ad, but as Sven-Goran Eriksson said: 'He's very cold when he gets a chance and he's very quick.'"

> "Last week I watched some do-it-yourself programme where a couple of refugee presenters from the makeover toolbox showed you how to have a kitsch Christmas."

These three cases are not from newspaper articles which are concerned with actual refugees. Instead, the phrase (*like*) [determiner] *refugee from* . . . is used to allude to a person's similarity to something else. However, this is a construction which contains an implicitly negative evaluation—the fact that such people are described as refugees at all accesses an existing negative discourse of actual refugees, but it also implies that they are not viewed as possessing the identity they are supposed to have, possibly because they weren't competent at it, or because they look as if they should be

Table D10.6 Crime and nuisance in the News Corpus

Newsman Fisk stoned by Afghan	refugees	
uries after being pelted with stones by up to 100	refugees	
ufacture the explosive in laboratories hidden in	refugee	camps. Mr Reid is said to have
an unknown number of Somali and Djibouti	refugees	have been arrested in the past week.
There have been complaints the	refugees	have caused a steep rise in petty crime and pushed down house prices
Four of the	refugees	who led the Chunnel charge were jailed for four months
Palestinians in the Gaza and West Bank	refugee	camps resent their lavish lives.
Israelis attacked the Rafah	refugee	camp – thought to be a stronghold of militants
ushtuns who were stranded in nearby	refugee	camps when the Taliban fled may be hiding arms and plotting revenge.
A RED CROSS boss kept secret a	refugee	plot to storm the Channel Tunnel
e in petty crime and pushed down house prices.	"They	are a pest," says a woman in th

**Paul Baker
and Tony
McEnery**

something else. So Michael Owen (in the second example) is viewed not so much as a footballer, but a "refugee from a Hovis ad(vert)". Finally, the identity they are supposed to resemble is constructed negatively—so the phrase implies that the person isn't even competent to perform a stigmatised identity properly, and instead is a refugee from it.

Conclusion

The News Corpus is (particularly) concerned with the impact of refugees on the UK rather than taking a global perspective. Attitudes are presented in (an) ambivalent and complex way, with refugees constructed as tragic victims, an out-of-control mass, pests or potential invaders. Metaphors of water or packages serve to dehumanise refugees further. The News Corpus also refers to official attempts to help refugees, but this is simply one discourse type among many which are present. The fact that the term *refugee* is used in metaphorical constructions "like some refugee from the Ricky Lake Show", reveals the negative connotation embedded within the word. . . .

Many of the linguistic strategies used to refer to refugees and asylum seekers—such as referring to them as an indistinguishable mass or vague quantity, using metaphors, describing them as bogus or referring to unspecified 'fears'—serve several purposes which are linked to the notion of racist discourse. As van Dijk (1987: 58) describes, there are four topic classes for racist discourses: they are different, they do not adapt, they are involved in negative acts and they threaten our socio-economic interests. Hardt-Mautner (1995:179) points out, "National identity emerges very much as a relational concept, the construction of 'self' being heavily dependent on the construction of 'other'". The racist constructions of refugees and asylum seekers, therefore, not only construct a threat to the status quo and national identity (which incidentally helps to sell newspapers), they also help to construct national identity by articulating what it is not.

However, more encouraging aspects of the corpus data suggest a less prejudiced picture than earlier researchers have found when looking at newspaper data. Stereotypes of refugees as criminal nuisances and constructions of asylum seekers as 'bogus' were still present in the corpora, yet they were relatively rare. Discourses which focused on the problems encountered by refugees and asylum seekers and/or attempts to help them were relatively more common, suggesting that in 2003 at least, there was a growing awareness of the need for sensitivity when discussing issues connected to immigration in the UK. As Law et al. (1997: 18) found in a recent study, about three quarters of news articles concerned with race contained media frames

> "which seek to expose and criticise racist attitudes, statements, actions and policies, which address the concerns of immigrant and minority ethnic groups and show their contribution to British society, and which embrace an inclusive view of multi-cultural British identity".

A study by Jessika ter Wal concluded that "the British tabloid press no longer seem to merit the overly racist tag that they were given by studies in the early 1980s." (2002: 407).

A corpus-based approach is therefore useful, in that it helps to give a wider view of the range of possible ways of discussing refugees and asylum seekers. A more

Paul Baker
and Tony
McEnery

qualitative approach to analysis may mean that saliency is perceived as more important than frequency—whereby texts which present shocking or extreme positions are focussed on more than those which are more frequent, yet neutral. While it is important to examine extreme cases, it is also useful to put them into perspective alongside other cases. In addition, corpus data can help us to establish which sorts of language strategies are most frequent or popular. For example, the refugees as water metaphor was found to be much more frequent than other metaphors, such as refugees as illegal packages or as invaders. Rather than simply listing the metaphors which appear in the data then, we are able to get a more accurate sense of which ones are naturalised, and which ones may be particularly salient *because* they are so infrequent.

In addition, the corpus-based approach enables the researcher to arrive at a more complete understanding of the meanings and functions of certain word choices in texts about refugees and asylum seekers. The connotative use of language in critical discourse analysis is one of the most fruitful areas of analysis available to researchers—and by looking at the collocational strength of lexical items in a corpus of general language, we are given an objective sense of the themes and associations that are embedded in words due to their continual pairing with other words. By 'exposing' the hidden collocations of certain words, we can explain that a certain word or phrase contains a hint of bias, but have not been able to specify why.

Issues to consider
❏ Baker and McEnery show how the cumulative patterning of lexical features in a corpus of texts can be used to posit the existence of a particular 'Discourse'. Can you think of features other than lexical choice that might also contribute to the construction of 'Discourses'? How might corpus analysis assist in detecting these features?
❏ Baker and McEnery combine a number of different analytical techniques, both qualitative and quantitative, in their analysis. How does this combination of techniques help to make their analysis more convincing?

FURTHER READING

Strand 1: What is discourse?

There are many good overviews of discourse analysis including Brown and Yule (1983), Carter (1997), Paltridge (2006) and Widdowson (2007). Good edited collections are Schiffrin *et al.* (2004) and Hyland and Paltridge (2011). Bhatia *et al.* (2007) focus on more recent developments in the field. Jaworski and Coupland (2006) is a fine compilation of key readings. For an elaboration of the three approaches to discourse, see Schiffrin (1994). For more on 'capital D Discourses', see Gee (2010).

Strand 2: Texts and texture

For a thorough treatment of cohesion and other aspects of texture, see Martin (1992). Stoddard (1991) is also a good introduction. Eggins (1994) provides a more general overview of systemic functional linguistics. A classic compilation of papers on coherence in discourse is Tannen (1984). Another important work on the structure and comprehension of narrative are Labov and Waletzky (1967) and Kintsch (1977). Carrell (1984) discusses the effects of schema on second language readers. Van Dijk and Kintsch (1983) provide another perspective on discourse coherence. Liu and O'Halloran (2009) discuss cohesion from a multimodal perspective.

Strand 3: Texts and their social functions

Apart from Bhatia (1993) and Swales (1990), Berkenkotter and Huckin (1995) is a good introduction to genre analysis. Johns (1997) and Swales (2004) focus more on academic genres. Bhatia (2004) gives a more up-to-date treatment of the field of genre analysis. See Christie and Martin (1997) for a systemic functional view of genre. Bateman (2008) takes a multimodal approach to genre analysis. Besides Blood (2000), Herring *et al.* (2004) is a good analysis of the genre of the weblog.

Strand 4: Discourse and ideology

The Routledge English Language Introduction which focuses most on discourse and ideology is Simpson and Mayr (2009) *Language and Power: A resource book for students*. A Routledge English Language Introduction which offers more information on aspects of grammar covered in this strand is Jackson (2002) *Grammar and Vocabulary: A resource book for students.* Hodge and Kress (1988) and Fairclough (1992) are classic works in the critical analysis of discourse. Good collections of papers on critical discourse analysis are Fairclough (1995) and Wodak and Meyer (2001). Fairclough (2003) gives an excellent practical introduction to the critical analysis of texts, and van Leeuwen (2008) provides a more practice-based approach to critical discourse analysis.

Strand 5: Spoken discourse

The Routledge English Language Introduction which focuses most on spoken discourse is Cutting (2007) *Pragmatics and Discourse: A resource book for students.* Coulthard (1992) is a classic edited collection on the analysis of spoken language. Austin's speech act theory was further developed by Searle (1966). Good introductions to pragmatics include Mey (2001) and Verschueren (1999), and good introductions to conversation analysis include Hutchby and Wooffitt (2008), Schegloff (2007), and ten Have (2007). The lectures of Harvey Sacks are collected in Sacks (1992). Drew and Heritage (1993) deals with talk in institutional settings.

Strand 6: Strategic interaction

The classic work on face strategies is Brown and Levinson (1987). A more recent book on face and politeness is Watts (2003). For more information on framing in interaction see Tannen (1993). Tannen (2005) is a good overview of conversational strategies. An excellent collection on discourse and identity from an interactional sociolinguistic perspective is De Fina *et al.* (2006). A collection dealing with speech styles and social languages is Auer (2007). For another approach to conversational strategies, see the work of Harré and van Langenhove (1999) on positioning theory. For studies on conversational strategies in computer-mediated communication, see Morand and Ocker (2003), Losh (2008) and Talamo and Ligorio (2001).

Strand 7: Context, culture and communication

Duranti and Goodwin's (1992) edited collection provides multiple perspectives on the problem of context. van Dijk (2008) examines context from a sociocognitive perspective. A very accessible introduction to culture and conversation is Agar (1994). Bauman and Sherzer (1989) presents an overview of the principles and practices associated with the ethnography of communication, and Philipsen (1975) is a good example of an application of this method. For more information on ethnographic research methods see Agar (1996) and Hammersley and Atkinson (1995).

Strand 8: Mediated discourse analysis

Wertsch (1993) provides a good introduction to the socio-cultural theory on which mediated discourse analysis is based. The seminal texts on mediated discourse analysis and nexus analysis are Scollon (2001) and Scollon and Scollon (2004). Norris and Jones (2005) is a collection which shows the wide range of contexts to which mediated discourse analysis can be applied. It also contains a clear explanation of the principles and terminology used in MDA. An alternative approach to the analysis of computer-mediated discourse can be found in Herring (2001).

Strand 9: Multimodal discourse analysis

Kress and van Leeuwen (2001) is a good theoretical introduction to multimodal discourse analysis. O'Halloran (2004) and Royce and Bowcher (2006) are good collections of studies from a systemic functional perspective. The papers in Jewitt (2009) present a more varied range of perspectives. Machin (2007) takes a critical approach to multimodality, and Forceville and Urios-Aparisi (2009) present an approach informed by cognitive linguistics. For more information on the transcription of multimodal data, see Baldry and Thibault (2005) and Norris (2004).

Strand 10: Corpus-assisted discourse analysis

The Routledge resource book which focuses on corpus-based analysis is McEnery and Xiao (2006) *Corpus-based Language Studies: An advanced resource book*. Stubbs (1996) is a well-known introductory text for corpus-based linguistics. Other good introductions are Biber *et al.* (1998) and Hunston (2002). Baker (2006) provides a clear overview of using corpora in discourse analysis. A classic application of corpus-based methods to critical discourse analysis is Orpin (2005).

REFERENCES

Agar, M.H. (1994). *Language shock: Understanding the culture of conversation.* New York: William Morrow. (Further reading)

Agar, M. (1996). *The professional stranger: An informal introduction to ethnography,* 2nd edition. New York: Academic Press. (Further reading)

Auer, P. (ed.) (2007). *Style and social identities: Alternative approaches to linguistic heterogeneity.* Berlin: Mouton de Gruyter. (Further reading)

Austin, J.L. (1976). *How to do things with words,* 2nd edition. (J.O. Urmson and M. Sbisa, eds) Oxford: Oxford University Press. (B1, B5, D5)

Baker, P. (2005). *Public discourses of gay men.* London: Routledge. (A10)

Baker, P. (2006). *Using corpora in discourse analysis.* London: Continuum. (A10, B10 Further reading)

Baker, P. and McEnery, T. (2005). A corpus-based approach to discourses of refugees and asylum seekers in UN and newspaper texts. *Journal of Language and Politics* 4(2), 197–226. (D10)

Bakhtin, M. (1981). *The dialogic imagination.* (C. Emerson and M. Holquist, eds, and V.W. McGee, Trans.) Austin, TX: University of Texas Press. (A4, D4)

Bakhtin, M. (1986). *Speech genres and other late essays.* (C. Emerson and M. Holquist, eds, and V. W. McGee, Trans.) Austin, TX: University of Texas Press. (D4)

Baldry, A. and Thibault, P. (2005). *Multimodal transcription and text analysis.* Oakville, CT: Equinox. (Further reading)

Barthes, R. (1967). *Elements of semiology.* London: Cape.

Barthes, R. (1977). *Image–music–text.* London: Fontana.

Basso, K. (1970). To give up on words: Silence in Western Apache culture. *Southwestern Journal of Anthropology* 26(3): 213–230. (B7)

Bateman, J. (2008). *Multimodality and genre: A foundation for the systematic analysis of multimodal documents.* Basingstoke: Palgrave Macmillan. (Further reading)

Bateson, G. (1972). *Steps to ecology of mind: Collected essays in anthropology, psychiatry, evolution, and epistemology.* Chicago: University of Chicago Press. (D8)

Bauman, R. and Sherzer, J. (1989). *Explorations in the ethnography of speaking.* 2nd edition. Cambridge: Cambridge University Press. (Further reading)

Berkenkotter, C. and Huckin, T.N. (1995). *Genre knowledge in disciplinary communication – cognition/culture/power.* New Jersey: Lawrence Erlbaum Associates. (D3)

Bhatia, V.K. (1993). *Analysing genre: Language use in professional settings.* London: Longman. (A3)

Bhatia, V.K. (1994). Generic integrity in professional discourse. In B-L. Gunnarsson, P. Linell and B. Nordberg (eds), *Text and talk in professional contexts.* ASLA: sskriftsrie 6, Uppsala, Sweden. (D3)

Bhatia, V.K. (1995). Genre-mixing and in professional communication: The case of 'private intentions' v. 'socially recognized purposes.' In P. Bruthiaux, T. Boswood and B. du Babcock (eds) *Explorations in English for professional communication.* Hong Kong: Department of English, City University of Hong Kong. (D3)

Bhatia, V.K. (1997). The power and politics of genre. *World Englishes, 16*(3), 359–371. (B3, D3)

Bhatia, V.K. (2004). *Worlds of written discourse: A genre based view.* London: Continuum. (Further reading)

Bhatia, V.K., Flowerdew, J. and Jones, R. (eds) (2007). *Advances in discourse studies.* London: Routledge. (Further reading)

Biber, D., Conrad, S. and Reppen, R. (1998). *Corpus linguistics: Investigating language structure and use.* Cambridge: Cambridge University Press. (Further reading)

Birch, D. (1989). *Language, literature and critical practice: Ways of analyzing texts.* London: Routledge. (D4)

Bizzell, P. (1987). Some uses of the concept of 'discourse community'. Paper presented at the Penn State Conference on Composition, July. (D3)

Bizzell, P. (1992). *Academic discourse and critical consciousness.* Pittsburgh, PA: University of Pittsburgh Press. (D3)

Blood, R. (2000, September 7). *Weblogs: A history and perspective.* Retrieved 22 February 2011, from Rebecca's Pocket: http://www.rebeccablood.net/essays/weblog_history.html (C3)

Brown, P. and Levinson, S. (1987). *Politeness: Some universals in language usage.* Cambridge: Cambridge University Press. (A6, Further reading)

Bourdieu, P. (1977). *Outline of a theory of practice.* Richard Nice, trans. Cambridge: Cambridge University Press.

Bourdieu, P. (1990). *Photography: A middle-brow art.* Cambridge: Polity Press.

Brown, G. and Yule, G. (1983). *Discourse analysis.* Cambridge: Cambridge University Press. (Further reading)

Burr, V. (1995). *An introduction to social constructionism.* London: Routledge. (D10)

Butler, J. (1990/2006). *Gender trouble: Feminism and the subversion of identity.* London: Routledge. (D5)

Byram, M. (1997). Teaching and assessing intercultural communicative competence. Clevedon, Avon: Multilingual Matters. (D7)

Carrell, P.L. (1984). The effects of rhetorical organization on ESL readers. *TESOL Quarterly, 18*(3), 441–469. (Further reading)

Carter, R. (1997) *Investigating English discourse.* London: Routledge. (Further reading)

China shuns U.S. mediation in its island dispute with Japan. (2010, November 10). Retrieved from http://articles.cnn.com/2010-11-03/world/china.japan.disputed. islands_1_island-dispute-diaoyu-islands-beijing-and-tokyo?_s=PM:WORLD (C4)

China: Trilateral talks merely US wishful thinking. (2010, November 2). Retrieved from http://www.chinadaily.com.cn/china/2010-11/02/content_11491199.htm (C4)

Chomsky, N. (1965). *Aspects of the theory of syntax.* Cambridge, MA: MIT Press. (D7)

Chouliaraki, L. and Fairclough, N. (1999). *Discourse in late modernity: Rethinking critical discourse analysis.* Edinburgh: Edinburgh University Press. (D8)

Christie, F. and Martin, J.R. (1997). *Genre and institutions: Social processes in the workplace and school.* London: Cassell. (Further reading)

Cohen, A.D., Olshtain, E. and Rosenstein, D.S. (1986). Advanced EFL apologies: What remains to be learned. *International Journal of the Sociology of Language, 62,* 52–74. (C5)

Coulthard, M. (ed.) (1992). *Advances in spoken discourse analysis.* London: Routledge. (Further reading)

Coupland, J. (1996). Dating advertisements: Discourses of the commodified self. *Discourse and Society 7*(2), 187–207. (B3)

Cutting, J. (2007). *Pragmatics and discourse: A resource book for students,* 2nd edition. Abingdon: Routledge. (Further reading)

Danet, B., Ruedenberg, L. and Rosenbaum-Tamari, Y. (1997). "Hmmm . . . Where's that smoke coming from?" Writing, play and performance on Internet Relay Chat. In S. Rafaeli, F. Sudweeks and M. McLaughlin (eds) *Network and netplay: Virtual groups on the Internet* (pp. 119–157). Cambridge, MA: AAAI/ MIT Press. (C6)

De Fina, A., Schiffrin, D. and Bamberg, M. (eds) (2006). *Discourse and identity.* Cambridge: Cambridge University Press. (Further reading)

Djonov, E. (2007). Website hierarchy and the interaction between content organization, webpage and navigation design: A systemic functional hypermedia discourse analysis perspective. *Information Design Journal 15*(2), 144–162. (A9)

Douglas, M. (1970). *Natural symbols: explorations in cosmology.* New York: Pantheon Books. (D7)

Drew, P. and Heritage, J. (1993). Talk at work: Interaction in institutional settings Cambridge: Cambridge University Press. (Further reading)

Dubrow, H. (1982). *Genre.* London: Methuen and Co. Ltd. (D3)

Duranti, A. (1988). Ethnography of speaking: Toward a linguistics of the praxis. In F.J. Newmeyer (ed.), *Language: The socio-cultural context* (pp. 210–228). Cambridge: Cambridge University Press. (D7)

Duranti, A. and Goodwin, C. (eds) (1992). *Rethinking context: Language as an interactive phenomenon.* Cambridge: Cambridge University Press. (Further reading)

Eggins, S. (1994). *An introduction to systemic functional linguistics.* London: Pinter Pub. (B2, Further reading)

Fairclough, N. (1992). *Discourse and social change.* London: Polity. (D3, D4, Further reading)

Fairclough, N. (1993). Critical discourse analysis and the marketization of public discourse: The universities. *Discourse and Society 4*(2), 133–168. (D3)

Fairclough, N. (ed.) (1995). *Critical discourse analysis: The critical study of language.* London; New York: Longman. (B1, Further reading)

Fairclough, N. (2003). *Analysing discourse: Textual analysis for social research.* London: Routledge. (Further reading)

Featherstone, M. (1991). *Consumer culture and postmodernism.* London: Sage. (D3)

Ferguson, C.A. (1985). Editor's introduction. Special language registers, Special issue of *Discourse Processes 8*: 391–394. (D6)

Fillmore, C. (1975). An alterntive to checklist theories of meaning. In C. Cogen, H. Thompson, K. Wistler and J. Wright (eds) *Proceedings of the first annual meeting of the Berkeley Linguistics Society* (pp. 123–131). Berkeley, CA: University of California Press. (D4)

Firth, J.R. (1957). *Papers in linguistics 1934–1951*. London: Oxford University Press. (A7, B10)

Forceville, C.J. and Urios-Aparisi, E. (eds) (2009). *Multimodal metaphor*. Berlin and New York: Mouton de Gruyter. (Further reading)

Foucault, M. (1972). *The archaeology of knowledge*. New York: Pantheon. (A4, B1)

Fowler, A. (1982). *Kinds of literature*. Oxford: Oxford University Press. (D3)

Gee, J.P. (1996). *Social linguistics and literacies: Ideology in discourses*. London; Bristol, PA: Taylor and Francis. (A4, B1, D4)

Gee, J.P. (2010). *Introduction to discourse analysis: Theory and method*, 3rd edition. London: Routledge. (D1, B2, B4 Further reading)

Geertz, C. (1973). *The interpretation of cultures*. New York: Basic Books. (D7)

Gershon, I. (2010). *The breakup 2.0: Disconnecting over new media*. Ithaca, NY: Cornell University Press. (C8)

Goffman, E. (1959). *The presentation of self in everyday life*. New York: Anchor Books. (A6)

Goffman, E. (1967). *Interaction ritual: Essays on face-to-face behavior*. Chicago: Aldine. (A6)

Goffman, E. (1974). *Frame analysis*. New York: Harper and Row. (A6, D6)

Goffman, E. (1981). *Forms of talk*. Philadelphia, PA: University of Pennsylvania Press. (D6)

Goodwin, C. (2000). Action and embodiment within situated human interaction. *Journal of Pragmatics, 32*, 1489–522. (Further reading)

Grice, H.P. (1975). Logic and conversation. In Cole, P. and Morgan, J. (eds) *Syntax and semantics*, Vol 3. New York: Academic Press. (B5)

Grice, H.P. (1991). *Studies in the way of words*. Cambridge, MA; London: Harvard University Press. (B1)

Gumperz, J.J. (1982a). *Discourse strategies*. Cambridge: Cambridge University Press. (B6)

Gumperz, J.J. (ed.) (1982b). *Language and social identity*. Cambridge: Cambridge University Press. (A6)

Gumperz, J.J. (1984). Communicative competence revisited. In D. Schiffrin (ed.), *Meaning, form, and use in context: Linguistic applications* (pp. 278–289). Washington, DC: Georgetown University Press. (D7)

Halliday, M.A.K. (1968). Notes on transitivity and theme in English. *Journal of Linguistics 4*(1): 179–215. (B2)

Halliday, M.A.K. (1976). The teacher taught the student English: An essay in Applied Linguistics. In P.A. Reich (ed.) *The Second LACUS Forum* (pp. 344–349). Columbia: Hornbeam Press. (D4)

Halliday, M.A.K. (1978). *Language as social semiotic: The social interpretation of language and meaning*. London: Edward Arnold. (A2, A7)

Halliday, M.A.K. (1994). *An introduction to functional grammar*. London: Edward Arnold. (B1, A2, A4)

Halliday, M.A.K. and Hasan, R. (1976). *Cohesion in English*. London: Longman. (B2, D1, D2)

Hammersley, M. and Atkinson, P. (1995). *Ethnography: Principles in practice*, 2nd edition. London: Routledge. (Further reading)

Hardt-Mautner, G. (1995). 'Only connect': Critical discourse analysis and corpus linguistics (Technical Papers vol. 6), Department of Linguistics, Lancaster University: UCREL. (A10)

Harré, R. and van Langenhove, L. (eds) (1999). *Positioning theory*. Oxford: Blackwell. (Further reading)

Harris, Z. (1952). Discourse analysis. *Language, 28*(1), 1–30. (D1)

Herring, S. (2001). Computer-mediated discourse. In D. Tannen, D. Schiffrin and H.E. Hamilton (eds) *Handbook of discourse analysis* (pp. 612–634). Oxford: Blackwell. (C6, Further reading)

Herring, S.C., Scheidt, L.A., Bonus, S. and Wright, E. (2004). Bridging the gap: A genre analysis of weblogs. *Proceedings of HICSS-37*. Los Alamitos: IEEE Press. (Further reading)

Hodge, R. and Kress, G. (1988). *Social semiotics*. Cambridge: Polity Press. (B4, Further reading)

Hoey, M. (1983). *On the surface of discourse*. London: Allen and Unwin. (B2)

Hofstadter, D. and the Fluid Analogies Research Group (1995). *Fluid concepts and creative analogies: Computer models for the fundamental mechanisms of thought*. New York: Basic Books. (D4)

Hogben, S. and Coupland, J. (2000). Egg seeks sperm. End of story . . .? Articulating gay parenting in small ads for reproductive partners. *Discourse and Society 11*(4), 459–485. (B3)

Holyoak, K.J. and Thagard, P. (1995). *Mental leaps: Analogy in creative thought*. Cambridge, MA: MIT Press. (D4)

Hudson, K. (1979). *The jargon of the professions*. London: The Macmillan Press Ltd. (D3)

Hunston, S. (2002). *Corpora in applied linguistics*. Cambridge: Cambridge University Press. (D10, Further reading)

Hutchby, I. and Wooffitt, R. (2008). *Conversation analysis*. Malden, MA: Polity Press. (Further reading)

Hyland, K. and Paltridge, B. (eds) (2011). *Continuum companion to discourse analysis*. London: Continuum. (Further reading)

Hymes, D. (1966). Two types of linguistic relativity. In W. Bright (ed.), *Sociolinguistics* (pp. 114–67). The Hague: Mouton. (D7)

Hymes, D. (1974). *Foundations in sociolinguistics: An ethnographic approach*. Philadelphia: University of Pennsylvania Press. (A7, D7)

Hymes, D. (1979). Sapir, competence, voices. In C.J. Fillmore, D. Kempler and W.S-Y Wang (eds) *Individual differences in language ability and language behavior* (pp. 33–45). New York: Academic Press. (D7)

Hymes, D. (1986). Models of the interaction of language and social life. In J.J. Gumperz and D. Hymes (eds) *Directions in sociolinguistics* (pp. 296–336). Oxford: Basil Blackwell. (D7)

Hymes, D. (1987). Communicative competence. In U. Ammon, N. Dittmar and K.J. Mattheier (eds) *Sociolinguistics: An international handbook of the science of language and society* (pp. 219–229). Berlin: Walter de Gruyter. (D7)

Hymes, D. (1993). Anthropological linguistics: A retrospective. *Anthropological Linguistics 35*, 9–14. (D7)

Iedema, R. (2001). Resemiotization. *Semiotica 137*(1/4): 23–39. (A9)

Jackson, H. (2002). *Grammar and vocabulary: A resource book for students.* Abingdon: Routledge. (Further reading)

Jakobson, R. (1990). *Roman Jakobson on language.* (L.R. Waugh and M. Halle, eds). Cambridge, MA: Harvard University Press. (B7)

Jaworski, A. and Coupland, N. (eds) (2006). *The discourse reader,* 2nd edition. London: Routledge. (Further reading)

Jewitt, C. (ed.) (2009). *Handbook of multimodal analysis.* London: Routledge. (Further reading)

Johns, A.M. (1997) *Text, role and context: Developing academic literacies.* Cambridge: Cambridge University Press. (Further reading)

Jones, R. (2000). Potato seeking rice: Language culture and identity in gay personal ads in Hong Kong. *International Journal of the Sociology of Language 143,* 33–61. (B3)

Jones, R. (2005). 'You show me yours, I'll show you mine': The negotiation of shifts from textual to visual modes in computer mediated interaction among gay men. *Visual Communication 4*(1): 69–92. (A9)

Jones, R. (2008). Rewriting the city: Discourses of Hong Kong skateboarders. *A paper presented at Sociolinguistics Symposium 17,* April 3–5, Amsterdam. (C7)

Jones, R. (2009a). Technology and sites of display. In C. Jewitt (ed.), *Handbook of multimodal analysis* (pp. 114–146). London: Routledge. (A3, A9, B3)

Jones, R. (2009b). Inter-activity: How new media can help us understand old media. In C. Rowe and E. Wyss (eds) *New media and linguistic change* (pp. 11–29). Cresskill, NJ: Hampton Press. (A9)

Jones, R. (2011). Sport and re/creation: What skateboarders can teach us about learning. *Sport, Education and Society 16*(5): 593–611.

Kendon, A. (1990). *Conducting interaction.* Cambridge: Cambridge University Press. (Further reading)

Kiesler, S. (1986). Thinking ahead: The hidden messages in computer networks. *Harvard Business Review 64:* 46–60. (C6)

Kim, Y.Y. (1991). Intercultural communicative competence: a systems-theoretic view. In S. Ting-Toomey and F. Korzenny (eds) *Cross-cultural interpersonal communication* (pp. 259–275). Newbury Park, CA: Sage. (D7)

Kintsch, W. (1977). On comprehending stories. In M. Just and P. Carpenter (eds) *Cognitive processes in comprehension.* Hillsdale, NJ: Lawrence Erlbaum Associates.

Kress, G. and van Leeuwen, T. (2001). *Multimodal discourse: The modes and media of contemporary communication.* London: Edward Arnold. (Further reading)

Kress, G. and van Leeuwen, T. (1996, 2006). *Reading images: The grammar of visual design,* 2nd edition, London and New York: Routledge. (A9, D9)

Kristeva, J. (1986). Word, dialogue and novel. In T. Moi (ed.) *The Kristeva reader.* Oxford: Basil Blackwell, 24–33. (D4)

Labov, W. (1972). *Sociolinguistic patterns.* Philadelphia, PA: University of Pennsylvania Press. (D1)

Labov, W. and Waletzky, J. (1967). Narrative analysis. In J. Helm (ed.) *Essays on the verbal and visual arts* (pp. 12–44). Seattle: University of Washington Press. (Further reading)

Ladegaard, H.J. (2011). 'Doing power' at work: Responding to male and female management styles in a global business corporation. *Journal of Pragmatics 43*, 4–19. (B6)

Lakoff, G. and Johnson, M. (1980). *Metaphors we live by*. Chicago: University of Chicago Press. (B9, D4)

Landow, G.P. (1992). *Hypertext: The convergence of contemporary critical theory and technology*. Baltimore, MD: Johns Hopkins University Press. (C6)

Law, I., Svennevig, M. and Morrison, D.E. (1997). Privilege and silence. 'Race' in the British news during the general election campaign, 1997. *Research report for the Commission for Racial Equality*. Leeds: University of Leeds Press. (D10)

Lin, A.M.Y. (1996). Bilingualism or linguistic segregation: Symbolic domination, resistance and code-switching in Hong Kong schools. *Linguistics and Education 8*(1), 49–84. (B6)

Liu, J. (2001). *Asian students' classroom communication patterns in U.S. universities: An emic perspective*. Westport, CT: Ablex. (D7)

Liu, Y. and O'Halloran, K.L. (2009). Intersemiotic texture: Analyzing cohesive devices between language and images, *Social Semiotics, 19*(4), 367–387. (Further reading)

Losh, E. (2008). In polite company: Rules of play in five Facebook games. *ACE '08 Proceedings of the 2008 International Conference on Advances in Computer Entertainment Technology*. Available online at https://eee.uci.edu/faculty/losh/LoshPoliteCompany.pdf (Further reading)

Machin, D. (2007). *Introduction to multimodal analysis*. London and New York: Hodder Arnold. (Further reading)

Malinowski, B. (1923). The problem of meaning in primitive languages. In C.K. Ogden and I.A. Richards (eds) *The meaning of meaning: A study of influence of language upon thought and of the science of symbolism* (pp. 296–336). New York: Harcourt, Brace and World. (A7)

Martin, J.R. (1985). Process and text: Two aspects of human semiosis. In J.D. Benson and W.S. Greaves (eds) *Systemic perspectives on discourse*, vol. 1. Norwood, NJ: Ablex. (A3, D3)

Martin, J.R. (1992). *English text: System and structure*. Amsterdam: John Benjamins. (Further reading)

McEnery, A. and Xiao, R. (2006). *Corpus-based language studies: An advanced resource book*. London: Routledge. (Further reading)

McLuhan, M. (1964/2001). *Understanding media: The extensions of man*. Cambridge, MA: MIT Press. (B8)

Mey, J.L. (2001). *Pragmatics: An introduction*, 2nd edition, Oxford: Wiley-Blackwell. (Further reading)

Milroy, L. (1987). *Language and social networks*, 2nd edition, Oxford: Basil Blackwell. (D7)

Morand, D.A. and Ocker, R.J. (2003). Politeness theory and computer-mediated communication: A sociolinguistic approach to analyzing relational messages,

Proceedings of the 36th Annual Hawaii International Conference on System Sciences (HICSS'03) – Track1 (p.17.2), January 06–09. (Further reading)

Murphey, T. (1992). The discourse of pop songs. *TESOL Quarterly 26*(4), 770–774. (C10)

Nanda, S. (2000). Arranging a marriage in India. In P.R. Devita (ed.) *Stumbling toward truth: Anthropologists at work*. Prospect Heights, IL: Waveland Press. (B3)

Nishida, K. (1958). *Intelligibility and the philosophy of nothingness*. Tokyo: Maruzen Co. Ltd.

Norris, S. (2004). *Analyzing multimodal interaction: A methodological framework*. London: Routledge. (A9, D9, Further reading)

Norris, S. and Jones, R.H. (eds) (2005). *Discourse in action: Introducing mediated discourse analysis*. London: Routledge. (Further reading)

O'Halloran, K. (ed.) (2004). *Multimodal discourse analysis: Systemic functional perspectives*. New York and London: Continuum. (Further reading)

O'Halloran, K. (2005). *Mathematical discourse: Language, symbolism and visual images*. London: Continuum. (A9)

Oldenberg, A. (2010). Lady Gaga explains her VMA raw meat dress. *USA Today*, 13 September 2010. Retrieved 12 March 2011 from: http://content.usatoday.com/communities/entertainment/post/2010/09/lady-gaga-explains-her-vma-raw-meat-dress/1?csp=hfn (B2)

Orpin, D. (2005). Corpus linguistics and critical discourse analysis: Examining the ideology of sleaze. *International Journal of Corpus Linguistics 10*, 37–61. (Further reading)

Ortega y Gasset, J. (1959). The difficulty of reading. *Diogenes 28*, 1–17. (D6)

O'Toole, M. (1994). *The language of displayed art*. London: Leicester University. (A9)

Owen, M. (1983). *Apologies and remedial interchanges: Study of language use in social interaction*. Berlin: Mouton Publishers. (C5)

Paltridge, B. (2006). *Discourse analysis: An introduction*. London, New York: Continuum. (Further reading)

Parker, I. (1992). *Discourse dynamics: Critical analysis for social and individual psychology*. London: Routledge. (D10)

People for the Ethical Treatment of Animals (2010). The PETA Files, Lady Gaga's meat dress, 13 September 2010. Retrieved 31 March 2011 from: http://www.peta.org/b/thepetafiles/archive/2010/09/13/Lady-Gagas-Meat-Dress.aspx (C2)

Philips, S.U. (1983). An ethnographic approach to bilingual language proficiency assessment. In C. Rivera (ed.) *An ethnographic/sociolinguistic approach to language proficiency assessment* (pp. 88–106). Clevedon, Avon: Multilingual Matters. (D7)

Philipsen, G. (1975). Speaking 'like a man' in Teamsterville: Culture patterns of role enactment in an urban neighborhood, *Quarterly Journal of Speech 61*, 13–22. (Further reading)

Press Trust of India (2010). Lady Gaga's 'meat dress' voted most iconic outfit. *The Times of India* 19 December 2010. Retrieved 31 March 2011 from: http://articles.timesofindia.indiatimes.com/2010-12-19/uk/28252870_1_meat-dress-outfit-lady-gaga (C2)

Propp, V. (1986). *Morphology of the folktale*. (L. Scott, Trans.) Austin, TX: University of Texas Press. (B1)

Quinn, N. and Holland, D. (1987). Culture and cognition. In D. Holland and N. Quinn (eds) *Cultural models in language and thought* (pp. 3–40). Cambridge: Cambridge University Press. (D4)

Reddy, M. (1979). The conduit metaphor – a case of conflict in our language about language. In A. Ortony (ed.) *Metaphor and thought* (pp. 384–324). Cambridge: Cambridge University Press. (D4)

Refaie, E. (2001). Metaphors we discriminate by: Naturalized themes in Austrian newspaper articles about asylum seekers. *Journal of Sociolinguistics 5*(3), 352–371. (D10)

Reisigl, M. and Wodak, R. (2001). *Discourse and discrimination: Rhetorics of racism and anti-Semitism*. London: Routledge. (D10)

Rey, J.M. (2001). Changing gender roles in popular culture: Dialogue in *Star Trek* episodes from 1966 to 1993. In D. Biber and S. Conrad (eds) *Variation in English: Multi-dimensional studies* (pp. 138–156). London: Longman. (A10)

Royce, T.D. and Bowcher, W. (eds) (2006). *New directions in the analysis of multimodal discourse*. London: Routledge. (Further reading)

Ruesch, J. and Bateson, G. (1968 [1951]). *Communication: The social matrix of psychiatry*. New York: W.W. Norton and Company. (C7)

Rumelhart, D. (1975). Notes on a schema for stories. In D. Bobrow and A. Collins (eds) *Representation and understanding: Studies in cognitive science*. New York: Academic Press. (B2, D2)

Sacks, H. (1992). *Lectures on conversation* (G. Jefferson and E.A. Schegloff, eds). Oxford and Cambridge, MA: Basil Blackwell. (Further reading)

Saville-Troike, M. (2003). *The ethnography of communication*. Oxford: Blackwell. (D7)

Schank, R.C. and Abelson, R.P. (1977). *Scripts, plans, goals, and understanding: An inquiry into human knowledge structures*. Hillsdale, NJ: Lawrence Erlbaum Associates. (B2)

Schegloff, E.A. (1968). Sequencing in conversational openings. *American Anthropologist 70*, 1075–1095. (B5)

Schegloff, E.A. (1988). Goffman and the analysis of conversation. In P. Drew and T. Wootton (eds) *Erving Goffman: Exploring the interaction order*. Cambridge: Polity Press, 9–35. (C5)

Schegloff, E. (2007). *Sequence organization in interaction: A primer in conversation analysis*. Cambridge: Cambridge University Press. (Further reading)

Schegloff, E.A. and Sacks, H. (1973). Opening up closings. *Semiotica 7*, 289–327. (B5, D5)

Schiffrin, D. (1994). *Approaches to discourse*. Oxford: Basil Blackwell. (Further reading)

Schiffrin, D., Tannen, D. and Hamilton, H.E. (eds) (2004). *The handbook of discourse analysis*. Oxford: Wiley-Blackwell. (Further reading)

Scollon, R. (1998). *Mediated discourse as social interaction: A study of news discourse*. New York: Longman. (D8, Further reading)

Scollon, R. (1999). Mediated discourse and social interaction. *Research on Language and Social Interaction 32*(1 and 2), 149–154. (D8)

Scollon, R. (2001). *Mediated discourse: The nexus of practice*. London: Routledge. (D8, Further reading)

Scollon, R. (2007). *Analyzing public discourse: Discourse analysis and the making of public policy*. London: Routledge. (Further reading)

Scollon, R. and Scollon, S.W. (2004). *Nexus analysis: Discourse and the emerging Internet*. New York: Routledge. (B8, Further reading)

Scollon, R., Scollon, S.W. and Jones, R.H. (2012). *Intercultural communication: A discourse approach*, 3rd edition, Oxford: Blackwell. (A6, B7)

Searle, J. (1966). *Speech acts*. Cambridge: Cambridge University Press. (Further reading)

Shuy, R. (1993). *Language crimes: The use and abuse of language evidence in the courtroom*. Oxford: Blackwell. (C5)

Simpson, P. and Mayr, A. (2009). *Language and power: A resource book for students*. Abingdon: Routledge. (Further reading)

Sinclair, J. (1991). *Corpus, concordance and collocation*. Oxford: Oxford University Press. (B10)

Stoddard, S. (1991). *Text and texture: Patterns of cohesion*. Norwood, NJ: Ablex. (Further reading)

Stubbs, M. (1996). *Text and corpus analysis*. Oxford: Blackwell.

Swales, J.M. (1981). *Aspects of article introductions*. LSU Research Report. University of Aston in Birmingham. (D3)

Swales, J.M. (1990). *Genre analysis: English in academic and research settings*. Cambridge: Cambridge University Press. (A3, B3, D3)

Swales, J.M. (2004). Research genres: Explorations and applications. Cambridge: Cambridge University Press. (Further reading)

Talamo, A. and Ligorio, B. (2001). Strategic identities in cyberspace. *Cyberpsychology and Behavior* 4(1), 109–122. (Further reading)

Tannen, D. (ed.) (1984). *Coherence in spoken and written discourse*. Norwood, NJ: Ablex Publishing Corporation. (Further reading)

Tannen, D. (1993). *Framing in discourse*. New York: Oxford University Press. (Further reading)

Tannen, D. (2005). *Conversational style: Analyzing talk among friends*. 2nd edition, Norwood, NJ: Ablex Publishing.

Tannen, D. and Wallat, C. (1987). Interactive frames and knowledge schemas in interaction: Examples from a medical examination/interview. *Social Psychology Quarterly 50*(2), 205–216. (D6)

ten Have, P. (2007). *Doing conversational analysis*, 2nd edition, London: Sage. (Further reading)

ter Wal, J. (2002). *Racism and cultural diversity in the mass media*. Vienna: European Research Center on Migration and Ethnic Relations.

Troike, R.C. (1970). Receptive competence, productive competence, and performance. In J.E. Alatis (ed.) *Linguistics and the teaching of standard English to speakers of other languages or dialects* (pp. 63–74). Washington, DC: Georgetown University Press.

United States Government (2001). Letter of two sorries. Retrieved on 5 March 2011 from: http://en.wikisource.org/wiki/Letter_of_the_two_sorries.

van Dijk, T. (1987). *Communicating racism: Ethnic prejudice in thought and talk*. London: Sage. (D10)

van Dijk, T.A. (2008). *Discourse and context: A sociocognitive approach*. Cambridge: Cambridge University Press. (A7) van Dijk, T. and Kintsch, W. (1983). *Strategies of discourse comprehension*. New York: Academic Press. (Further reading)

van Leeuwen, T. (1999). *Speech, music, sound*. Basingstoke: Macmillan. (A9)

van Leeuwen, T. (2008). *Discourse and practice: New tools for critical discourse analysis*. Oxford: Oxford University Press. (Further reading)

van Leeuwen, T. (2011). *The language of color: An introduction*. London: Routledge. (A9)

Verschueren, J. (1999). *Understanding pragmatics*. London: Arnold. (Further reading)

von Humboldt, W. (1836). Über die Verschiedenheit des menschlichen Sprachbaues und ihren Einfluss auf die geistige Entwicklung des Menschengeschlects. *Royal Academy of Sciences of Berlin*. (Reprinted as *Linguistic variability and intellectual development* (1971), trans by G.C. Buck and F.A. Raben. Miami, FL: University of Miami Press.) (D7)

Vygotsky, L.S. (1981). The instrumental method in psychology. In J.V. Wertsch (ed.) *The concept of activity in Soviet psychology* (pp. 134–143). Armonk, NY: M.E. Sharpe. (B8)

Walther, J.B. (1996). Computer-mediated communication: Impersonal, interpersonal and hyperpersonal interaction. *Communication Research 23*(1), 3–43. (C6)

Watts, R. (2003). *Politeness*. Cambridge: Cambridge University Press. (Further reading)

Wertsch, J.V. (1993). *Voices of the mind: A sociocultural approach to mediated action*. Cambridge, MA: Harvard University Press. (Further reading)

Wertsch, J.V. (1998). *Mind as action*. Oxford: Oxford University Press. (D8, Further reading)

Widdowson, H.G. (1973). *An applied linguistic approach to discourse analysis*. (Unpublished doctoral dissertation). Department of Linguistics, University of Edinburgh. (D1)

Widdowson, H.G. (2007). *Discourse analysis*. New York: Oxford University Press. (B1, Further reading)

Wodak, R. and Meyer, M. (eds) (2001). *Methods of critical discourse analysis*. London: Sage. (Further reading)

AUTHOR INDEX

GLOSSARIAL INDEX